A Question of Innocence

A Question of Innocence

A True Story of False Accusation

Lawrence D. Spiegel

Afterword by Douglas J. Besharov, J.D., LL.M.

The Unicorn Publishing House
New Jersey

Jean L. Scrocco
The Unicorn Publishing House, Inc.
1148 Parsippany Blvd., Parsippany, NJ 07054.

Distributed in Canada by Doubleday Canada, Ltd., Toronto, ON M5B 1Y3, Canada

Edited by William J. McGuire

Afterword © by Douglas J. Besharov, J.D., LL.M.,

Photographs by Robyn Craig, John Bell, Karen Touhey of the *Daily Record*, Morristown

Printed in the United States of America

Typography by L&B Typo., Inc. of N.Y.C.

Special thanks to Bob Rebach and John H. F. Enteman, Esq.

Thanks to Lance Booth, Pete Rossi, Theresa DeLuna and Ceil Robinson

Printing History 15 14 13 12 11 10 9 8 7 6 5 4 3 2 1

Library of Congress Cataloging-in-Publication Data

Spiegel, Lawrence, 1945–

A Question of Innocence.

1. Child molesting — United States — Case studies.
2. Visitation rights (Domestic relations) — United States — Case studies. I. McGuire, William, 1950-II Title.
HQ72.U53S65 1986   362.7'044   86-11239
ISBN-O88101-055-3QQ

To Jessica

ACKNOWLEDGMENTS

I wish to express my heartfelt love to my parents, family and friends, especially those who are mentioned within the text, for their patience, understanding and support. I would also like to express my gratitude to others who never lost their faith in me and were there when I needed them throughout my ordeal. They include: Eleanor Bush, Alan Mackerley Sr., Mark Spiegel, Lew and Selma Krever, Robert Brenner, Martin Mayer, Dr. and Mrs. Roger Casulli, Dr. Peter Sabolch, Dr. Walter Bilotta, Dr. Robert Beshar, Ric and Pat Wynn, Mary Fitzpatrick and Jimmy Di Bernard.

My deepest appreciation to those professionals whose care, concern and talents formed the backbone of my support system. Without them, I could not have endured.

To Dr. Gary Safier and Dr. Stanley Machlin for their medical expertise and compassion and to Dr. Ralph Underwager and Dr. William McIver for their consultation.

To Katharine Sweeney, Esq. for truly caring for and safeguarding Jessica's best interests.

To my attorneys, Herbert M. Korn and Steven P. Haft, for their dedication and devotion, and to their assistants, Bobby and Liz, for putting up with my constant phone calls.

To Jack Ford, Esq., and Robert Cherry, Esq., for their consultation.

To Judge Charles Egan, Judge Daniel Coburn and Judge Donald Collester for their wisdom, integrity and true pursuit of justice.

To those members of the media, especially Jay Mathews, Penny Pinsker, Brian Murray, Bill Riley and Paul Wyckoff for their help in bringing my plight to public attention.

To everyone at The Unicorn Publishing House, in particular my Publishers, Jean Scrocco and Joseph Scrocco for taking a chance on me, and my editor, Bill McGuire, whose talents were instrumental in enabling me to express what truly needed to be said.

To Janeen Love, who is truly the incarnation of her last name, and without whom I could not have survived at all.

AUTHOR'S NOTE

For me, this book is an attempt to set the record straight and express the many feelings which I could not externalize during the ordeal. It is also a gesture of gratitude to those who have stood beside me.

Most importantly, this book is meant as the highest expression of love and caring for my little girl, Jessica, lest she feel any guilt or blame for the occurrences described here. One day, when she is old enough to read this, it may lay to rest any psychological residue she may be carrying and serve to reassure her that no matter what has happened, my love for her is unequivocal and everlasting.

After two years of suffering and separation from my only child, I have finally gained enough distance to recognize my unique position. I am a father who has been falsely accused of sexually molesting my own daughter. I am also a practicing clinical psychologist. Therefore, I have developed a dual perspective on this problem — first as a parent, then as a professional.

This accusation, which nearly ruined my personal and professional life, involved me in what has been termed, The False Accusation Syndrome. Its eight stages, as I have observed them, are listed as subtitles to each chapter. When my case drew national attention through the media, people throughout the country in similar situations sought my professional assistance. The sheer number of people experiencing this problem was as startling as were the cases. Through my struggles and theirs, I have come to understand the plight of the falsely accused.

The purpose of this book is threefold:

First, to bring to public awareness the tragedy and misery of the parents, children and others victimized by false accusations. This focus will point out the vulnerability of everyone to this hysteria.

Second, to help those in divorce and/or custody disputes, and those who are already the victims of false accusations discover valuable information that will assist them on their own pathways out of their troubled situations.

Third, to provide the mental health professionals and the falsely accused with insights into the complex and emotionally-charged False Accusation Syndrome.

I have included copies of original documents, news articles, certifications and court orders. These documentations, in addition to verifying the facts, trace my tracks. I have underlined specific sentences to highlight the crucial facts. Nothing has been altered.

Until our social service agencies and legal system can distinguish between false and true accusations and prevent this problem, we all must understand the Syndrome and learn to minimize its impact. For now, our best hope rests in the mutual understanding of the Syndrome by the mental health practitioners and the falsely accused.

Above all, I believe this story, despite how bizarre it may seem, is true and factual.

L.S.

August 11, 1986

PART ONE

A True Story Of False Accusation

1

NICENESS AND NAIVETE

Stage 1: The Set-Up

At first glance, one would say the story began the day I was arrested in the parking lot of my office in Morris County, New Jersey. That day, December 9, 1983, I was a successful clinical psychologist with a growing private practice. That afternoon, I was escorted to a waiting police car, charged with sexually molesting my then two and a half-year-old daughter, handcuffed and taken to police headquarters. Suddenly my work, my dreams, my life — everything I had struggled for — were shattered. The confusion, disbelief, fear and anguish I experienced at that moment became an ongoing nightmare which continued for over two years. This charge was filed by my ex-wife about two weeks after our divorce was finalized. Yet the stage was actually set more than two years prior to that.

March 3, 1981 was the date of my marriage to Valori Mulvey. The ceremony was performed by a judge in the Morris County Courthouse with Valori eight months pregnant. My two closest friends, Tony and Patti Blaser, were the only guests. This same judge had presided over my no fault divorce from Pauline, my first wife of ten years. We had divorced, not because of problems or discord, but as a result of a mutual decision. Our lives were headed in opposite directions. She had wanted a more conventional relationship with regular working hours and a normal family life. I, on the other hand, was submersed in my teaching, writing and clinical practice.

I met Valori when she was a student in one of the college classes I had taught. We began dating when the semester ended. I was strongly attracted to her. She had green, penetrating eyes, and long thick brown hair. Being very thin, almost skinny, she appeared taller than five foot four. She was extremely alluring and sensual in an exotic, quasi-Oriental manner. We saw each other at every opportunity and discovered that we shared many things in common. I developed deep feelings for her and Valori's feelings for me were mutual.

Valori then became pregnant. Her pregnancy was more than unexpected. I had been told by my urologist a few years prior that the motility of my sperm was low and it would be highly unlikely that I would father a child. Although my first wife had hoped to become pregnant, we were never able to have a child.

Suffice to say, our marriage did not start out under optimum conditions. But we believed our love for each other would see us through. The birth of our daughter, Jessica, on April 6, 1981, provided significant hope that our marriage would strengthen. Sadly, such was not the case. Though our little girl was beautiful and we both loved her intensely, our relationship fell into deep trouble. For almost two years, we both tried to make our marriage work.

We went for marriage counseling and psychotherapy in the fall of 1982, but it was to no avail. We began a trial separation in December of that year. Valori and Jessie remained in our luxury apartment and I moved out. I still saw them daily. Valori and I continued our counseling for the benefit of Jessie.

I had thought long and hard about the affect of a separation upon Jessie and had discussed the issue on several occasions with our psychotherapist. Ultimately, I determined that the constant conflicts and arguments between Valori and me would be more detrimental to Jessie than a separation. I felt that Jessie was still young enough to acclimate herself to a change of that kind.

The more time I spent with Valori, the more unhappy we both became. Frequently, our discussions would center on her fears over a number of things — my fidelity was a primary issue. Her sense of my unhappiness, coupled with her own insecurities, produced a continuous stream of threats as to what she would do IF .... I grew intolerant of her unfounded accusations. At a point of severe emotional strain, when our relationship lacked real communication, I felt lonely and depressed. One night, while away at a conference, I momentarily escaped and had a brief encounter — a one night stand with a woman I had never seen before or since. I soon told Valori about my indiscretion, which forced her to confront her own threats and ultimatums.

January 1983

At first it seemed as though Valori accepted my indiscretion. But by the beginning of January, it was clear that her anger and rigidity were going to prevail. Without warning, on January 23, she obtained a temporary restraining order, denying me access to our apartment and child. She then changed the locks.

Two days later, she left for parts unknown with our child. That same day my brother's wife, Debra, who was one of Valori's closest friends, called me at my office. She said Valori had called to say good-bye, but would not say where she was headed. Debra said Valori sounded irrational and disoriented. I then received a call from another of our close friends, Betty Lentchner, my partner's wife, who added that Valori may be acting irrationally as a result of using drugs and medication. She thought Valori had found the key to my locked gun cabinet and may have been sleeping with a loaded gun under her pillow with Jessica in the same bed. Both callers were frightened for Valori and Jessie's welfare.

I immediately called my friend and attorney, Arnold Miniman. He succeeded in getting the restraining order lifted and persuading the superintendent to allow me into my apartment.

Before entering the apartment, I was greeted by a note taped to the door, which appears as Exhibit A. (The 1982 date on Valori's note was a mistake of habit, since 1983 had just begun.)

EXHIBIT A

> Anyone ~~also~~ found on these premises
> B-33, Apt 3 will be prosecuted
> for breaking + entering
>
> This notice is posted on the
> request of Oakwood Village Management
>
> Signed
> V. Spiegel
> 1/25/82

When the superintendent opened the door, all that Debra and Betty had told me about Valori's increasingly irrational behavior was confirmed. Every window, blind, shade and curtain was completely shut. Not one speck of light or outside air could penetrate. The large living room bookcase had been moved and used to barricade the door. Every name and number had been erased from the bulletin board and the phone had been left off the hook. I remembered Debra saying that Valori thought people were "after her."

I walked into the bedroom and looked under Valori's pillow. As I raised it an inch or two, I saw the brown, carved wood of the revolver's handle. In a panic, I called Debra and Betty to tell them what I had found. I asked both of them to come over, despite the fact that it was snowing quite heavily. I was hoping they could help me determine where Valori might have gone. I then called a psychiatrist to consult with him about the prospective danger. I was told by his answering service that he was away on vacation. Did I wish to have the covering doctor call me back? I had no idea who that was, but "Yes," I said, "And it is an emergency."

I sat down in the dark kitchen at the empty table in the first of what were to be many, a state of shock and bewilderment. I saw Jessie's highchair, food warmer and some of her toys on the kitchen counter. Will she be all right? Where could they be? Tears of fear and anguish began to flow down my cheeks.

Shortly thereafter, Debra and Betty arrived. I answered the door, still wiping the tears from my eyes. Together we sat down and tried to think of the various places where Valori might have gone. Some fifteen minutes later, the phone rang. "This is Dr. Hamlin calling," the voice said, "I'm covering for Dr. Frowirth during his vacation. Can you tell me what the problem is?"

I explained the situation to him, thinking to myself all the while, what is the point of this? He doesn't know me from Adam, why should he care? What could he do to help? How will he know that I'm telling the truth and recognize the seriousness of the situation?

When I finished telling him what had happened, I waited for his reply, hoping that he could add some insight or offer some helpful advice. Instead, he asked, "What's your address?" Mechanically, without even thinking about why he had asked that question, I recited my address.

"I know where that is," he said crisply. "I'll be there in about twenty minutes. Leave everything as it is."

I looked out the window. It was still snowing heavily. Would this psychiatrist make a house call in the middle of a snow storm? "There are three or four inches of snow on the ground," I said.

"No problem," he responded in the same professional tone. "I have four-wheel drive." I heard the click from the other end, lowered the phone and hung it up. I turned back to the dining room table where Betty and Debra sat with expectant looks on their faces.

"Well, what did he say?" asked Debra.

"He's coming over here," I replied.

Meanwhile, my mind was racing. Not only had I been shocked when he said he would come over, but in a strange way I found it pleasantly unusual that a psychiatrist, whom I did not even know, was coming to this apartment as a professional courtesy. Then the real impact of Dr. Hamlin's response hit me. It brought me back to the reality that my child may be in serious danger. Again I felt that sinking feeling of fear in the pit of my stomach.

Twenty minutes later, a young man with horn-rimmed glasses and smoking a pipe arrived at the apartment. Dr. Hamlin surveyed the situation — closed blinds, erased bulletin board, etc., then sat with the three of us for nearly two hours, questioning and discussing the problem. Finally he stood up. "If you can't locate her, call the police and the Division of Youth and Family Services, then call your attorney. I will prepare a report detailing this situation. You can pick it up first thing Monday morning at my office. Good luck. If you need anything else, call me." He was gone as quickly as he arrived.

After Dr. Hamlin left, I called another of our close friends, Nancy Reber. She is one of those rare individuals who possesses an extraordinary sense of intuition as well as a sharp analytical mind. She and Debra were very similar in that way, and they were Valori's two best friends. I knew the two of them might figure out where Valori had gone.

Late that night, after calls to the airlines and bus terminals provided no leads, Debra remembered that one of Valori's sisters had just moved to southern New Jersey with her family. That's when Nancy took over. She went back to her home, poured over South Jersey phone books and came back with the phone number and address of Valori's sister. She and her family lived in Indian Mills, New Jersey. We figured that Valori might have gone there. Our assumption turned out to be true.

On Monday morning, I picked up an initial draft of Dr. Hamlin's report. I had worried the entire weekend and, after reading his report, my fears were reinforced again. A final copy was sent to my attorney some time later. An excerpt appears here as Exhibit B.

Then I went directly to my lawyer's office. I was determined to get Jessica back immediately. Arnold and I spent the day putting together an emergent order to show cause. This is a legal document which requires a spouse to appear in court to explain certain actions. We filed it in Family Court late that afternoon. It did not help matters to have Arnold tell me that I could not just go get Jessica. If Valori had not left the State, then she had not broken any law. Therefore, the best we could do was to file the motion requiring her to justify her actions.

EXHIBIT B

Psychiatric Associates of New Jersey, P.A.

161 Madison Avenue
Morristown, New Jersey 07960
(201) 540-9550

February 14, 1983

Steven P. Haft, Esq.
1200 Route 46
Suite 208
Parsippany, N.J.   07054

RE: Valori Spiegel

Dear Mr. Haft:

Dr. Lawrence Speigel has asked me to write a letter about my opinion of the mental condition of his estranged wife, Valori, and whether there is any danger to the welfare of their daughter Jessica, age 18 months, who is under the care of Valori.

Disorder. Obviously, first hand evidence is necessary to form a conclusive diagnostic impression, however, innocent lives hang in the balance. I suggest that the child be placed in protective custody, and that the court also hold her in a protective environment until the nature of her problem and the extent of the danger can be more precisely ascertained.

Very truly yours,

Cary L. Hamlin, M.D.

CLH:v

February and March 1983

We filed that motion, but we were not prepared for the response. It seemed that Valori's father, a fairly wealthy corporate executive, had sent her money to retain a well-known lawyer in the area, Anthony Wahl. On Wednesday of that week, Arnold called me to his office once again. Valori's new attorney had filed answering papers, which, among other things, accused me of being an alcoholic, a homosexual and a drug addict. I became infuriated at such absurd accusations. I wondered who had given Valori this idea.

Arnold proceeded to explain to me that, if this separation and divorce were going to be as messy as it seemed, I was better off with another lawyer. He and I were too close to one another for him to be able to represent me in an objective manner. Overriding my protests, he said, "I want you to meet Steven Haft."

"Never heard of him," I replied. It would be fine, Arnold explained. I would like Steven and he would do a good job for me. We would meet for lunch tomorrow.

At one o'clock the next day, I walked into the Par-Troy Diner, looked around and spotted Arnold sitting in a corner booth with a tall, good-looking man about my age. When we were introduced, I was surprised and impressed to hear his deep, booming voice. I instinctively liked him. Arnold had made a good choice.

Once the introductions were completed, Arnold said we had a court date the following week. At that time, our motion and Valori's response to it would be heard. He had already explained the situation to Steven. All I had to do was sign the change of attorney form. Arnold finished his sandwich and departed, leaving Steven and me to talk.

The longer we conversed, the more I liked Steven. He was more my style than Arnold, who was a laid-back, rather conservative and soft-spoken man. Steven was confident, assertive and, despite his proper "objective attorney composure," was a more radical and freethinking individual. Neither of us could have possibly realized then how close we would become, nor how bizarre our adventures would be throughout the next two years.

Our first day in court that February morning, was to be one of the most bewildering, yet satisfying days of my life. It was a strange scene. It seemed at the outset, more like a wedding or funeral or some other type of family occasion. Valori's parents had flown up from Georgia. Two of her sisters with their husbands and her aunt were there. They were all milling around in a small crowd outside the courthouse when Steven and I arrived. On the opposite side of the entrance was a small contingent of my relatives and friends — Rick, my brother, and Debra; Tony and Patti Blaser, as; well as Betty and her husband, Dr. Lawrence Lentchner, who was at that time my friend and professional partner.

Once inside the courtroom, the two sides squared off. Like a wedding or other formal family occasions, her family sat on one side of the room, while my friends and family sat on the other. Within a short time, the battle lines had been clearly drawn. Valori and her father came well prepared with their expensive lawyer and show of family solidarity. They were not prepared, however, for the psychiatric testimony from Dr. Hamlin's report, certifications from Debra and Betty, and a few other facts we had in store. Judge Daniel Coburn presided.

We had submitted our papers, asking that there be a temporary change of custody until Valori went through a psychiatric examination. Valori submitted her papers which accused me of being an alcoholic, homosexual and drug addict. She asked for sole custody of Jessica. She also requested that my visitation be restricted and supervised.

Since we had brought the motion, Steven put me on the stand first. After soliciting my version of the story and professional psychological assessment, he introduced Dr. Hamlin's letter. Then he produced the other facts. First was the handwritten note Valori had taped to the apartment door. Then came the second note which was written by Valori following one of our marital discussions. I had saved it because it distressed me greatly. She had listed what she thought we should give to each other and what she believed each of us wanted. In both Valori's give and want columns, she had written, "drugs." The lists are shown in Exhibit C.

When the judge looked at the handwritten notes, his eyebrows raised. He asked the court clerk to show them to Valori.

"Is that your handwriting, Mrs. Spiegel?" the judge asked.

"Yes, Your Honor," was the reply. My wife's attorney, Anthony Wahl, went white.

"Mr. Wahl, would you like a brief recess to confer with your client?" queried the judge.

"Yes, your Honor, I would," responded Mr. Wahl in a shaking voice.

EXHIBIT C

Val wants	Larry gives	Larry wants	Valori gives
Intell. stim.	Give support $1,9,all	Intell. stim.	Compassion - Support - emotional
② Love Play + learn out play (us)	Love - honest	Play + learn to 1 play (us)	Romance
① Truth (Drugs)	Romance	● Truth	LOVE
Patience	Sexuality (historic)	② Patience	Devotion to your growth —
Understanding from you that what specific functions I do are from love not duty.	Caring - protection Professional supp. Cooperate A Parenting	Cut hair Do laundry Understand etc. Delve deeply as possible	your genius Sexuality (seduction)
You to delve into me as deeply as is possible for both of us.	Intell. stim. Play?	Recog. have been etc.	Cooperate in parenting Intell. stim.
Recog. that I have a capability out of love	Patience		Play (Drugs) Patience

Fidelity

Suddenly, we were out in the hall, both sides milling around and conferring among themselves.

"Come with me," said Steven.

He and I, along with Tony, quickly found a small conference room. Steven explained that we could probably, at this point, take temporary custody of Jessie. Did I really want to do that? Was that going to mean even more trauma for her? As an alternative, Steven suggested that, in Jessie's best interest, we could leave temporary custodial care with Valori but dictate our own stringent terms. Steven said we could go back into the courtroom and withdraw our custody motion. That would take everyone by surprise and allow us to dictate terms which would give me ample visitation and, at the same time, protect the welfare of my child. The court would certainly agree to our plan. I looked to Tony, whose intuition and wisdom I trusted. He nodded his approval.

"Okay," I said to Steven, "but let's make certain of the safe-guards for my child." He was already busily scribbling our demands on his note pad. "Don't say a word when we go in," said Steven. "Let me handle it. Got it?"

"Yes," I said, still reviewing the details of our strategy.

The remainder of the proceedings couldn't have gone better if I had written the script myself. The judge quickly brushed aside all of Valori's allegations of drug usage, homosexuality, etc. and severely chastised her for her actions and accusations. The hearing ended with the judge awarding me weekly visitation with Jessie, plus every other weekend. Valori was to meet me each time at her aunt's home in New Brunswick, which was about a half hour away from our apartment. The thought of the frequent rides for Jessie disturbed me a little, but I knew she loved riding in the car, so it seemed all right.

The judge concluded by giving me a visitation that afternoon. Jessie was to be ready at Valori's aunt's home at 4:00 p.m. We all exited the courtroom. Once outside, the two groups stood separately. Glancing over, the distress and anger on the part of Valori's family was quite apparent. They were fighting and arguing among themselves.

Anthony Wahl had made it clear to us during the recess that Valori's father was paying for her legal expenses and engineering the moves. People began drifting away. Steven was already waiting for me at my car. I started toward Valori to firm up arrangements to see Jessie that afternoon. Valori's father intercepted me and pulled me off to the side. The look on his face was similar to the one I had seen when I had told him Valori and I were getting married. Back then, he blustered around for about forty-five minutes, then finally resigned himself to the situation. His last words to me at that time were, "Just what I needed, a Jew for a son-in-law."

"I'm not overjoyed with an Irish Catholic father-in-law, either," I replied, trying to keep it light.

This time, however, as he led me close to the side of the court-house away from the others, his tone was much graver. "Okay," he said, "how much will it cost to get you out of their lives?"

I was stunned! I looked at his face to determine if he was really serious. He was. I did not know what to say. As a result of not getting his way in court, he was really trying to buy me off. I looked him in the eyes and said, "You know, Ed, you are more of an ass than I thought you were." I turned and walked away.

"You're going to be sorry for that," he screamed after me.

I turned my head to look at him. His face was beet red; he was fuming. I continued walking to my car where Steven was waiting. He saw the interchange but was too far away to hear what had transpired. "What was that all about," he asked as I got into the car. I told him. "Are you serious?" he asked. I assured him I was. He nodded his head and waited for me to start the car.

The remainder of February and the month of March were scarred by chronic disputes and violations of my visitation rights which landed us back in Family Court several times. It was apparent the judge was getting tired of the situation. Each time, he would chastise Valori and admonish her for violating my right to visitation. Each time, she would leave the courtroom seeming very repentant and, shortly thereafter, do the same thing again. The constant strain was taking its toll on Jessie. She developed hives and rashes, became moody and always put up a struggle when it was time for me to take her back to her mother.

April through August 1983

The chronic bitterness finally came to a head on April 6, Jessie's second birthday. It was a Wednesday, the day of my weekly visit. I had intended to bring her home for the day and have a birthday party with her cousins, Jeremy and Heather. I never got the chance.

Early that morning, Valori called to say she couldn't drive to New Brunswick because something was wrong with her car. I told her I would pay to have it fixed and I would drive down to her sister's home that day. She told me not to bother, that she was not going to let me see Jessie anyway and hung up. I went immediately to Steven's office and told him what happened. Steven called her attorney, Mr. Wahl, who said he would speak with her and call us back. A few minutes later, he called and told Steven that Valori had said the same thing to him. She was not going to let me see Jessie. He tried to reason with her, but she would not listen.

I told Steven I was going to the home of Valori's sister anyway. He gave me a copy of Judge Coburn's court order which specified the visitation schedule. He cautioned me not to do anything drastic. If I had any trouble, I was to call the police or Sheriff's Office. I began the drive in my camper with the court order and a map of New Jersey. It took more than three hours of steady driving to reach Indian Mills, New Jersey.

As I arrived at her sister's home, I saw Valori drive away in her car which "did not work." She had been informed that I was coming. I had stopped at the State Police barracks to have an officer call ahead. State Trooper Moose had called Valori and she reiterated that she would not let me see Jessie. When he had cited the court order, she hung up. He suggested that I try going over there. If there was any more trouble, I should call the Sheriff's Office, since this was a civil, not a criminal, matter.

When I saw Valori leave the house, I drove to town and immediately called the Sheriff's Office. They told me it would take a while, but they would have an officer meet me. After waiting in a gas station parking lot for about two hours, Officer Joseph Horn pulled up and identified himself. I showed him the court order and told him what had happened.

"Follow me," he said. He got into his car and drove toward the home of Valori's sister while I followed in my camper. His certification, submitted to the court and labeled here as Exhibit D, tells the rest of that day's events.

EXHIBIT D

Steven P. Haft, Esq.
1200 Route 46, Suite 208
Parsippany, New Jersey 07054
(201) 334-2444
Attorney for Defendant

VALORI M. SPIEGEL   :
 	
         Plaintiff   :
 	
    vs.   :
 	
LAWRENCE D. SPIEGEL   :
 	
         Defendant   :
	SUPERIOR COURT OF NEW JERSEY
	 CHANCERY DIVSION: MORRIS COUNTY
	
	 Docket No. M-03149-83
	
	     Civil Action
	
	     <u>CERTIFICATION</u>

Joseph Horn, of full age, certifies as follows:

1. I am a Sheriff's Officer with the Burlington County Sheriff's Department and make this Certification on behalf of Lawrence D. Spiegel, the Defendant in the above matter.

2. On Wednesday, April 6, 1983, <u>I was dispatched by the Burlington County Sheriff's Office to assist Mr. Spiegel in obtaining visitation with his child.</u>

3. I met Mr. Spiegel and proceeded to the residence where Mrs. Spiegel is residing, 105 Holly Drive, Vincentown, New Jersey.

4. Upon arriving there, Mr. Spiegel waited outside the car and I walked up to the door. A woman came to the door who was later identified as Mrs. Little, the Plaintiff's sister.

5. <u>I identified myself and showed Mrs. Little a copy of the March 24th Order issued out of the Superior Court by Judge Coburn.</u>

6. Mrs. Little then went into the house and a man then appeared at the door identified as Mr. Little. By this time, Mr. Spiegel had walked up to join me near the door.

7. When Mr. Little came out he started yelling and screaming that we had no business being there and that we should get off his property. I tried to explain to him that I was merely attempting to assist Mr. Spiegel in seeing his child on her birthday.

8. Mr. Little continued to scream that Mr. Spiegel had no business being there and that we should get off his property. He thereafter threatened to call the police. At this point Mr. Spiegel requested that he be allowed to see his child for a period of one hour. Mr. Little then turned his back and went into the house.

9. A few minutes later another woman came out of the house who was identified as the Plaintiff, Valori Spiegel. She appeared to be very nervous and uptight and immediately began ranting and raving over the fact that her husband had appeared. She flatly refused to allow Mr. Spiegel to see his child. I tried to explain to her that since the Order allowed for visitation for Wednesdays and she did not provide the visitation because of transporation problems that I felt it was proper for Mr. Spiegel to come to Vincentown to see his child. She refused to listen to me and while I was talking she began to rehash her entire life history as it related to Mr. Spiegel. She was yelling and screaming and ordering us to leave the property. She told me that her lawyer advised her not to allow her husband to see their child.

10. Mr. Little then reappeared and sent Mrs. Spiegel back inside the house. He asked for my name and badge number which I proudly gave him. I again requested that they allow Mr. Spiegel

the opportunity to see his child and wish her a Happy Birthday, even if for only a few minutes.

11. Mrs. Spiegel then reappeared at the door and continued to refuse to allow any visitation with the child. She was insulting and abusive in her tone and attitude.

12. Mrs. Spiegel appeared irrational and it is my opinion that she cannot deal with her problems and is not a fit person to care for an infant child.

13. After approximately 40 to 45 minutes Mr. Spiegel and I left the premises and went to the local State Police barracks.

14. At no time while I was there did Mr. Spiegel have an opportunity to see or talk to his child.

15. At no time did I ever make any threats to any of the parties or persons present but merely advised them that it was my opinion that they were violating a valid Court Order. I did, indicate to Mrs. Spiegel, that I thought that a warrant for her arrest could be issued as a result of her behavior and actions.

16. I hereby certify that the foregoing statements made by me are true. I am aware that if any of the foregoing statements made by me are willfully false that I am subject to punishment.

/s/ Joseph Horn
JOSEPH HORN

Dated April   , 1983.

April 9 found us back in court once more. The papers submitted by both sides for this hearing were almost exact duplications of those submitted for our first court date back in February. Again, Valori submitted her certifications asserting that I was an alcoholic, drug addict and homosexual. I again asked for a temporary change of custody and a psychiatric examination for Valori. I expressed my concerns, echoing those of the Sheriff's Officer, for the health and safety of Jessica.

Judge Coburn severely admonished Valori, who sat with her head hanging down staring at the courtroom floor. He informed her he would not tolerate any more violations of the visitation agreement. He said to Valori, "I don't care if you do not have a car, I don't care if you have to walk, I don't care if they storm the Bastille. You be where you are supposed to be."

Though the judge did not change the custody ruling, he did ask Valori and me to have psychiatric examinations. He instructed her to find an apartment no further away than New Brunswick and to make certain she adhered to the "letter of the agreement" with regard to visitation. If there was one more violation, he would issue a warrant for her arrest. I told the court I would pay for an apartment for Valori, in order to bring her closer and out of the environment of her sister's home. The judge then instructed our attorneys to begin work on a divorce settlement, since we were obviously headed in that direction.

Valori and Jessie moved into an apartment in New Brunswick. We signed a temporary settlement agreement. The situation got considerably better. Valori went back to school at Rutgers, I helped take care of Jessie and we both began dating other people. The woman I began to see, Janeen Love, was a compassionate and warm individual. Life settled down to an almost comfortable routine.

The latter part of spring and through the summer was a placid time in Valori's and my relationship. Suddenly, Valori had become tolerant, understanding and amiable — so amiable, that I suppose I should have had my doubts. Everyone else did and cautioned me not to trust this new personality. Perhaps, I was simply too close to the trees to see the forest or, perhaps, I just wanted peace so badly. In actuality, as I look back, I think it was just plain naivete. I was too trusting of people. Soon that became abundantly clear.

During this period, I paid Valori's college tuition and Jessie's nursery school and baby-sitters. Though I was already strained financially, Valori asked me to pay for a trip to Georgia to visit her parents late in August. I was concerned about the trip, but I thought her father's anger would have subsided with our separation and pending divorce. I was soon to learn, I was never so wrong about anything in my life.

Things between Valori and me continued to go "unbelievably" well. I bought the plane tickets, drove Valori and Jessie to the airport and picked them up about a week later. The trip to Georgia, an event which could have upset the apple cart, seemed instead to hold few negative affects. In retrospect, I realize that these cooperative times were actually part of the "Set-up" stage of The False Accusation Syndrome.

September 1983

After picking them up at the airport, I dropped Valori at her apartment to unpack and I spent the day with Jessie. We went to the park and then to McDonald's. Jessie, however, returned from Georgia with some strange questions.

Jessie at 2½ years old. We were several months away from the tragedy that would separate us for nearly 2½ years.

Niceness And Naivete

"Do you love Mommy?" she asked, as we drove toward McDonald's after an hour on the swings.

"Yes," I replied.

"Poppa" (her name for Valori's father) "says you don't," she said seriously.

"Well, there are lots of different kinds of love, Jessie."

"Mommy says she doesn't love you," she said persistently. She was extremely verbal for a two-year-old. In fact, she started talking early, about thirteen months old, and hadn't stopped since.

"Do you love Poppa?" she continued.

"Yes," I replied.

"Poppa doesn't love you." She was making a game out of it now. She then launched into her child gibberish, which she did when she was uncomfortable or upset. I made a game out of it with her and she seemed to forget it when we arrived at McDonald's.

The effect of Valori's parents on Jessie, luckily, seemed short-lived. She soon stopped asking questions about love. Valori continued to be "unbelievably" cooperative. Throughout September, I began to feel that things would really be okay. Jessie was back in nursery school and Valori began classes at Rutgers to complete her BA degree in psychology. I was still Department Chairman in psychology at the local county college. My private practice and the Integrative Psychology Institute which I had begun with my colleague, Dr. Lentchner, were doing exceptionally well.

For the first time in 13 years, I seriously considered resigning from my teaching position at the college so that I could do full time clinical work and seminars at the Institute. Dr Lentchner, who had also taught at the same college, had resigned in late June to devote himself to our new Institute. I began the new term at the college, nonetheless. Teaching was something I loved so much, I couldn't give much credence to the thoughts of quitting, notwithstanding the urgings of my partner to do so. Anyway, I needed both the teaching and the Institute to make enough money to support Valori, Jessie and me now that we were maintaining two separate households. Besides, there were payments on more than $15,000 which I had borrowed to cover my legal fees and lost income from my clinical practice due to court hearings and legal meetings.

On September 22, I drove Valori to court for our divorce hearing. The past three weeks, Valori had been consistently pleasant. We had seemingly begun to accept and reconcile ourselves to the dichotomy of getting divorced and developing a friendship, simultaneously. I was convinced we would make it and the worst was over. Despite the continuing words of caution and suspicion from many of my close friends, I was unaware of the "Set-up."

October 1983

October continued to encourage my blissful naivete. On October 3, Valori gave me a birthday party, something she had never done in the two years we had spent together. On October 20, the court granted us a final judgment of divorce. Valori withdrew from the record all her charges that I was an alcoholic, drug addict, etc., admitting they were not true.

These were the most tranquil and easygoing weeks we had experienced for a long time. The three of us began doing things together. On various occasions, Valori and I took Jessica to the park and several times we went out to eat together. We seemed to be getting along better now than during our short-lived marriage. Everything felt so genuine and I had high hopes. It really seemed we would become friends. There was a sense of true cooperation between Valori and me. The impact on Jessie was obvious. She was very happy, laughing a lot and constantly talking to both Valori and me. That is why I was not at all prepared for what happened next.

November 1983

On November 4, the trouble started again. An excerpt from the certification I submitted to the Family Court, marked Exhibit E, tells the story.

EXHIBIT E

REC'D

NOV 16 1983

MAT-30

~~~~~ Clerk

FILED

NOV 1983

BITNER & HAFT
1200 Route 46
Parsippany, New Jersey 07054
(201) 334-1400
ATTORNEYS FOR Defendant

VALORI M. SPIEGEL	SUPERIOR COURT OF NEW JERSEY CHANCERY DIVISION: MORRIS COUNTY
Plaintiff ,	
vs.	**Docket No.** M-03149-83
LAWRENCE D. SPIEGEL	**CIVIL ACTION**
Defendant .	CERTIFICATION

Lawrence D. Spiegel, of full age, certifies as follows:

1. The parties appeared before the Court on ~~~~~ 22,

~~~~ classes. There did ~~~~~~~~~ to be any problems of

any nature.

8. On Friday evening November 4th (my visitation weekend)

my phone service at my office received a call from Valori. She

left a message that she had a family emergency and had to leave

town. She did not say where she was going nor did she request

my permission to take Jessica with her.

9. I waited throughout the weekend for some word from Valori, but received no message.

10. By Wednesday, November 9 the date of my next scheduled visitation I still had not heard a word from or about Valori. Finally, later that afternoon, Valori called me. My first reaction was that she was home and I asked to speak with Jessica. Jessica and I spoke on the phone and she was as loving as always. When I then continued my conversation with Valori she apologized for not calling me sooner and informed me that she was at her sister's home in the Cincinnati Ohio area. Valori told me that her sister was ill and had gone there to help out and had simply forgotten to call me. She sounded sincerely sorry and gave me her sister's phone number. I spoke with Valori about coming to Ohio to visit with Jessica during the weekend of November 12 and 13 since Valori indicated that she might be there for a few weeks. Valori was amenable to my visitation. Our conversation ended with my telling Valori that I would call again on Friday evening to let her know what my flight plans would be. This entire conversation was very amicable.

11. When I called Valori on Friday evening November 11, I spoke with her and told her that I would fly out to Cincinnati on Sunday. She told me that her sister did not want me to come to the house and it was her suggestion that she meet me at the airport with Jessica. Since I had not yet firmed up a flight schedule I told Valori that I would call her on Saturday to make

- -

final plans.

12. At approximately 10:00 a.m. on Saturday, November 12, Valori called my home and seemed completely irrational. She said I was not to come to Cincinnati. She also said that she had "found out what was going on" and was going to put a stop to it. When I asked her what she meant she said "you know exactly what I mean". I told her that I did not have the vaguest idea of what she was talking about. She responded again by saying "you know what I am talking about". She then told me not to bother coming to Ohio because she would be gone by the time I got there.

13. ... de arrangements

Since Valori refused to say where she was taking Jessie next, I had to reach them before they departed Ohio. I had professional obligations that required me to remain in New Jersey that day, so I immediately sent my assistant, Lou Popek, to Ohio by plane. At least he could begin the task of finding Valori and Jessie's exact location. I would arrive the following day.

Before leaving New Jersey, I contacted the Hamilton County Police Department in Ohio and explained the situation to Sergeant Boeing. He returned my call a short while later and told me that he had spoken to someone at the house. He suggested that Valori not leave Ohio since she may have violated a New Jersey court order. Any further actions on her part may make matters worse.

I joined Lou in Ohio the next day. He had found Valori's sister's home, but Valori and Jessie had already departed. I called her sister, Ronnie, and begged her to tell me where Valori had taken my child. She said she could not tell me, but would try to contact Valori. Someone would call me back.

About an hour later, the phone rang. It was Valori's father. He said Valori and Jessica were at his home in Georgia. Without waiting for my reply he said, "We know what you are doing and we're going to stop you. You will never see that child again." With that he hung up. From the expression on my face, Lou didn't have to ask the news. There was nothing to do but return to New Jersey. I knew I would have to call Steven and go into court to get Valori and Jessie back. Throughout our return trip I remained silent. I couldn't grasp what Valori or her father were talking about. What was it that was happening here?

On November 16, Valori and Jessie were returned by court order to the State of New Jersey and ordered to appear before a different judge, the Honorable Donald Collester in Morris County Family Court. This hearing would set the stage for what was to come for the next two years. I did not, of course, at that time realize the significance of this day in court.

When Steven and I walked into the courthouse waiting room, Jessie was there along with her grandmother and Valori. A man, who turned out to be one of Valori's father's hired hands, stood near by. Though I had not seen Jessie for over two weeks, she came running to me the moment she saw me. She jumped on my lap and played with my tie. She seemed largely unaffected by the furor surrounding her.

Once inside the courtroom, the judge asked for an explanation for Valori's most recent violation of court orders. Her attorney stood up ready to respond. We were prepared for more of the old story. I was harassing her, I was an alcoholic or a drug addict. What he said, however, stunned me.

He informed the judge that the reason Valori ran away to Ohio was because she thought that I had sexually abused Jessica. Steven and I looked at each other in complete astonishment. The judge glanced toward our table where Jessica sat contentedly on my lap playing with my tie and my beard. He looked back at Mr. Wahl and asked if there was any evidence to support such a claim. Mr. Wahl said there was a doctor Valori had taken Jessica to see, who had said that he would verify the complaint. But when contacted by Mr. Wahl, the doctor would not verify the complaint.

The judge seemed outraged by such a wild and unsupported allegation. He stopped the proceedings and summoned both attorneys to his chambers. Jessie and I went out to play. The attorneys came out approximately twenty minutes later. Anthony Wahl looked pale and sheepish and Steven looked confident and happy. I did not have to ask, I knew things had gone well. A moment later we were all summoned back into the courtroom.

"All rise," droned the clerk. The judge returned to the bench with a somber look on his face. Once again, Valori was severely chastised for her behavior, told that the court would not tolerate any further violation of its orders and would listen to no more wild accusations. This time the judge did alter the custody arrangement, giving me joint legal custody of Jessie, as I had requested my first time in court over six months before. This meant that I had equal say in any and all major decisions regarding Jessie's welfare. The judge advised me that, now if Valori left the state with Jessie again, I had the legal right to go bring her back. He then instructed that I could take Jessie home with me for our visitation, which we had been deprived of for two weeks.

On the way out of the courtroom, I heard Valori ask her attorney, "Why does he always win?"

"Because you always break the law, my dear," was the response.

As I left the courtroom with Jessie, Valori said, "This will be the last time you see your daughter." I ignored it and kept walking. This remark, however, had Steven concerned.

Once outside the courthouse Steven said, "I want you to be very careful from this point on. Valori is not going to drop this idea. I want you to document in writing all of the time you spend with Jessie and try not to be alone with her."

"Yes, yes," I replied as I strapped Jessie into her seat. She was still too young to really understand what we were saying.

"Don't 'yes' me," Steven said emphatically. "I'm not kidding. She will pursue this!"

"Okay, okay," I said, as I pulled away. Steven just stood there shaking his head. I, on the other hand, was happy about the day's outcome, certain that the worst was over and looking forward to the rest of the afternoon with Jessie and Janeen. I was still convinced that justice always triumphed. I had no hint of what was ahead.

More violations of my visitation, more days in court and another warning from my lawyer, Steven Haft.

2

THE AX FALLS

Stage 2: The Shock

The weeks following November 16, when the accusations of sexual abuse first surfaced in court, were extremely stressful. A cold war existed between Valori and me. She no longer allowed me into her apartment, insisting I wait outside when coming for Jessie. My attorney continued to emphasize the seriousness of the charge and again urged me to keep a journal documenting my visits. Jessica clearly sensed the air of tension and cried each time I took her back to Valori.

The constant emotional strain was unraveling my life. I was unable to continue in my teaching position at the college. I had missed too many classes as a consequence of the numerous days in court or chasing Valori around when she violated my court-ordered visitations. It had reached the point where I was being unfair to my students. I had no choice but to reluctantly tender my resignation. For the first time in fourteen years, I was no longer a member of the faculty at the college.

The cold war raged throughout November with Jessie caught in the middle. I tried to reason with Valori, stressing the need for cooperation. At first she refused to talk at all, but gradually she loosened up a bit and became more cooperative. She still, however, would not permit me to enter her apartment. On one of my usual Wednesday evening visits with Jessie, Valori asked me to drive her to a class because her car was not running properly again.

She suggested I pick them up, drop her off at school and take Jessie to McDonald's playland. After class we would meet again. We did exactly that and on the way back to her apartment, we talked openly with one another. Perhaps the cold war was thawing a bit. I told Valori to fix her car and I would pay for it. She thanked me, yet when we arrived at the apartment door, I was not invited in.

We'll give it some time, I thought to myself on the drive home. Even with the warning from my friends and the constant cautions from Steven, I remained optimistic. I had no clue that Valori's change of demeanor, along with her request that I drive her to class, was part of the execution of the "Set-up." Now that the facts have come to light, I know the "Set-up" had been planned even before her unannounced departure for Ohio. As early as September, Valori had contacted a psychologist for Jessie. By early November, Valori had taken Jessie for an examination. So the sexual abuse scheme had been well under way in September and October when Valori and I were enjoying what I thought were tranquil and cooperative times. This fact was confirmed later in testimony given by Dr. Walter Frankel. An excerpt of his testimony, confirming the dates when Valori contacted the clinic, appears here as Exhibit A.

EXHIBIT A

```
 Frankel                                                        26

1    D R.   W A L T E R   B.   F R A N K E L, having been duly

2         sworn by the Officer, testified as follows:

3

4    EXAMINATION BY MR. RUBBINACCIO:

5             Q       Please tell the members of the Grand Jury your
```

6   name and how you are employed.

7   A   My name is Walter B. Frankel, and I'm a psychologist.

8   I work at the Richard Hall Community Mental Health Center in

9   Somerset County.

10   Q   Are you employed there as a clinical

11   psychologist?

12   A   Yes, I am.

13   Q   How long have you been so employed there?

14   A   Since October of 1983.

15   Q   Is it correct to call you Dr. Frankel?

16   A   Yes.

17   Q   Dr. Frankel, did you have occasion to see a

18   Jessica Spiegel?

19   A   Yes, I did.

20   Q   Can you tell the members of the Grand Jury on

21   what day or dates did you see Jessica?

22   A   If I can refer to some notes here, that would be

23   helpful. I saw Jessica on one occasion, November 4, 1983.

24   Q   And can you tell the members of the Grand Jury

25   how that contact was made?

Frankel   27

1   A   Well, I had been previously contacted by Jessica's

2   mother, Valori Mulvey Spiegel. She had come in originally

3   to our clinic in September, prior to my being employed there,

4   and was seen by another psychologist on staff for an initial

5   interview.

6   Q   Did that interview take place with Jessica

7   Spiegel also?

8   A   No. She was not present at that time. She indicated

9   that she could wait for services. She was put on a waiting

10   list, which we have. She contacted the center again on her

11   own initiative on October 31st. I fielded that phone call.

12   I then assumed the case from the first psychologist, who was

13   leaving the clinic and had transferred the case to me.

14   Q   Had that particular psychologist seen Jessica

15   at all?

16   A   I don't believe he had. If I could just look at his

17   notes here, I could verify that. It does not appear that

18   Jessica was at the initial interview, just the mother, Valori

19   Spiegel.

20   Q   When did you have occasion to speak with Jessica

21   Spiegel?

22   A   Not until November 4th, as I indicated.

23   Q   On November 4th did you see her in person at

24   your clinic?

25   A   Yes, I did.

The Ax Falls

Still engulfed in my cloud of naivete, I proceeded with my regularly scheduled visits with Jessie. On Saturday I picked her up at 10:00 a.m. accompanied by my baby-sitter Claudine, who was Dr. Lentchner's stepdaughter. In keeping with Steven Haft's instructions, I tried to have Janeen or Claudine with Jessie and me at all times, so as not to be vulnerable to more accusations of sexual misconduct, should they be in the offing. Until that Saturday, I truly believed we would not hear any more of that nonsense.

That morning when Jessie, Claudine and I stopped at the diner for breakfast, I had a clear indication that the nonsense had not stopped. As we were eating, Jessie suddenly said, "Daddy, don't put your face in my pagina." Claudine and I looked at each other as though we had just seen a Martian.

"Jessie, what did you say?" I asked.

"I said, don't put your face in my pagina," she repeated. Both times the statement was made with absolutely no emotion or upset. It was clear she was repeating something she had heard. She did not know what it meant.

"Jessie, where did you hear that word?" I asked. She replied she didn't know and lapsed into baby talk, asking for ice cream. I let it drop. I was embarrassed and unsure how to handle this with Claudine there. For the rest of the meal, we just ignored it.

That afternoon as Jessie was about to take her afternoon nap, she said, "Daddy, you hurt my bummy." She then used the word "pagina" again but told me this was part of a dream. I asked her to show me where her "pagina" was and she pointed to her buttocks. When I tried to question her further, she became silly and would not respond. Five minutes later she was asleep.

I walked into the kitchen, Janeen and Claudine were talking about Jessie's new vocabulary. "What are you going to do?" Janeen asked.

"I have no idea," I replied. "I guess I better call Steven." Although it was Saturday, I was so bewildered I had to call him at home. I told him the circumstances and he reiterated his feeling that Valori intended to persist with the sexual abuse allegations. Jessie's words confirmed that. He again told me not to be alone with her and continue to keep a journal as to where we were and what we did. I assured him I was doing so and told him Janeen and

Claudine were here with us. He suggested I call Valori and try to reason with her about this.

I called and told her what Jessie had said to me. She replied, "I know, she told me the same thing and I believe her." I asked Valori if she had taught Jessie the word "vagina" and she said "Yes." Then she told me she had taken Jessie to a psychologist, but would not tell me his name. I explained that we should both be involved when it comes to doctors, but she refused to discuss that and said, "We're waiting and we're going to put a stop to it."

I immediately responded, "Waiting for what?"

"I don't know yet," she paradoxically replied.

Despite my fervent pleas to resolve this for the sake of our child, she hung up. I stood looking at the telephone in total frustration and dismay. I had no idea how to handle this.

The situation deteriorated even more in the following weeks. Jessie continued to say the same two phrases, "Daddy hurt my bummy," and "Daddy put his face in my pagina." Each time, they were said with no conviction, no emotion and with no sense that she understood what they meant. Though I repeatedly tried to talk with Valori about this, I got nowhere.

On Wednesday evening, November 30, Janeen and I took Jessie to her favorite Chinese restaurant. I did not let Valori know that Janeen was with me simply because I did not want to aggravate things. I was following Steven's instructions and not spending time alone with Jessie. Sitting at the table, Jessie said, "Daddy, don't put your face in my pagina," and "Do they have ice cream here?" Both statements were made in the same breath with no difference in emotional tone. Janeen and I sat silently. Several minutes later, I ordered Jessie her favorite ice cream.

We finished dinner and returned Jessie to Valori's apartment at approximately 8:00 p.m. As usual, Valori met us at the bottom of the steps. As was also the norm, Jessie began to cry and complain when I attempted to give her to Valori. She literally clung to my shirt screaming. I convinced her it was okay, that Daddy would be back Saturday. I told Valori I needed to discuss the continuing situation and asked if I could call her later.

She said, "Call me at 10:00." She turned and walked up the stairs with Jessie still whimpering. Unknown to Valori, Janeen had been sitting in the back of my camper watching the entire episode.

At precisely 10:00 p.m. I called Valori's apartment. There was no answer. I called periodically until midnight. By now I was truly worried. Had Valori decided not to answer? Had she taken off with Jessie again? Not knowing what else to do, I called the police department in her municipality, Franklin Township. I explained the situation to the officer and asked if a patrol car could stop at the apartment to see if they were home and everything was okay. I gave my phone number and asked the police to call me back after they checked.

Twenty minutes later, Officer Joe Serotowitz called, saying he had gone to the apartment. Valori had answered the door and told the officer she had been sleeping. Officer Serotowitz informed me that Valori said she had not seen me for more than a week, that I was harassing her and constantly calling the police. In addition, he intended to file charges against me for filing a false police report and harassing Valori. I suggested that before he did so he would be wise to check the police department records to see if I had ever called the Franklin Township Police before. We agreed to speak the next day.

When I spoke to Officer Serotowitz the following day, his whole attitude had changed. I told him I had a witness with me the day before, as well as a receipt signed and dated by Valori for the support payment I had given her. I guess he also checked his records and found I had never called the police before. I then asked him to repeat what Valori had told him. "She told me point blank, Doc, she hadn't seen you for a week." Following his apology, he told me he certainly would not file charges against me and would testify for me should it be needed.

These events, including those still to come, were all part of Valori's apparently predetermined, complex plan. Also unknown to me, Valori had already taken Jessie to several medical doctors, hoping to convince one of them that Jessie had been abused. She wanted the doctor to file a sexual abuse report with the Division of Youth and Family Services or DYFS (die fuss). That would set in motion an investigation which could easily ally Valori with the authorities. But none of the doctors would file such a report because they found nothing unusual. Valori's plan was stalemated.

Valori's accusation separated me from my daughter, ruined my career and drained my bank account. It also hung a 15 year jail term over my head.

The actions of an accuser like Valori, are not just extreme examples of revenge, but stem from severe psychological problems which may lie inactive for some time. No sane mother could consciously sacrifice the health and well-being of her child, by using the child as a tool for revenge. Often these problems are triggered by perceived rejection, personal failure or a person's inability to come to terms with his/her own emotions. Accusers manufacture false charges rather than deal with their own emotional shortcomings. In Valori's case, the trigger was her perceived rejection by me.

December 1983

On Saturday, December 3, Claudine and I drove to Valori's apartment to pick up Jessie. It was my practice to try to have Claudine with me each time I visited with Jessie. This was especially true on the weekends when Jessie stayed overnight. I had a standing arrangement with Claudine to baby-sit every other weekend and on overnight visits.

We would drive to Valori's, pick up Jessie, go out for breakfast and then ride back to my apartment. Most often, Janeen would arrive later because she worked very late on Friday evenings and lived a good distance away. She would stay over on Saturday evenings. It worked out well. The three of them often went shopping after breakfast, giving me time for writing or chores around the house. We would spend the rest of Saturday and Sunday together.

Now I realize, I too frequently made Jessie's needs the responsibility of Janeen and Claudine. If I could do it over again, I know I would spend every moment I could with my little girl. Unfortunately, I did not recognize it then. At any rate, this particular weekend was one of those rare weekends when Janeen stayed over both Friday and Saturday night. There was a special reason for it.

The previous week Janeen and I talked seriously about marriage. Although we knew it was soon for such a decision and both of our families and friends would no doubt hold that view, we felt that was what we wanted. I was beginning to accept the fact that Valori would persist in causing problems and I had already decided to ask for custody of Jessie unless Valori completely cooperated. Knowing how genuine our love felt, I didn't want my problems with Valori to overshadow my relationship with Janeen.

Janeen and I decided to get married with only a few of our close friends knowing. We would tell others after the fact. That way, we could be spared the advice from well-meaning friends and relatives. We also decided to tell Claudine that weekend, since she would be there and hear our discussions. When she arrived, Janeen and I told her. In many ways, Claudine was a wise thirteen-year-old and she was very happy to hear the news. We made it clear to her that we did not want Jessie to know yet. She had enough to deal with as it was. Claudine understood this.

It was usual for Claudine and me to pick up Jessie without Janeen, even when she was at my apartment. Naturally, I tried to avoid having Janeen and Valori together, even though they tried to be cordial with each other. This morning, breakfast was uneventful.

Jessie, Claudine and I ate at the diner near Valori's as we usually did. On the drive to my apartment, Jessie was strapped in her car seat up front. Claudine was all the way in the back of the camper. I don't think she heard the following conversation. I was glad she didn't.

"Daddy, you are not supposed to hurt my pagina," said Jessie out of nowhere.

I must admit, I was getting very frustrated and tired of hearing this. I was quite sharp and confronted her directly. "Jessie, why are you saying this? You know Daddy doesn't hurt you."

"Yes Daddy does," she said.

"Jessie, did someone tell you to say this to me?" I asked.

"Mommy says I should tell you not to hurt me," she replied.

I was angry. We went around again with me saying, Mommy must have made a mistake and Jessie insisting that she was supposed to say what Mommy told her or she would get smacked.

A few hours after we arrived at my apartment, Janeen took Jessie and Claudine to the mall to buy Jessie some new shoes. That gave me the opportunity to call Valori. By now, I had had enough of this nonsense and I intended to confront Valori. I did exactly that. I asked her directly if she had told Jessie to say that to me. To my surprise she admitted talking to Jessie about it. Valori said, "I told her if you hurt her that she should tell you not to."

She again reiterated her belief that Jessie was telling the truth. It was impossible for me to conceive how a two and a half-year-old could alone make up such a thing. Valori said Jessica was in therapy, then retracted it, then later made reference to it again, still refusing to give me the doctor's name. She repeated that Jessica was telling the truth and said again, "We're going to put a stop to it."

Finally, I brought things to a head. I told her that unless she cooperated, I would file a motion for custody of Jessica. I restated this intention in a note to her which I sent at Steven's suggestion. The note, appearing as Exhibit B, asks for Valori's cooperation and implies that I would begin custody actions if I didn't get it.

EXHIBIT B

12/5/83

Val,

Since our phone conversations don't seem to be going so well, and since you feel I am harrassing you I've decided to write instead. I am hoping that this medium will enable us to develop a cooperative relationship which heretofore (since Cincinnatti) has been lacking.

Rather than going through courts and/or lawyers; I am asking that you respond with what Judge Collester has called "reasonableness" and please provide me with the names of the Drs. to whom you took Jese. As a joint legal parent I am entitled to know. I would also like the name of her school and teacher.

I hope you will see your way clear to respond affirmitively. If I don't receive a response by mail by a week from today I will assume your response to be negative.

Lawrence Spiegel
Larry

A Question of Innocence

When Janeen, Jessie and Claudine came home from shopping, my first wife, Pauline, also arrived for a visit. Pauline and I had remained friends despite our divorce. For several hours all of us talked in the kitchen about the situation while Jessie and Claudine played in the other room. Pauline left about 8:00 p.m. While I put Jessie to bed, I wondered if Valori had surmised that Janeen and I would soon marry. Could the situation with Jessie be Valori's way of striking back?

Jessie interrupted my thoughts when she said, "Daddy, sometimes I'm afraid of my dreams." I did not know if this had anything to do with the statements Valori had taught her to say or whether it was related to bedtime fears. I assured her, however, that Daddy was here and there was nothing to fear. After a few minutes of allaying her fears, her head was on my chest and she was fast asleep.

On Sunday morning, our friends and neighbors, John and Nancy Reber, visited for a short time. Later that afternoon, my brother Rick, his wife Debra and their two children arrived. We had planned to go out to dinner together. The kids played in Jessie's room for a few hours, while the adults sat and talked. About 3:00 p.m. Claudine's father, Larry Lentchner, came to take her home.

Janeen and I told Debra and Rick of our decision to marry. They, too, were excited and wished us the best. About 5:00 p.m., we all went to eat. Then Janeen and I took Jessie back to Valori's. This time Jessie began to complain about returning to her mother before we were even out of the restaurant. It was all I could do to summon the strength to be firm with her. She cried all the way back and refused to talk to me. She was still crying when I gave her to Valori at the bottom of the steps. My last words to Jessie were, "Daddy will come to see you on Wednesday, honey."

Little did I know that I would not see her for nearly seven months until she was carried in hysterics into the foreboding environment of a criminal courtroom to testify against her Daddy.

On Wednesday afternoon, December 7, I arrived at Valori's apartment to pick up Jessie for my afternoon visit. It was the first time since October that I had come alone to see her. I saw Steven that Monday and helped him prepare the motion for custody. I put in writing what I told her on the phone, stating that her attorney should contact Steven by the end of the week to resolve the difficulties or we would file our motion for custody. I was not playing this game anymore.

As I pulled into the parking lot of Valori's apartment, I immediately noticed her car was not there. I went to the door and rang the bell. There was no answer. Here we go again, I thought, certain that Valori was up to her old tricks, denying my visitation with Jessie. It did not dawn on me that she was up to some new tricks.

I sat in my camper in the parking lot for over an hour. Still there was no sign of them. Then I drove around the college campus and past Valori's aunt's house looking for her. I went back to the parking lot. Depression overcame me and I began to cry. I realized these incidents must be causing great confusion for Jessica. I looked in the rearview mirror at my own reflection. The strain of these incidents was beginning to take its toll. I was looking very worn and tired. I realized Valori would come home at some point and I was determined to wait. My sadness was replaced by anger and frustration at Valori. I called my office and had my secretary reschedule my appointments. I wanted to see Jessie, at least to say "hello." I also had to confront Valori.

About six hours later, her car pulled into the parking lot. She got out carrying Jessie, who was fast asleep. Valori whispered that she would take Jessie upstairs to bed, then come back down to talk with me. She preferred I not wake Jessie. She went upstairs and I stupidly stood outside waiting. Finally, she returned.

I confronted her with this violation of my rights. To my surprise, she appeared extremely apologetic. She told me her car broke down again. Yet I had already given her money for a new car which her father was to have bought in Georgia because it was less expensive there. Though Valori's story was difficult to swallow, she did sound sincere. She ended by telling me the gas station fixed it temporarily so she could get home, but she was not supposed to use it until it was really fixed.

Like a blithering fool, I fell hook, line and sinker. I gave her my Exxon credit card to have the car repaired. She appeared grateful. I shrugged off my anger without the slightest notion that I was less than forty-eight hours away from disaster.

Friday, December 9, was another of those clear winter days.

Despite my problems, I felt good. I worked at home in the morning and went to my dentist appointment in the afternoon. By 3:30 p.m. I was headed toward the Institute. I wanted to call Steven and update him on Wednesday's incident with Valori before my first patient arrived. The feelings of resignation and fatigue still engulfed me. As I drove to the office, I had no intuition of what awaited me.

I pulled into the parking lot, noticing nothing out of the ordinary. I parked in my usual spot at the rear of the building, took my briefcase, locked the camper and started for the office building. Taking a few steps from the camper, I noticed two men emerge from a dark blue car at the end of the lot. They walked directly toward me, showed me their badges and identified themselves as members of the county police department. They asked me to get into their car, saying they needed to talk with me. I got into the back seat.

A woman showed me her badge and said I was under arrest for sexual penetration of my infant daughter which occurred on or about the third of December within the borough of Flanders, County of Morris. Meanwhile, one of the male officers came around to my side of the car and proceeded to handcuff me. The look of astonishment, bewilderment and shock on my face was indicative of my feelings. This experience and those that followed were a nightmare.

At the police station, after being booked and fingerprinted, I was permitted to call my attorney. It was after 5:00 p.m. and I just caught Steven leaving his office. When I told him what had happened, he was as shocked as I was. He explained that this was a criminal charge and he did not want to handle it himself. He would call Herbert Korn, a criminal lawyer. Mr. Korn would call back. I sat alone in a detention room shaken and still in a state of shock.

About fifteen minutes later, Mr. Korn called. He told me not to say anything to anyone. He would send his associate, Bernie Recenello, to the police station to take care of things. By the time Bernie arrived, bail had been set at $10,000. Bernie attempted to get a reduction in bail for my release, but had little success. He said he would return to his office and have Herb Korn talk to the judge. Meanwhile, I had to stay in jail. He also said he would call Janeen at

At the police station — shock, fear, confusion — all at once.

my office and let her know the circumstances, since I had patients waiting to see me.

It was not until nearly 11:00 p.m. that Mr. Korn succeeded in having Judge Shelton lower the bail. I wrote a $1,000 bail check. Before my release, I was told my camper had been impounded to be searched for "evidence." I was also informed of a "temporary" condition of bail: I was not permitted to see or communicate with "the victim," my own infant daughter. Janeen, who had been waiting for the past several hours at my home, drove with Debra to the police station. They took me home.

As soon as we got there, I called Herb Korn at his home, which he had instructed me to do when I spoke to him from the police station. I was extremely upset, especially at the condition of bail that prevented me from seeing my little girl. When he answered the phone, I expressed my gratitude for his efforts and immediately told him of my concern about the condition of bail. His said nothing could be done now or through the weekend, but on Monday we could move to have the condition modified. That relieved my anxiety somewhat, though at the time I had no notion of how complex this one issue would become. Even though Herb was an experienced defense attorney, he had no idea of what lay ahead either. There was nothing to do but wait for Monday.

3

THE TRIALS AND THE TRAUMA

Stage 3: The Denial

Upon awakening in the morning, I was unaware of my state of shock. Aimlessly, I wandered about my home in a trance. I did not want to speak to anyone. I wouldn't answer the phone when it rang. My mind vacillated between blankness and the repeated racing thoughts of my arrest, thoughts of denial, thoughts of worry for Jessie and myself. I was functioning in the darkness of a living nightmare. Nothing could snap me out of it. I couldn't concentrate on anything for more than a few seconds. The phone rang incessantly. It all seemed unreal.

Even now, I have difficulty recalling details from that weekend and the final weeks of 1983. It is, of course, during this period of acute trauma, that the victim of a false accusation experiences the most disorientation. I functioned mechanically until the beginning of January. There were sporadic outbursts of rage followed by depression, but my basic feeling was one of overwhelming shock and denial. I couldn't believe this happened. I wished it was just a bad dream.

December 11, 1983

On Sunday morning my self-imposed isolation was abruptly ended. My colleague, Larry Lentchner and his wife, Betty, were banging loudly on my apartment door at 9:00 a.m. They had brought the morning papers and showed me the newspaper article which appears as Exhibit A. As I discovered, it was one of many articles in the papers.

EXHIBIT A

Therapist denies sex charge

A psychologist accused by Morris County authorities of sexually molesting a 2½-year-old girl issued a denial of the charges yesterday, claiming he was "set up" by someone.

Lawrence D. Spiegel, 35, a former County College of Morris psychology professor who now works in a Randolph clinic, issued the statement through his attorney, Herbert Korn.

"The charges are nothing more than the figment of a very pitiful, sick and distorted mind," Korn quoted his client.

"At this point, we know nothing about the charges, who made them and what facts they are based on," Korn said, stating Spiegel's patients are concerned with the allegations lodged Friday night by the Morris County Prosecutor's Office Sex Crimes Unit.

A statement issued Saturday by Prosecutor Lee Trumbull said the charges stemmed from a complaint filed with the state Division of Youth and Family Services. The child was examined by a doctor who confirmed a sexual assault, the prosecutor said.

Seeing the headline sparked a flurry of confused, disoriented thoughts. How did the papers find out so soon? How could they have talked to Herb Korn even before I had a chance to sit down with him? Most importantly came the realization that my arrest was public knowledge. How could I show my face in public? I wanted to run away.

From that point, the situation went from bad to worse. Before I could process the impact of the newspaper articles, the next blow struck. I could hardly believe my ears as my partner of thirteen years told me he had decided to leave the Institute for a position with a nearby psychiatric group. This, he said, had nothing whatsoever to do with my arrest and its exposure.

I was livid. Even if I gave him the benefit of the doubt, accepting the fact his decision had nothing to do with my arrest, his timing stunk. I could imagine how many others at the Institute would desert the sinking ship, once they were informed of Dr. Lentchner's resignation.

As Executive Director of the Institute, I demanded his resignation in writing as soon as possible. Dr. Lentchner exited quickly. Although his resignation was made known, Dr. Lentchner took nearly six weeks to conclude his business at the Institute. His letter of resignation, Exhibit B, would become even more significant before my ordeal actually ended.

EXHIBIT B

Psychiatric Associates of New Jersey, P.A.

20 Community Place
Morristown, New Jersey 07960
(201) 540-9550

1/30/84

To the Board of Trustees, Integrative Psychology Institute:

As of this day I resign any and all associations with the Integrative Psychology Institute, including the Special Vice President position, the Clinical Directorship and any staff position.

Sincerely,

Lawrence H. Lentchner, Ph.D.

A Question of Innocence

I fell into a long, sulking, depressed silence. In two days my whole world had collapsed. My former friend's resignation made the Institute's future very uncertain. Although there were thirteen other therapists and interns, it was Dr. Lentchner and I who were the primary driving force behind the Institute. I had horrid visions of the next board meeting, answering the questions about my arrest, and informing them of the resignation. I knew the chairman of the Board of Directors would call an emergency meeting the moment he saw the newspapers. I was already in debt from the long divorce and I no longer had the income from my teaching position. Now I was fearful that my income from the Institute was in jeopardy.

Janeen, who was very perceptive to my needs, always had found a way to help me through my problems. Now there was nothing she could do to ease my pain and worry. She, too, was in a state of shock and could only sit and helplessly watch. I remained depressed and alone. I grew anxious for the Monday meeting at Herb Korn's office.

That Sunday night I was extremely restless and filled with anxiety. I had brief, intermittent periods of light sleep, mixed with constant awakenings. At one point I heard Jessie's voice yelling, "Daddy, Daddy," as she normally did when she had a bad dream. Half asleep, I stumbled into her room, only to be confronted by her empty bed, toys, clothes and pictures. It was too much for me. I broke down and cried, remembering the times I held her in my arms, soothing her fears from a nightmare. I recalled her infant years, the many nights of rocking her in my arms as I gave her a bottle and changing her diaper.

I glanced at the clock. It was 3:25 a.m. Janeen was fast asleep. I went back to bed only to awaken again at 4:15 a.m. There was no point in trying to sleep. I got up and went into the kitchen to make some coffee. Reaching into the cabinet, my fingers automatically grasped the child safety locks I had installed. Getting milk from the refrigerator caused me to see the little magnetic pots and pans I had bought for Jessie. She was all around me, yet she was not here.

Anxiety peaked in me. I kept telling myself I would see Herb today and something would be done. They couldn't separate my little girl from me without proof of wrongdoing. This was Valori's scheme, I thought, a way to prevent me from seeing Jessie, to punish me for what she felt I had done to her, not to Jessie.

December 12 through December 15, 1983

Since the police had my camper, I drove my 1971 Cougar that morning. It took a little while to locate my lawyer's office and find a place to park. At 9:20 a.m., tired, anxious and worn, I approached a glass door with the inscription which read:

Herbert M. Korn
Attorney At Law.

He was located in an office building just a block away from the Morris County Courthouse. I gave the receptionist my name. She asked me to have a seat, she would tell Mr. Korn I was there. I was offered some coffee. "No thank you," I said automatically.

I was wondering about the man I was about to see. Although I had never met him, we had spoken on the phone once or twice in our professional capacities prior to my arrest. One of my patients was also one of his clients. My impression was of a young, competent, and somewhat abrupt, man. He sounded confident, even arrogant, yet somehow polite and friendly. It's a peculiar posture, yet one I have noticed among good trial attorneys. I had no mental picture of him and was too tired and worried to conjure one up.

I waited five minutes, then the receptionist pointed to a door, telling me to go in. Behind a desk, in a high-backed swivel chair, sat a man about my age. He was good-looking in a rugged sort of way. As we shook hands, he introduced himself in an excellent speaking voice. With an air of confidence about him, he got right down to business. "I asked Steven Haft to come over here this morning," he said. "I thought he could help fill me in."

"That's fine with me," I replied. The security of knowing Steven was coming helped me calm down a bit. Soon he arrived. He took one look at me and said, "You look like hell."

"What do you think you would look like if you had been through what I have?" I responded.

For a variety of reasons, it was fortunate that Steven had come. His legal mind was always an asset and certainly he articulated the legal history much better than I could have. But the most important thing Steven did, which never even dawned on me until that moment, was to assure Herb of my innocence. Luckily, Steven had seen Jessie and me interact often enough to have a good sense of the relationship. Just three weeks prior in Family Court, he had seen Jessie come running to me and throw herself on my lap.

We spent almost three hours trying to piece together what had transpired. How did Valori lodge the complaint with DYFS, if indeed it was Valori? How did the case get to the Prosecutor so quickly? Why had no one contacted or questioned me before an arrest was made? In asking these questions of Steve and Herb, I got my first real lesson in law. But we would not get our answers until my arraignment, when the Prosecutor would reveal them in what was called "discovery." Until then, nothing could be done.

I was outraged that we had to sit idle and wait. What about getting to see Jessie? I had told her last week, "Daddy will see you next week." If I didn't see her, she would get very upset. Through the next hour of planning, I calmed down. We finally developed a plan.

Steven would file a motion in Family Court to attempt to get information from DYFS and the Prosecutor. He would also ask the judge to modify the condition of bail, so that I might be allowed to see Jessie. Herb would do the same in criminal court. Both motions would be worded to give the judges three options: removing the restriction on visitation, allowing supervised visits or holding a hearing about the visitation question. How long would this take? Ten to fourteen days, I was told.

I sat dumbfounded. "You mean for two weeks I can't see my child and we can't even get any information?" "That's right" was the answer. At that point, I burst into another rage. I wanted to go to the Prosecutor's office, grab him by the tie and make him tell us what this was all about. I wanted to call the Governor, my state senator, etc.

It took a good deal of time for Steven and Herb to calm me down. Finally, it was agreed I would make an appointment with the social worker at DYFS who was in charge of my case. Meanwhile, my staff and friends, especially Debra and Nancy, would track down the doctors mentioned in the newspaper articles. Also Janeen, Debra, Claudine and my first wife, Pauline, would give Steven sworn statements concerning the events of the December 3 weekend. Both Herb and Steven warned me not to violate the condition of bail. I was not to communicate with Jessie.

The final item of the meeting concerned the press. The newspaper articles did not mention that this was a family matter. It sounded as though I had molested some strange two-year-old baby. Herb was adamant that I not talk to the press. All statements would have to come from Herb or Steven. I reluctantly agreed.

For the next several days we were busy getting ready for court. Even so, I was still in a daze, functioning mostly on automatic, alternating between a total denial of the situation and obsessive worry about Jessie. Herb and Steven got their motions underway and I made an appointment to see Kay Curtiss, the DYFS social worker in Somerset County where Valori lived.

Once again, I had to cancel my patients for the week. I was too upset to see anyone. I spent most of my time at home with Janeen, Debra and Nancy, pouring over Somerset County phone books for medical associations listing the pediatricians and child psychologists. I wanted to locate the doctors involved, if indeed there were any. I also had countless telephone conversations with friends, relatives and members of the Board of Directors of the Institute. Time and again, I had to recount the events; what we knew and what we didn't. I succeeded in getting the President of our Institute to postpone a meeting for a few weeks until we knew more.

On Wednesday, I drove to the Somerset County office of the Division of Youth and Family Services. I knew this agency was fraught with incompetence from my own past professional relationship with them. Yet, I assumed it was an agency which served the family when it could. It wasn't long before I got my first taste of the bureaucratic, almost arrogant, disposition of this agency. When I finally saw Kay Curtiss, a very cold, distant and insensitive woman, her manner clearly indicated that she held me guilty until proven innocent. I asked many questions; I got no answers. She would not tell me who filed the charge, though I assumed it was, of course, Valori.

When I discussed the matter of a two-year-old being programmed by her mother, I received the standard reply, "Children don't lie." She would not give the names of the doctors involved, but did admit that DYFS had not taken Jessie for a medical examination. They had only Valori's word that a doctor had confirmed abuse.

I asked why DYFS had violated its own procedural manual, which calls for a medical exam in suspected abuse cases. Kay Curtiss said she felt it unnecessary, as though she had some special training that enabled her to make such a judgement. Why wasn't I notified and why was the case referred to the Prosecutor on such a flimsy allegation? I was told it was standard procedure. I asked for a copy of the files. I was refused, more agency standard procedure. There was no point continuing the discussion.

I invoked my prerogatives as a licensed psychologist and asked to see the supervisor. I presented him with a formal Authorization for Release of Records form which I normally used in my practice. Obviously, he had not confronted a situation like this before, and not knowing what to do, he ordered Kay Curtiss to give me the records. They included the drawings of human figures shown here as Exhibits C1 and C2. On one figure, Jessie had been asked to put a mark every place Daddy kissed her and on the second figure, every place Daddy had touched her. Jessie put marks on many parts of the body, with the exception of the genital areas. She concluded her work by scribbling on the paper.

EXHIBIT C1

- 3 -

B. DIAGRAM AND LIST OF ALL MARKINGS ON CHILD

PART I - diagram

CHILD'S NAME _____

#1 asked Jessica to circle everywhere on figures that her father had kissed her it. it received. Ref Kay Curtiss, DYFS, and finished

Please indicate the lesion or marking on the drawing
with numbers corresponding to marking description on
the next page.

JESSICA Spiegel

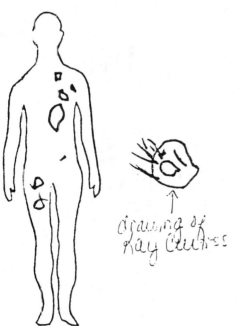

drawing of Kay Curtiss

10-7-83

Physician's Signature

EXHIBIT C2

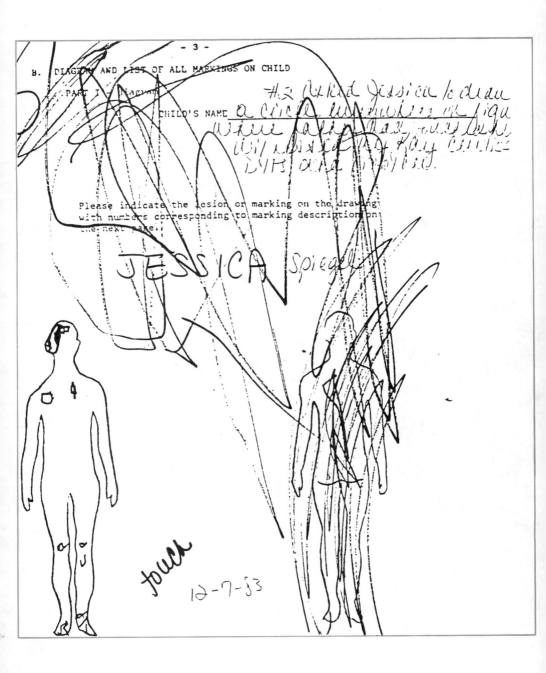

The Trials And Trauma

I returned to my apartment and sat down with the records. Actually, they were just scribbled notes by Kay Curtiss. Their contents served to make the events even more incomprehensible. They merely verified the fact that Valori had gone to see Kay Curtiss, on Wednesday, December 7, the day she and Jessica were not home for my visitation. Ms. Curtiss had seen them together that day and, in addition to Valori's statements, she also elicited the statement from Jessie, "Daddy put his face in my pagina." Still, it seemed impossible that the charges were filed so quickly and I was arrested the second day after Valori went to DYFS. There had to be more to this. But what?

Meanwhile, we continued our attempt to locate the doctor who examined Jessie. As I sat in my bedroom looking at the DYFS records, I heard shouts from the kitchen. Nancy was yelling, "I found him, I found him!"

Nancy had done it again! She had spoken to a secretary at the Richard Hall Mental Health Center in Bridgewater, New Jersey, who confirmed Valori's visits with Dr. Frankel. Of all the physicians and psychologists in the congested Somerset area, Nancy had found the doctor on her second phone call. I grabbed the number from her hand, kissed her and ran to the phone.

Dr. Frankel said DYFS had contacted him and he was not supposed to give me any information. As a professional courtesy, however, he would informally speak briefly with me. He said Valori had been there three times. The first visit was in September when she saw a psychologist who was no longer with the center. At that time, Valori said she thought that I was hypnotizing Jessie. He then saw Valori once alone and once with Jessie. He was writing a report to DYFS, and though he could not talk in specifics, he felt his report would "help" my case. We later received a copy of that report, which appears here as Exhibit D.

EXHIBIT D

Richard Hall Community Mental Health Center
of Somerset County

500 North Bridge Street & Vogt Drive
Bridgewater, New Jersey 08807
(201) 725-2800

Mr. Anthony G. Wahl
Attorney at Law   December 27, 1983
Hanover and Ridgedale Avenues
P.O. Box 1309-R
Morristown, NJ 07920-1309   RE: MULVEY, (SPIEGEL) VALORI

Dear Mr. Wahl:

I have assembled the following "events profile" which may be of help in your legal efforts on behalf of Valori Mulvey Spiegel. (AKA Valori Mulvey).

1. ' am a psychologist licensed to practice in the state of New Jersey and am associated with the Richard Hall Community Mental Health Center in Bridgewater Township, Somerset County, New Jersey.

2. Valori Mulvey (aka Valori Spiegel) first contacted this clinic on 09-19-83, and was seen by Charles Mark, Psy.D. - a licensed psychologist - on 09-29-83. Dr. Mark's note indicates that Ms. Mulvey's main concern at that time was her belief that her ex-husband, a psychologist, had been hypnotizing their 2½ year old daughter, Jessica, to dislike her maternal grandparents (i.e., Mrs. Mulvey's parents). Dr. Mark commented in his note that, "the veracity of this accusation could not be determined. . . ". Ms. Mulvey indicated that she and her daughter were otherwise doing well and agreed to some supportive therapy. She was informed that there was a waiting list but said she could wait or get in touch sooner if the situation became urgent. She was given the phone number of Guideline, the Center's 24-hour crisis unit. In light of their discussion that day, Dr. Mark was reserved in making any clinical judgement regarding Mrs. Mulvey other than to comment that Ms. Mulvey is an "anxious woman" who had been contending with some very stressful separation and divorce issues.

3. On 10-31-83 I received a phone call from Valori Mulvey in which she expressed concern that her daughter, Jessica, age 2½, may have been inappropriately touched by her father during a recent overnight visitation with him. Ms. Mulvey's concerns were based on the following observations:

    (a) Jessica was said to have stated that father, Larry Spiegel, had "hurt my bummy", "bummy" being Jessica's word for the vaginal area.
    (b) Jessica was said to have had a nightmare at her father's the evening of the alleged "touching" and for five nights subsequent to that visit when she was returned to Ms. Mulvey's. This was an unusual occurrence, according to Ms. Mulvey.

The Trials And Trauma

(c) Ms. Mulvey stated she had taken Jessica to Dr. Michael Lapkin, her pediatrician, and that he observed a "minor irritation" in the vaginal area. She said he felt that such a finding could be consistent with any number of causes and did not comprise evidence of abuse. A meeting was scheduled with me for the following day in view of the urgent sounding nature of the matter. Ms. Mulvey sounded concerned and sincere in relaying of the details.

4. On 11-01-83 Ms. Mulvey was seen individually. Above information was reviewed, as was relevant history concerning separation and divorce. When asked how she learned of the aforementioned alleged inappropriate touching by her ex-husband, Ms. Mulvey indicated that, only after she allayed Jessica's irrational fears that she would be punished for telling, did Jessica speak of Daddy's hurting "my bummy". Ms. Mulvey said that after they spoke Jessica seemed relieved and became her usual playful and happy self, whereas before she had appeared somewhat distracted and inattentive. Two plans were agreed on: (a) that I would talk to Dr. Lapkin to get his impressions (b) that Ms. Mulvey would talk to her ex-husband about whether he had experienced any difficulty re: toilet training issues with Jessica that might have resulted in some overly harsh but not abuse-intending treatment of Jessica's vaginal area.

5. Although called on 11-01-83, Dr. Lapkin was not reached by me until 11-02-83. His report was somewhat at variance with Ms. Mulvey's. He maintained in our conversation that, in the visit referred to above, there was no indication of Jessica's having any vaginal trauma or irritation. He said he relayed this clearly to Ms. Mulvey but conceded that if Jessica was complaining it might be consisten with harsh wiping surrounding toileting activities.

6. 11-04-83 - Ms. Mulvey came to the clinic with Jessica. She stated that the previous morning, i.e., (11-03-83) the day after an afternoon with her father, i.e., (11-02-83) Jessica said the following: "Can we get up? My bummy hurts. Daddy put his face in my bummy". When asked "what part?" by her mother, Jessica was said to have responded "his nose". Ms. Mulvey told me she took Jessica back to Dr. Lapkin yesterday and he confirmed the presence of an external vaginal irritation.

I spent considerable time engaging Jessica individually in play in an attempt to secure further information and/or insight into the situation. Jessica separated easily from her mother who left the playroom after several minutes. She was neither withdrawn, anxious about her mother's whereabouts, or overly active, despite the fact that she was alone with me, an adult male stranger. We played with some dolls, albeit not anatomically detailed ones. Despite considerable questioning on my part, Jessica provided minimal information. At one point, she said "Daddy hurt Jessica's bummy". She would not or could not elaborate. At another point a male adult doll was said to have done "something bad" to a child doll. Again elaboration was not forthcoming.

I discussed these findings with Ms. Mulvey and told her I would like to further confer with Dr. Lapkin about their last visit. It is possible

Mr. Anthony G. Wahl
December 27, 1983

Page 3
RE: MULVEY - (SPIEGEL)

that Ms. Mulvey received the impression that I was going to call DYFS, although I did not categorically state such. I made clear that my decision would not be made until after consulting with Dr. Lapkin.

7. 11-04-83 in a telephone conversation Dr. Lapkin confirmed some minor external irritation of Jessica's labia minora. He stressed that such irritations are not uncommon in children and could stem from unintended harsh wiping, a child's self-stimulatory rubbing, and so on. He did not seem to feel that the matter warranted a DYFS investigation.

The decision on my part not to inform DYFS was made on several grounds.

(a) Most of the data suggesting abuse was from Ms. Mulvey, and there seemed to be a number of factors alluded to above which might be considered mitigating.

(b) Jessica's own verbal input was slight and equivocal. But most of all she did not appear to be a child who exhibited any of the classic signs of psychological distress, e.g., withdrawal, anxiety, hyperactivity, clinging behavior, etc.

(c) Dr. Lapkin, an experienced pediatrician, struck a very cautionary tone with regard to forming an impression of sexual abuse.

I did try to telephone Mrs. Abby Gallagher, Ms. Mulvey's aunt, on two occasions during the week of 11-07-83 - 11-11-83 but there was no answer. I was given her number as the means by which to communicate with Ms. Mulvey. My intent was to inform Ms. Mulvey of my decision "not to report" but to encourage her to take this initiative on her own should she genuinely deem it in Jessica's and her own best interest. I also wanted to encourage Ms. Mulvey to continue therapy involvement with someone, albeit not necessarily with me.

It is my professional opinion, despite differences in the "reading" of a highly complicated and ambiguous situation that Ms. Mulvey, like myself, was acting sincerely and with the best interests of her child at heart. Her expressions of concern were, I believe, bonafide and she seemed to genuinely believe there was some type of improper conduct going on. The information available to me at the time did not prove compelling enough to make a report to DYFS, however, it is impossible to rule out the actual occurrence of improper conduct.

I certify that the facts stated above are true to the best of my knowledge, information, and belief.

Walter B. Frankel, Ph.D.
Walter B. Frankel, Ph.D.
Senior Psychologist
Licensed New Jersey and Pennsylvania

WBF:drc

Was Dr. Frankel the one that notified DYFS? His answer was an emphatic, "NO!" But he did give me the name of the pediatrician he had spoken with, whom Valori had taken Jessie to see, a Dr. Michael Lapkin of the Somerset Pediatric Group. The moment Dr. Frankel hung up, I called Lapkin.

Dr. Lapkin had also been contacted by DYFS and told not to release any information. But he was even more willing to talk to me than Dr. Frankel. He told me specifically that Valori had brought Jessica to see him on two occasions, concerning possible sexual abuse. He related that on both occasions he found nothing to substantiate these accusations. I asked him if he had notified DYFS and he said, "Absolutely not." He told me another physician called him a few weeks later, saying Valori had also brought Jessie there for an exam. Valori told this physician that Dr. Lapkin would substantiate her charges. Lapkin told this physician he found nothing and sincerely questioned Valori's motives. His report, Exhibit E, appears below.

EXHIBIT E

Somerset Pediatric Group P.A.   MICHAEL LAPKIN, M.D., F.A.A.P.

A Professional Association

155 UNION AVENUE, BRIDGEWATER, N.J. 08807
1-C NEW AMWELL ROAD, SOMERVILLE, (HILLSBOROUGH) N.J. 08876

To Whom It May Concern:

I saw Jessica Spiegel on two occasions, the dates were 10/31/83 and 11/3/83. The child was brought to my office because the mother was concerned that the child suffered trauma to her vagina by her father. On first examination there was no evidence of any abnormality. The second examination showed minimal irritation to the labia majora. However, the vaginal vault and no internal structures showed any signs of abnormality. I explained to the mother that the irritation to the labia could have been caused by clothing, toilet tissue, etc.

Under no circumstances did my examination reveal any evidence that this child was abused.

Sincerely,

M. L. Lapkin, M.D. LD NW

Some months later, Herb succeeded in getting the typed records from DYFS. They pretty much substantiated the scenario we suspected had taken place. When examined closely, however, several subtleties emerged, which left us in awe. The agency actually documented its apparent negligence and incompetence in its own report.

A section of the DYFS report by Kay Curtiss appears here. Clearly seen in paragraphs one to four, DYFS was aware of Jessie's visits to Dr. Lapkin and Dr. Frankel. Paragraph five indicates their awareness of a third physician, Dr. Rogers, the family physician Lapkin spoke about. The last sentence in paragraph five states that none of these professionals called DYFS to report any abuse.

One paragraph indicates that DYFS also spoke to Dr. Frankel. He reiterated that he found no substantiation of abuse. Paragraph seven shows that DYFS, nevertheless, contacted the prosecutor, despite the fact that three professionals would not substantiate any abuse. Therefore, the DYFS investigation, prior to making its referral to the prosecutor, consisted of one day of investigating. Below is an excerpt from the DYFS report, appearing as Exhibit F. Incidentally, it did not explicitly state who made the initial report to the agency. It seemed clear to us, however, that it must have been Valori.

EXHIBIT F

Jessica Spiegel _____ CASE # ___KC188150___ PAGE _____

Mother is an undergraduate psychology major at Rutgers and hopes to get her degree this year. Jessica attends nursery school. Father pays child support in cash directly to mother not through probation as mother had a problem with his checks bouncing in the past.

Mother brought her yearly date book which she started keeping after the divorce with her. She was able to relate specific events and dates by using this book.

On 10/26/83, Jessica had a nightmare after visiting father. Mother called father to tell him about the nightmare and find out how Jessica behaved during the day. Father told mother Jessica had had a nightmare the previous weekend when she was visiting him. That

The Trials And Trauma

2

morning Jessica told mother that she didn't want to go see father.
The next morning when mother was dressing Jessica, Jessica complained
that her pants were too tight and complained all day that her bummy
(buttocks) hurt. That night in the bath Jessica complained that
her bummy hurt. Mother observed her vaginal area to be red.

3

Jessica had nightmares every night following. On 10/31/83, mother
asked Jessica what was scaring her and causing her to have nightmares.
Jessica said she couldn't tell her mother because she would get angry.
Jessica then started to cry and shake all over and told her mother
that father was huring her bummy. Mother told Jessica she would take
care of it. The next day mother took Jessica to Dr. Lapkin, Somerset
Pediatric Group and Dr. Wally Frankel, Richard Hall Mental Health
Center. Mother had originally applied for counseling at Richard
Hall Mental Health Center in September as father was telling Jessica
who she could and couldn't love. Dr. Lapkin wanted to see Jessica
again after her next visit with father. Dr. Lapkin told mother that
something was probably happening considering vaginal redness and
nightmares. Indicated to mother that there was little evidence that
would stand up in court.

4

Mother also advised her attorney, Anthony Wahl, 540-8432, of
allegations. Attorney allegedly brought this information to
Judge Kollaster's attention at a hearing on 11/16/83. According
to mother, father has taken mother back into court on several
occasions and judge is fed up with situation.

5

Mother took Jessica to Cincinnati to get away from father and visit
her sister - also to Georgia to visit her mother. While at maternal
grandmother's, Jessica acted out the abuse, put her face in mother's
lap and wouldn't stop at mother's request. Mother finally had to
push her away. Jessica then asked mother "am I bad?" While in

---

Cincinnati the mother took Jessica to Margaret Sanger Clinic of Ohio
(513-721-2234) where they saw Joan Schenberg (sex counselor, marriage
enrichment and therapist) who talked with mother about teaching Jessica
that her body is her own, she has the right to say no, etc. Father filed
complaint against mother for taking Jessica out of state and followed them
to Ohio. Mother also took Jessica to Dr. Rogers, family physician,
828-5962 or 5314. Jessica reportedly told Dr. Rogers about sexual abuse.
Dr. Rogers saw Jessica on 11/28, 12/1 and 12/5 after visits with father.
Mother sought help from all these professionals - none of whom she felt
helped her. None of these professionals called DYFS to report possible
abuse.

Interviewed Jessica in presence of her mother as she seemed reluctant to
separate from her. Jessica very bright and verbal, knew her colors and
numbers, coordination excellent, able to draw circles and a face with eyes,

mouth and hair. Used anatomically correct dolls to interview Jessica. Jessica undressed dolls and immediately grabbed adult male doll's penis. Body parts identified correctly - Jessica called nipples "titties", buttocks "bum", vagina and penis were "birdie", later she referred to penis as "penis", pubic hair was "fuzz." Jessica was embarrassed when she called penis by correct term and went to her mother and sucked on her bottle for reassurance. We played going to visit daddy with the dolls. Jessica drove them to daddy's house in his van, undressed female doll for bed and put diaper on her. Jessica still wears a diaper at night. Jessica said that daddy wears panties to bed. Positioned dolls sleeping side by side, female doll's head on daddy's outstretched arm in bed. Jessica told me that daddy hurts her bum - demonstrated how by placing female doll on her stomach, then Jessica knelt over the doll and put her face on doll's buttocks. I then had Jessica draw circles on pictures of body outlines where father had kissed or touched her. Touch was the second drawing - when Jessica started to make circles on back of the figure she took magic marker and made large marks all over figure. —

Arrangements made for mother to take Jessica to Morris County Prosecutor's Office where they were to be interviewed by Inv. Janet Rapisardi. Telephone call to Ms. Rapisardi to relate allegations and interview.

7/83 Wally Frankel, Richard Hall Mental Health Center, called and spoke to Suzanne Maggiore. He had seen mother and Jessica and decided not to report to DYFS as he could not substantiate abuse.

9/83 Telephone call to Janet Rapisardi, Morris County Prosecutor's Office. Jessica's account of abuse the same as what she told me. Jessica also told Janet that daddy licks her birdie. Father did not visit with Jessica on 12/7. Visit rescheduled for 12/11. Father will be arrested today on charges of sexual assault.

Telephone call to mother. Wants to take Jessica to counseling. Doesn't want to return to Dr. Frankel who they saw once as he did not support them. Referred mother to Rutgers Community Mental Health Center.

/15/83 Telephone call to Dr. John Rogers. Saw Jessica on 11/29/83 for suspected sexual abuse. No evidence any trauma on this date. Jessica had been seen prior to this by Dr. Lapkin who found inflammation around vaginal area. Also seen by Wally Frankel, Richard Hall Mental Health Center. Dr. Rogers

(type this side first)

It must have escaped Ms. Curtiss' attention that Jessie was complaining about nightmares not reality, even though the word "nightmare" appears five times on the first page of her report. It is also clear from the DYFS notes that Valori had lied about Dr. Lapkin's findings when he examined Jessie. It appears that Ms. Curtiss simply accepted Valori's word as fact.

The Trials And Trauma

The apparent ineptitude and incompetence of DYFS was demonstrated again about a year later in a separate incident in May of 1985. At that time, I was working with a couple in my clinical practice who had a three and a half-year-old girl. One evening, as a consequence of a series of events, the mother created such a disturbance that the police and DYFS were called. My business card was on the bulletin board in their apartment, so the police called my office. I went there immediately.

When I arrived, the DYFS worker was preparing papers to remove the child from the home. I interceded and volunteered to take the child to her relatives out of state, rather than have her placed in a foster home. The DYFS worker said he would check on that, but the child would have to spend the night in a foster home. The following day, I sent Janeen to the DYFS headquarters to request that the child be released in my custody and be flown to her relatives in Detroit. As incredible as it sounds, this same agency which pressed child molestation against me — charges which were still pending in court — released this child into my custody. I received a letter, Exhibit G, from DYFS a few days later, thanking me for my help. Need I say more about the credibility and competence of this agency?

EXHIBIT G

State of New Jersey

DEPARTMENT OF HUMAN SERVICES
DIVISION OF YOUTH AND FAMILY SERVICES

Reply to:
Morris County District Office
Gateway Plaza
121 Center Grove Rd.
Randolph, New Jersey 07869
(201) 361-8400

May 28, 1985

Dr. Lawrence Spiegel
40 Baldwin Road
Parsippany, NJ   07054

Re: ▇▇▇

Dear Dr. Spiegel:

Please find enclosed the releases of information which Mr. and
Mrs. ▇▇▇ signed authorizing Alana ▇▇▇ to be released to you
and Janeen Love. Thank you for all of your help at the time of
Alanas' placement.

Sincerely

Emil DeRiggi
Social Worker

enclosures

EDR:mg

New Jersey Is An Equal Opportunity Employer

The Trials And Trauma

December 16, 1983

It was our first day in court since my arrest. Both Herb's and Steve's motions were heard at the Morris County Courthouse. At 9:00 a.m., Herb's motion to modify the condition of bail was heard in criminal court. Steven's motion, asking the family court judge to do the same, would be heard later that day. We viewed our chances in family court as slim, since I was faced with a criminal charge.

Both motions asked the judge to either modify the condition of bail so that I could see Jessie or hold a court hearing to review the condition of bail. Steven and his junior partner, Eric Kapnick, met me at Herb's office. I felt hopeful heading to the courthouse and was literally surrounded by lawyers as we entered the courtroom.

I had not met Eric before, though I had seen him on occasion at Steven's office. He was young, extremely motivated and eager to learn. We sat in the back of the courtroom with my friend, Tony. Steven and Herb milled around the front of the crowded courtroom, conversing with other lawyers and some of the prosecutors. This was my first exposure to criminal court. The entire day was set aside for Judge MacKenzie to hear bail motions.

It was a chilling scene, as Sheriff's officers led in an entire line of prisoners, handcuffed together in a long chain. They sat in the area normally occupied by the jury. The jail cases had priority. We sat for over an hour while the judge listened to the pleas of lawyer after lawyer. He seemed to be fair but somewhat abrupt, probably due to the large volume of cases. Finally, the court clerk called, "State versus Spiegel; bail modification motion."

Herb argued admirably. He related all the attendant and mitigating circumstances. He began by relating the stormy marital history. He advised the judge the condition of bail was imposed at 11:00 p.m. on a Friday by a judge who had no specific information about the incident. The condition of bail, Herb contended, was meant as a temporary measure, born out of the urgency of the circumstances. Surely, it could now be modified to allow supervised visitation or, at least, a hearing should be held. But our evidence, which included the reports of Dr. Hamlin and Officer Horn and certifications from everyone who had visited my home that weekend of December 3, seemed to be of no interest to the judge.

It was difficult to follow the interchange between Herb and the judge. But the concluding statement was clear. "Your motion for modification is hereby denied. It would not be appropriate for this court to modify Judge Shelton's order at this time."

All of us met outside the courtroom. Steve and Herb approached, engaged in legal strategies. Herb looked at me and shrugged his shoulders. As much as he was an expert at being an impartial defense attorney, the disappointment was in his face. "I'm sorry, there's nothing else I can say. Maybe Steven will have better luck this afternoon in family court."

"I know," I responded, "You did all you could." I knew he had argued from the heart.

I was shattered and on the verge of tears. It seemed this might be indicative of what would happen that afternoon in family court. The heavy feeling grew heavier. "C'mon," Herb said, "Let's go back to my office." Silently, the five of us walked away.

The scene that afternoon in family court seemed more bizarre than criminal court. This time, Herb and Tony sat in back with me. Eric seated himself in the first row. The small family courtroom was packed with attorneys. In addition to Herb, Steven and Eric, there were Valori's lawyer, Mr. Wahl, and Mr. Rubbinaccio of the prosecutor's office. There was also an attorney for DYFS and another representing one of the doctors. The tiny courtroom could hardly accommodate them all. These attorneys were clustered around the prosecutor's table, while Steven sat alone at the defense counsel's table.

The hearing lasted for over an hour. This time, I heard Steven's impassioned pleas answered by Judge Collester's reply. Although the judge certainly sympathized with the defendant's plight, so long as there was a concurrent criminal proceeding, it was not within his jurisdiction to modify the condition of bail. Neither could he compel DYFS and the doctors to provide any information or order a hearing. These matters would have to be decided in criminal court.

Tears began to flow down my cheeks. Now I realized no one would let me see Jessie. I completely lost control in the back of the courtroom and began sobbing. Herb took me by the arm, "Let's get out of here," he said. "This isn't going to help."

He led me out of the courtroom to the men's room and told me to pull myself together. Herb speaks with such authority, you can't help but do what he says. I splashed water on my face.

"Okay, are you ready?" he asked.

"Okay," I replied. We walked out of the men's room and I started toward the courtroom.

"No, No," said Herb, "You don't need to go back in there." He took me back to his office.

I was shocked and dissociated. I could not believe this was really happening. My mind played back the court events over and over. Something was missing. Maybe we didn't know some important fact. In Steven's words, "Something wasn't kosher."

I have no idea how long it was until Steven, Eric and Tony returned. Steven told me to go home; there was nothing more I could do. He was going to talk to Herb for awhile. He would see me on Monday. I could tell he was hurting, too. I just nodded my head and left.

December 17 through December 31, 1983

As time passed, I began slipping into the third stage of The False Accusation Syndrome. I could feel myself sliding deeper and deeper into depression as the denial stage began to wear thin. I was experiencing many of the physical symptoms of depression, including daily stomach cramps and headaches. Janeen put away any reminders of Jessie. Although the door to Jessie's room was kept closed, it didn't help. The closed door was a constant reminder of the nightmare at hand.

Christmas was approaching. Everything I heard and saw brought the picture of Jessie to my mind and tears to my eyes. I couldn't stop thinking about her. She must have wondered where her Daddy was and why he didn't come to see her. I cried more in that two-week period than in all my thirty-seven years. Nothing had ever impacted me so hard in my entire life.

I still experienced short episodes of dissociation and disbelief, but the reality of the situation had begun to sink in. I was falling into the acute, chronic depression which is characteristic of the next stage of the Syndrome. At night I had vivid dreams, often about Jessie. It was hard to tell which was worse, the days or the nights. I could not work, I could not think. Sometimes, in the mornings, I felt so heavy I could hardly pull myself from the bed.

Janeen stayed with me, supporting and soothing me. She intuitively knew there were times I needed to be alone. On several occasions, I opened the door to Jessie's room, sat on her bed and simply wept. Janeen knew it was important to allow my grief to express itself. After awhile, she would come into the room and comfort me.

On December 22, insult was added to injury. Valori had filed a motion for permission to take Jessie to her parent's home in Georgia for the holiday. When Steven called and told me, I was furious. How could the court even consider such a thing at such a sensitive time? Steven and I quickly composed and filed an opposing motion, objecting to Valori's request to take Jessie to Georgia. Never in our wildest dreams did we think Judge Collester would seriously entertain a request to permit Jessie to be taken out of state in the midst of all the furor. That day I learned never to attempt to predict what a judge might do.

Steven and I looked at each other in utter astonishment as Judge Collester said, "I am going to grant the Plaintiff's request to go to Georgia. She must, however, return to New Jersey by January 2." He did not explain his reasons for the decision.

Steven stood and screamed his objections, but the judge would not listen. He declared the hearing over and walked from the courtroom. What happened next seemed like something out of a movie. Steven grabbed his papers and ran from the courtroom, stuffing them in his briefcase as he moved. Not knowing what else to do, I ran after him.

By the time I got out of the courtroom, Steven was out of sight. I rounded the corner and saw him running down the corridor toward the elevators, still shoving papers into his briefcase. I ran and finally caught him at the elevator. "Where are you going?" I asked, trying to catch my breath.

"I don't know," he replied. The elevator reached our floor. The doors opened with no one inside. He walked in and I followed.

"Really Steven, where are you going?" I queried again.

"I don't know," he stated again, "but I'm going to find someone and do something. They are not going to get away with this!"

"Steven," I said, "Who exactly do you think you are going to find at 4:45 p.m. in the afternoon in late December?"

"Maybe an Appellate Court Justice, maybe a State Supreme Court Justice, I don't know, but I'm going to find someone!" He pushed button three and we got off on the third floor.

"What's up here?" I asked.

"I don't know," Steven said, "I've never been here before."

He went running off down the hall, poking his nose into every open door. The place looked deserted to me. Finding this scene hard to believe, I could not help but laugh momentarily at what a sight we were. Steven stuck his head in the doorways, yelling, "Is anybody here?" I followed, repeatedly saying, "I don't believe this."

I was just about to give up and head back toward the elevator when I saw Steven disappear through a doorway. A light shone from the room. As I approached, I heard voices. A sign read:

Chambers
Supreme Court Justice Pollock.

I stood just outside the door, listening to the conversation. I couldn't hear all of it, but I did hear Steven saying something about an Appellate Judge and an emergent order staying Judge Collester's decision.

I could not believe Steven had simply burst into the chambers of a Justice of the State Supreme Court. When I heard the Justice say, "Let me see if I can help," and I heard him begin to dial the phone, I was in awe. Was this the way the American system of justice worked? My lawyer runs around the courthouse like a lunatic and finds a benevolent Supreme Court Justice who, for some reason, simply decides to help us in our plight. The Justice made six or seven phone calls and located an appellate court judge who agreed to issue a stay of Judge Collester's decision.

Steven would have to write the order and someone would have to drive to Judge Melvin Antell's home in Springfield that night, so he could sign it. Then the copies of the order had to be hand-delivered to Valori and her attorney immediately. Judge Antell would hold a hearing on the matter the following morning. Until then, Judge Collester's order was stayed and Valori was not to leave the State.

As Steven emerged from Justice Pollock's chambers, he looked as shocked as I was. We were jubilant, but kept ourselves quiet until we were safely in the elevator. The moment the doors closed, we screamed, laughed and talked at the same time. We had the following conversation — if you can call it that.

"Did that really happen," I said, "or am I dreaming?"

"It happened," said Steven.

"It didn't," I said.

"It did," he replied.

"That didn't really just happen," I said again.

"It did," said Steven ... ad infinitum.

Outside the courthouse, Steven said, "We better get back to the office and prepare this order. You are going to have to go to Judge Antell's home tonight and then serve Tony Wahl and Valori with the papers. If I stay out too late again with you tonight, my wife will kill me."

I telephoned Janeen at the apartment and asked her to meet us at Steven's office. I did not bother to explain what had happened. I knew we would need her to type the order. Steven and I immediately drove to his office.

He began writing the order. I telephoned the airlines to find out Valori's travel plans. She was booked on a 10:00 a.m. flight. I was sure we had at least temporarily won this battle. The hearing was scheduled for 9:00 a.m. By the time it ended, Valori would never make the flight, no matter what the outcome of the hearing. At the very least, her plans would be delayed. That would give us even more time to respond to the situation.

Janeen arrived just as Steven completed the writing. She began typing without asking any questions. By 7:30 p.m. we were done. Steven gave us directions to Judge Antell's home. He instructed us to leave copies of the signed order in Tony Wahl's home mailbox and at Valori's apartment. He would be in Judge Antell's chambers in the morning and would call as soon as there was an outcome to the hearing.

The Trials And Trauma

People were preparing for the holiday, traveling to the homes of family and friends. Decorations hung everywhere. But for Janeen and me, it was a strange night. Here we were, heading to the home of an Appellate Court judge. It was past nine when we finally arrived. We walked up the front path and rang the bell of the expensive home. The daughter of the judge answered the door. A few moments later, the judge walked down the stairs in his robe and slippers. "I expected you somewhat earlier than this," he said, obviously not happy about our late arrival.

He was a distinguished-looking man in his early sixties with silver-grey hair. I apologized for being late and handed him the court order. His attitude was rather curt. He merely motioned for us to sit down while he read the paper. I never would have thought, not in my wildest imagination, that I would be sitting in the home of an appellate court judge at 10:00 p.m. just a few days before Christmas. It was so bizarre it actually added to my incoherence.

We sat on the couch waiting and wondering if he was going to sign the order. He studied it carefully, then picked up a pen and scribbled his signature. Janeen and I looked at each other and inwardly breathed a sigh of relief. When the Judge had signed all three copies, he stood and handed me the order.

"Tell the attorneys to be in my chambers tomorrow at 9:00 a.m. sharp." That was all he said, except for a quick good night as he started back up the stairs. His daughter let us out. We thanked her as we headed into the cold.

We spent the night delivering copies of the court order to Valori's apartment, her attorney's home and Steven's office. By the time we got home, it was past 3:00 a.m. We fell into bed in a state of exhaustion, hopeful we had accomplished something.

The phone rang at 10:00 a.m. and I answered it with eager anticipation. Instead, an avalanche slid through my head. Judge Antell reversed the stay and reinstated Judge Collester's order. Valori had been waiting at the Newark airport while the hearing was in progress. After she spoke to her attorney, she had just enough time to get on the plane. Steven could not believe the decision of the judge. He did not know what to say.

I hung up and told Janeen. She started to cry. I felt this court decision was an omen that any possibility for happiness in my life was gone. When I thought of Jessie spending Christmas so far away and having no explanation as to my absence, I sunk into the deepest depression yet. I really did not want to live, but my logical mind would not let me carry out my fantasies of suicide.

I gave up. Everything was so hopeless. I began to wonder, as many victims of false accusations do, what I had done to deserve this?

If someone had said Jessie's Christmas gifts would remain unopened for years, I'd have thought them crazy not prophetic.

$\boxed{4}$

GIVING UP

Stage 4: The Depression

Throughout January 1984, it took a major effort to do anything. My depression and physical exhaustion often debilitated me. I had to force myself to work and even the smallest details of living were nearly impossible to perform. What made it worse were the constant sights and sounds of children, be they at the local supermarket or on television. There was no escaping the ever-present reality of Jessica's absence.

My work as a psychologist was both a blessing and a curse. At times, I could get beyond my own problems to become absorbed in helping my patients with theirs. Other times, I was less effective with my patients — sitting with them, yet being distracted with my own situation.

My mind was occupied with two basic matters. One was my possible indictment by a Grand Jury. The indictment process was a legal matter I knew little about. Steven and Herb were very candid with me. They said an indictment was a formality. It was when the Prosecutor presented his case to a Grand Jury. Yet the Grand Jury process was actually an arm of the Prosecutor. Only the Prosecutor decided what evidence was to be presented. Neither I nor my attorney was allowed to be present. Only if I was indicted, would I receive the Prosecutor's case file.

This only served to increase my feeling of helplessness. Steven and Herb encouraged me to get on with my life and leave the legal matters to them. Other than putting Nancy's powers to work to try to find the third physician who ostensibly examined Jessie, I made every effort to free myself from depression and continue on with my life.

The other matter which occupied my daily thoughts concerned my position at the Institute. In early January, I faced the Board of Directors of the Institute. The atmosphere was strained when I entered the conference room. I spent two hours answering questions and trying to allay the Board's fears. The issue of my taking a voluntary leave of absence was raised. I was pleasantly surprised to find almost all the Board members were unequivocally behind me. They felt that unless I was proven guilty, there was no need to take a leave.

We then discussed Dr. Lentchner's resignation. The Board pledged their full support to the continued operation of the Institute. I remained uncertain about our survival without Dr. Lentchner, but I intended to call a meeting of the entire staff to ask their cooperation. We would do the best we could. I promised the Board a complete report in February and the meeting ended.

Many members spoke to me individually, offering to help in whatever way they could. Several volunteered to lend me significant sums of money for my legal fees. I thanked each of them and said I would keep their kindness in mind. By the end of January, the legal fees, support payments and missed time at the office had put me over $50,000 in debt. My financial problems continued to escalate. Eventually, I was forced to borrow some money from those Board members.

My spirits were a bit lifted the day after the Board meeting when Nancy arrived at my apartment. She walked in and handed me a piece of paper. It read, John Rogers, M.D., Family Physician. Nancy had found the third physician.

"How on earth . . ." I started to say.

She cut me off. "Those are the dates Valori brought Jessie to see him. Do you realize she brought Jessie to the doctor before and after each of her visits with you?"

Giving Up

I checked my notes against the dates Jessie had visited Dr. Lapkin. Then I checked my own diary of Jessie's visits. Sure enough, Nancy was right. Valori had taken Jessie to the doctors just before and just after each visitation with me. She obviously hoped one of the doctors would find something unusual, so she could attribute it to me. "Are you going to call?" asked Nancy, snapping me from these thoughts.

"Call?" I said, preoccupied with my thoughts.

"The doctor, the doctor!" she screamed.

"Oh yeah, I'll call right now."

I went into the bedroom and dialed the number. As it turned out, Dr. Rogers was not there, but his associate, Dr. Cohen, got on the line. After a good deal of coaxing, he verified the dates and findings of each office visit. On the December 5 visit, there was some redness around the vagina. This, he said, could be consistent with oral contact, but added like Dr. Lapkin had, that such redness was very common and could be caused by any number of things— tight underwear, rubbing with toilet paper or the child running around a lot. He said the redness was not an indication of abuse. He added a very interesting note by informing me of a medical test, which if performed within forty-eight to seventy-two hours of an incident, would document any such abuse.

I told him the alleged abuse had taken place on December 3 or 4 and inquired whether Dr. Rogers had performed such a test at the December 5 examination. Dr. Cohen's response was, "No, I don't see that he did. I have no idea why not."

I got off the phone and walked into the living room. I told Janeen and Nancy what Dr. Cohen had said. They were elated upon learning of his statements. I had no idea that Dr. Rogers would have a different interpretation of the examinations when he later testified before the Grand Jury. Back then I was happy Nancy had found the mysterious third physician.

My depression, however, remained intact. Other than work, I spent most of my time in isolation with Janeen. We seldom went out, rarely saw friends or family and often did not answer the phone. I was still afraid to show my face in public. I felt I was the only person in the world with this problem. It never occurred to me that others were experiencing equally bizarre and incredible situations. Unbeknown to me, false accusations were happening by the thousands throughout the country, especially when divorce and custody issues were present.

Mid-January brought several developments. The first occurred on January 24, when I learned of my indictment through the newspaper. Seeing it in print, Exhibit A, threw me for a loop. It reinstated my depression in full.

EXHIBIT A

Psychologist indicted on sex assault charge

A Mount Olive psychologist was indicted yesterday by a Morris County grand jury on charges he sexually assaulted a 2-year-old girl.

Lawrence D. Spiegel, 38, of 151 Route 206, Flanders, was charged with aggravated sexual assault against the child on Dec. 3 in Budd Lake. He is free on $3,500 bail pending further court action.

Spiegel, a former professor at the County College of Morris, was ar- rested in December at his office in Mount Freedom, Randolph.

The Morris County Prosecutor's Office had been tipped off to a possible criminal situation involving Spiegel by the state Division of Youth and Family Services in Somerset County, said police.

The prosecutor's office notified the family's doctor who confirmed the girl had been sexually assaulted, said police.

In one of the articles, I read that a "family" physician confirmed the abuse. That didn't follow with what I had been told by the doctors. It didn't take me long to realize, however, that despite what the newspapers said, I knew this was Valori's doing.

The Prosecutor had used his discretion to its limit in my case. The four certifications of Janeen, Debra, Pauline and Claudine, verifying the events of the weekend in question, were never shown to the Grand Jury. The letter from Dr. Lapkin, stating his examination "under no circumstances" revealed any evidence of child abuse was never presented. Dr. Lentchner, who had seen Valori for psychological counseling, also wrote a most revealing certification see here in Exhibit B. That was withheld by the Prosecutor also. In essence, the Grand Jury saw only the Prosecutor's side of the case.

EXHIBIT B

I, Lawrence Lentchner do hereby certify the following:

1. I make this deposition having been advised that prosecution has requested that Dr. Spiegel not see his child before there is an outcome of this case. In addressing this, I think the following facts are salient.

2. In the period of time for three weeks before Dr. and Mrs. Spiegel permanently separated, Mrs Spiegel chose to speak with me at regular times, as a friend, to discuss the difficult emotional stress she was experiencing. In this period of time, she advised me that _she had spent two days "convincing Jesse that it was al-right to hate daddy."_ It seemed quite clear to me that she was teaching their child to verbalize agreement with her on emotional and cognitive status. At that time, _she talked at length about her family's hatred of Larry Spiegel,_ her husband and how if they separated, Valori's father would do anything he could to avoid Larry's being the father of this child. Especially he would not let Jesse "be a Jew like her father."

3. On another occasion, _Mrs. Spiegel spoke openly about feeling a sense or knowledge that she had been sexually molested by her father._

4. It seems perfectly clear to me that _Mrs. Spiegel is capable of "projecting" her own emotional termoil, doubt and sexual pathology into her daughter_ and that these opinions of mine are born out by the above history.

Lawrence lentchner

A Question of Innocence

Other developments were more positive. The therapists at the Institute had rallied behind me. The Institute was holding its own. It seemed to remain untouched, despite the newspaper coverage of the indictment. I was happy about that and, for a short time at least, I could stop worrying about my job and source of income.

As a consequence of Dr. Lentchner's leaving, I had to contribute more of my own earnings to support the monthly office overhead. This, in conjunction with the mounting legal fees, cut deeply into my finances. I was unable to continue paying Valori the liberal sums of money agreed to at our divorce. As a result, she could no longer pay her rent. Having no choice, I agreed to a consent order allowing Valori and Jessica to live at her parent's home in Georgia for an indefinite, but temporary, period. She was to return when my condition of bail was modified. Valori took Jessie to Georgia.

To make matters worse, even after Valori took Jessie to Georgia, I was brought back to court on several occasions by the probation department. Although they were fully aware of the pending criminal charges and the fact that my private practice had all but collapsed, they, nonetheless, wanted me to continue paying full alimony and child support. So when I wasn't in criminal court with Herb, I was with Steven defending myself from the clutches of the persistent probation department. The oppression, indignation and hopelessness I experienced pushed me deeper into depression. I was being buried by the problems of Valori's false accusation.

February 1984

Late one evening in February, while I was with my last patient, Janeen buzzed me on the intercom. She had been working at the Institute full time in order to help ease the financial pressures. I grumbled "Yes," into the phone.

Janeen said, "Sorry to bother you, but I thought you would like to know Dr. Lentchner is here and would like to see you."

I immediately suspected he had come to ask for his job back. "Tell him to wait, I'll be done shortly."

I finished with my patient and asked Janeen to send in Dr. Lentchner. Sure enough, he entered with slumped shoulders and bowed head — the depressed stance I had come to know so well over the years. There was a large part of me that did not want to make this easy for him.

Dr. Lentchner had found his new position earned less money and more hours. He had seen that the Institute had survived the publicity of my arrest and indictment. His immediate decision to bail out and save his career had been a spontaneous one which he now regretted. We talked for some time and he eventually got around to his hasty decision to resign. I had not filled his vacated position and he knew it. His wife, Betty, who had never supported his resigning, had stayed on in her position as Administrative Director. I knew this had caused a good deal of conflict between them. He asked if he could return as Clinical Director.

I responded with, "Of course," sounding extremely charitable. It was not my good nature that made me so cooperative. I was thinking how much easier this would make things financially for all concerned. I had no inkling of the consequences his reinstatement would bring in the very near future.

I felt satisfaction announcing Dr. Lentchner's return at our next Board meeting. He assumed his previous position. We also approved a reorganization plan which made me Acting Executive Director, pending formal approval at our next meeting. Situations were improving. I felt my depression lift a little. Though the pain of missing Jessie was still very much with me, I began to experience a glimmer of hope that my life might return to normal.

March 1984

Since the Institute was functioning well, I could spend more time with Herb and Steven developing our legal strategies. Herb had consistently tried to get a modification of bail through formal motions in court and private conversations with judges and prosecutors. I could not see Jessica and no one wanted to stick their neck out for the sake of a parent/child relationship.

When we reviewed the transcript of the indictment, not only were Herb and Steven in awe, so were several other attorneys who reviewed it. None of the lawyers had ever seen such a flimsy excuse for an indictment. According to several of them, the Prosecutor's presentation of the case was indeed questionable. They said it bordered on prosecutorial misconduct.

We believed the Prosecutor did not substantiate that abuse had taken place. The only testimony which even implied impropriety came from Dr. John Rogers, the family physician. But Rogers, in fact, never checked with Dr. Frankel, even though he knew Frankel was the psychologist who had seen Jessica and Valori. In addition to that omission, his analysis of Jessica's examination was considerably different from what his associate, Dr. Cohen, had told me on the phone. Again, the pieces were not fitting together. Again, the question arose: Who was really making these pieces move?

Other "witnesses" included Valori's aunt, the Prosecutor's investigator, Janet Rapisardi, and Dr. Frankel. The latter's testimony was the only thing said on my behalf. The first social worker from DYFS to be involved did not even testify and neither did Valori. That, I thought, was strange.

The transcript created even more confusion for us. The following excerpt from the Grand Jury transcript demonstrates the nebulous language used by the Prosecutor in describing the crime. From his definition of sexual penetration, we could not even conclude what it was that I had allegedly done to Jessie.

> The statute that we're going to deal with is 2C:14-2. It states: "A person is guilty of aggravated sexual assault if he commits an act of sexual penetration with another person under any one of the following circumstances . . ."Sexual penetration is defined in the statute to mean: "Vaginal intercourse, cunnilingus, fellatio, or anal intercourse between persons or the insertion of the hand, finger, or object into the anus or vagina either by the actor or by the actor's insertion. The depth of the insertion shall not be relevant as to the question of the commission of the crime."

Another surprise was found in the testimony of the Prosecutor's investigator, Janet Rapisardi. She was the woman in the police car the day of my arrest. As seen in the transcript, members of the Grand Jury questioned her strenuously with regard to "who" filed the initial complaint. The jury obviously thought this was an important point. It clearly seemed they wanted to be sure the complaint did not come from a vindictive ex-wife.

After several minutes of evasive answers, the forewoman of the jury asked who brought this case to the attention of the Division of Youth and Family Services. Investigator Rapisardi said that the complaint had been filed by a priest named Father Frank. That was odd since Valori had not been to church for years. She must have suddenly become religious. Another Juror, wanting to be certain Valori did not initiate the charge to DYFS, asked the question again. The answer was, "The mother never contacted DYFS directly, no." An excerpt from the Grand Jury testimony appears here as Exhibit C.

EXHIBIT C

16	
17	
18	A JUROR: Could you give us just a little
19	inkling as to how this knowledge came about?
20	Q Could you tell the members of the Grand Jury
21	how did the Morris County Prosecutor's Office come to know
22	of Jessica Spiegel and how did the investigation begin?
23	A A referral regarding the alleged sexual assault was
24	referred to Somerset County DYFS. Somerset County DYFS in
25	turn contacted the mother, Ms. Valori Mulvey, to come in for

Rapisardi   10

1   an interview to speak with Jessica and also contacted Morris

2   County DYFS, because Morris County is the location of the

3	crime scene. Morris County DYFS in turn contacted the
4	Prosecutor's Office, and that is how we received the case.
5	Q What town did the alleged incident take place?
6	A In Flanders, which is the residence of Dr. Spiegel.
7	As I stated before, Flanders is in Morris County. However,
8	the victim lives in Somerset County, which is how Somerset
9	County DYFS is involved.
10	THE FOREWOMAN: Who brought it to the attention
11	of Somerset DYFS?
12	THE WITNESS: A person by the name of Father
13	Frank, who is affiliated in a church in that area.
14	A JUROR: And then how would the Father --
15	you're talking about a priest. How did he get --
16	Q How did he come to know the information?
17	He came to know the information because Ms. Mulvey
18	went to Father for guidance regarding this incident.
19	A JUROR: The original -- the child's mother
20	is not the one who brought the information out. Is
21	that it?
22	Q Did the mother contact DYFS?
23	A The mother never contacted DYFS directly, no.

We assumed Valori, having been unsuccessful in her attempts to get one of the three doctors to file the sexual abuse complaint, went to a priest. She must have convinced him to file the complaint, instead of doing it herself, or so we assumed. We had not, as yet, had an opportunity to go through the piles of notes and papers the Prosecutor had recently given us. When examined closely, we would eventually find that Investigator Rapisardi had given the Grand Jury misleading information. The Grand Jury, however, based upon their understanding of the facts, gave the Prosecutor his indictment.

In March, Herb filed a motion in Morris County Criminal Court to have the indictment thrown out. He based his argument on the lack of evidence, as well as the Prosecutor's biased handling of the Grand Jury hearing. But if the charge remained, Herb asked for a modification of the condition of bail, to allow me to see Jessie.

Although Judge Charles Egan denied our motions at that time, he instructed the Prosecutor to have more evidence than what surfaced during the Grand Jury proceedings if this was brought to trial. The stormy marital history pointed to a possibility of a vindictive ex-wife. Considering the weakness of the State's case and the disruption of a parent/child relationship, Egan wanted no stalling by the prosecution. He would move this case quickly. He set a pretrial hearing for March and told the Prosecutor to go head with a trial or dismiss the charges. Egan made it clear, he did not intend to let a two and a half-year-old testify if that was in the Prosecutor's mind. He added that he did not have the authority to reverse Judge MacKenzie's decision regarding the condition of bail.

To the best of my recollection, there followed a series of events between Herb and the Prosecutor's office. About a week later, the Assistant Prosecutor in charge of the case, Mr. Michael Rubbinaccio, told Herb he would discuss my case with his superior, Prosecutor Lee Trumbull. It was possible that the charges may be dismissed. He had indicated this at the pretrial hearing before Judge Egan. The judge, who was leaving for a vacation in Italy, expected the recommendations to be made expediently and assumed this matter would be clarified by the time of his return in May. Mr. Rubbinaccio had indicated he thought this was possible.

I was overjoyed and greatly relieved at this news. I called everyone, telling them the charges would be dropped shortly. The next day I called Herb to see if anything had been done and he said the Prosecutor was out of town. Any agreement to dismiss the charges would have to wait until the following week. Although I was impatient to see Jessie, I would have to wait a short time more.

When Mr. Trumbull returned to his office in that last week of March, I received a phone call from Herb. "I have bad news," he said, "Trumbull is not going to drop the charges."

It was like December 9, 1983, all over again. "Why? why?" I screamed into the phone.

"I have no idea, Larry," said Herb. "I thought it was a good shot, too. I guess we will have to wait for Judge Egan to come back, and then I'll file a motion to try the case or dismiss."

I felt myself slipping back into a state of shock. "How can this happen Herb?"

"I have no idea. I just don't know what to tell you," said Herb.

Prosecutor Lee Trumbull and Assistant Prosecutor Michael Rubbinaccio. Why was my case, my conviction so important to them?

I hung up the phone. Back came the haunting feeling that something was going on which we did not know about. Back came the question, why were "they" pushing this thing so hard? Steven began checking into Valori's father's connections. Did he know someone associated with the Prosecutor? We could find no such link. The whole thing simply transcended insanity. The shock and oppression was as bad, or worse, than ever. But this second trauma had just begun. There was some consolation in the fact that the efforts of the Prosecutor did not go unnoticed by the press or public, as evidenced in Exhibit D.

EXHIBIT D

More sex assault cases go to trial

By BRIAN MURRAY
Daily Record Courthouse Writer

"What are the options that I have other than to proceed with sexual assault cases that some may not think are trial sufficient. To do otherwise would open the door for those types of assaults," says Morris County Prosecutor Lee S. Trumbull.

That's part of the reason Morris County is witnessing what may appear to be a rash of sexual assault cases being brought before judges in the county courthouse and an astonishingly high number of cases in which young children are being molested.

In the past three weeks five sexual assault cases have gone to court. And they are only part of the 81 cases that were taken on by county prosecutors between Jan. 1 and May, as opposed to the 33 cases taken on during the same time period last year.

According to Superior Court Judge Charles M. Egan Jr., the criminal assignment judge in Morris County, the sexual assault caseload has increased tremendously in the past 10 years and "particularly in the last four or five years."

However, those high statistics do not mean Morris County is becoming a focal point for sexual crimes. On the contrary, prosecutors say residents could be witnessing the turning point where such crimes will begin to decrease in this area.

"We're not, all of a sudden, being besieged by a rash of sexual assaults," says Trumbull. "The same percentages are there. But the main factor is ... people are more willing to come foward and report them."

Interlocked with that, according to Investigator Colleen McMahon of the prosecutor's sex crimes unit, is the public's recognition that law enforcement officials in this area have become more sensitized to the dilemma of sexual assault victims.

Looking at recent cases in which a 3-year-old victim has been called to testify and where mentally retarded victims are also taking the stand, Trumbull admits his department is taking cases to the grand jury and proceeding with prosecutions where it may have at one time backed off.

"There used to be a test for trial sufficiency. That was a term I never heard before coming to Morris County two years ago," says Trumbull. "I understood you needed sufficient facts before you could move on a case ... but there was a time when some cases were considered a no-win situation and were never acted on."

Those cases included child molestations where the victims were extremely young or in cases where the victim appeared too mentally incompetent to be considered a strong trial witness.

"From day one on this job, the first sexual assault case I encountered was on my desk for dismissal. But I took the case and, with Assistant Prosecutor Michael Rubbinaccio, determined additional work had to be done," said Trumbull.

That work resulted in the conviction of a man highly respected in his community for repeatedly assaulting his teen-age daughter.

Diligence in other "no-win" situations since then has also paid off, if not in convictions and guilty pleas, at least in pushing offenders through the system and possibly getting a message across that the crime will not continue to go unnoticed, says Trumbull.

Judge Egan agreed that more cases have come to his bench recently.

"In the last year or two there seems to have been more coming before me involving children and sur-prisingly young children," he said. "Curiously, I've also seen fewer of the allegations of a forcible rape between two adults. It seems there used to be more of them."

Investigator McMahon says television programs centering on child molesting and incest have prompted people to report such incidents to a degree where most of the cases her office gets involve child molesting.

"The programs are bringing to light what the public was not aware of or just didn't want to accept at one time," she says, noting most children assaulted are victimized by their own relatives or adults they know and trust.

She emphasized that the increased number of cases is indicative of more incidents being reported by schools and relatives and not an increase in the actual number of assaults.

But the prosecution's willingness to push such cases has not been immune to criticism, especially in the cases of Lawrence Spiegel, a 38-year-old Flanders psychologist charged with child molestation, and John St. Luke, a 62-year-old orderly at Greystone Park Psychiatric Hospital charged with sexually assaulting two female patients.

In Spiegel's ongoing case, the alleged victim is 3 years old and prosecutors are fighting to use her as a witness.

Spiegel has maintained his innocence and factors, such as the credibility of the person who reported the alleged assault and whether the girl is capable of understanding enough to relate facts to a jury, raise some serious questions on the entire case.

St. Luke, who must face a new trial after a jury acquitted him on one charge and remained deadlocked on three others, is faced with the testimony of two mentally retarded women and, again, credibility is in question.

"There are those who criticize the options we've exercised in proceeding with such cases, but we have to take our victims as we find them," says Trumbull. "The situation is presented to us, we don't create them.

What other options do we have in some of these cases, to let the criminals go?"

Trumbull added that his office does not proceed with any case until it has been investigated and determined to be a legitimate complaint.

"What we're doing is bringing more of these cases to a grand jury and letting the people decide if a person should be prosecuted. When they decide, we go ahead," said Trumbull.

As if things were not bad enough, late in March I received a letter from my landlord which indicated he would not renew my apartment lease. I had lived there four years. The reasons cited in his letter never mentioned the sexual abuse charges. But he, like many others, had already convicted me of the crime. He simply did not want me around.

It took all my strength just to go to his office to discuss my lease. He pulled out a file and put it on his desk. I saw that it contained the newspaper clippings about my case. But he had no interest in discussing the matter with me. I left and decided I had better call Steven.

Steven was furious. He told me not to worry, he would take care of it. In the midst of my legal nightmare, I also had to be concerned about losing my home. My finances were such that if I lost my apartment, I literally had no place to go. Then in mid-August, after several letters had been exchanged between Steven and the landlord, the issue was finally resolved. I received a letter that guaranteed the renewal of my lease. Steven had succeeded in securing my apartment as my home.

April 1984

Each day I lived in depression surrounded by the uncertainty of the future. I had difficulty seeing my patients again and found it impossible to take solace in anything. Since Judge Egan was away for three weeks, I was encouraged by everyone to take a vacation.

A Question of Innocence

Larry and Betty Lentchner were most instrumental in urging me to "get away for awhile." Janeen's parents offered us the use of their camper since the police still held mine. Though I had some bad intuitive feelings about leaving at this point, I finally agreed to go.

Janeen and I drove to Florida to visit my parents. I had only spoken to them over the phone since this whole mess had begun back in December. They were in their sixties and lived in a retirement community. This was an opportunity to alleviate their worries somewhat. We left for Florida in mid-April. The Lentchners assured me that they would oversee the day to day responsibilities of the Institute.

While packing, I had resolved to make this as relaxing a vacation as possible. During our trip southward, I promised myself I would try to put thoughts of Jessie aside and make an effort to lift my feeling of oppression. I had to do this not only for my sake, but for Janeen's as well. The pressure of supporting me through my misery had begun to take its toll on her. It was my turn to do something for her. But as we drove south, everything I saw reminded me of Jessie. I continued to drift off into my depressive, obsessive thoughts. Every McDonald's we passed, every child I saw, even songs on the radio, evoked memories of her. She loved to ride in my camper and used to chatter constantly about everything she saw.

I kept these thoughts to myself and after a few days, I actually managed to pull myself out of it somewhat. As we reached northern Florida, I could see the trip was doing Janeen some good. Once we got into sunshine, she gained a tan and lost the worn look she had had back in New Jersey.

Driving for long periods of time was therapeutic for me. It also provided time for reflection. At Del Ray Beach, we spent a few days with my parents. It was obvious they were deeply concerned with the crisis and my well-being. But the more I explained the various circumstances, the more preposterous the entire situation seemed. My parents asked if someone had been paid off. Was there something I wasn't telling them? What were the facts as I knew them?

They sat on the sofa staring at me in total disbelief as I reviewed the details. No, there were no doctors who reported any abuse. No, there was no one else who said anything of the kind, just Valori and her aunt. Yes, I did explain to the court she was apparently unstable. My profoundly perplexed parents could not understand how such a thing could occur. But then again, neither could I. Finally I stopped trying to explain. It only made things worse.

The days passed quickly and soon I was watching my parents wave good-bye as we began the ride home. I felt I had done little or nothing to dispel their worries. In truth, there was less I could do to alleviate my own.

The drive soothed me a bit as we moved northward. We stopped at a restaurant in Virginia. I called my assistant and closest confidant, Lou Popek, just to check on things at the Institute. It took only a moment for me to know from the tone of his voice that something was very wrong. Lou was not given to unjustified expressions of alarm. He said he had tried to reach me at my parents, but had missed me by a few hours. I knew something was really wrong.

"What's going on?" I asked.

"I'm not sure," he replied. "But something is and I don't like it. We can't go into this on the phone," he continued. "Where are you?"

"Virginia."

"When can you get back?"

"When do I need to get back?" I asked.

"Now," said Lou, in his typically candid way.

"Do I need to leave tonight," I asked, "or can I wait and head back tomorrow?"

"Now," came the reply.

I walked back to the table where Janeen sat waiting for me. We had planned to stay in Virginia that night and take several days to drive home through the Blue Ridge Mountains and Skyline Drive. I knew she was looking forward to it. The vacation had really begun to revive her. I was reluctant to tell her the news, yet I had no choice. The disappointment was obvious on her face, but her level of strength, loyalty and selflessness was astounding.

"I understand," she said "We can come back to the Blue Ridge Mountains another time."

We finished our meal, got back in the camper and headed for New Jersey. "What now?" I thought, as we sped through the night. What had alarmed Lou so much? My mind raced, as did the camper up the interstate highways. We reached our apartment at 9:00 a.m. We were both exhausted. Janeen went to bed and I called Lou.

May 1984

It is a regrettable fact of human behavior that one individual's misfortune is used by another for personal gain. It is certainly true that during bad times, one learns who his friends really are. Oftentimes one's enemies turn out to be those least expected. This was exactly what I discovered upon my arrival home.

Lou had plenty of reason for his alarm. As we spoke on the phone, he said a Board meeting was suddenly scheduled for next week. Lentchner had been meeting secretly with members and staff, seemingly to influence them to pursue my resignation as Executive Director.

I listened in disbelief. Why would Larry Lentchner do this, especially after I had reinstated him as Clinical Director? Both Larry and Betty had been among my closest friends. Why would he do such a thing? It seemed to Lou that Lentchner was intimating that Valori's charges were true. Apparently, it was his way of gaining control of the Institute. I knew what motivated his actions.

Larry's envy of me had been festering for a long time. For ten years, he had been my subordinate at the college when I was chairman of the department. Now as Executive Director of the Institute, I was once again his direct superior. I knew it was eating away at him. He wanted to be number one, not number two. In addition, Larry had always been jealous of my close relationship to Betty and her children, Claudine and Jennifer. I had been a second father to them after Betty divorced her first husband. Her children seemed to relate to me better than to their stepfather, Larry. This had bothered him, perhaps more deeply than anyone had realized. His suppressed feelings against me had now surfaced and were converted into damaging actions.

The attempted takeover of the Institute by Lentchner proved to be only the tip of the iceberg. He had gone much further than that. Since his return to the Institute, Dr. Lentchner had jumped on Valori's bandwagon and had actually been cooperating with the prosecution behind my back. I found out he had contacted Mr. Rubbinaccio through a former patient who worked for the Prosecutor's office. Lentchner's involvement apparently halted the Prosecutor from reviewing the dismissal of the charge. Herb surmised that it was Lentchner's involvement which caused the Prosecutor to persist vigorously with the charges. This was later confirmed when the Prosecutor gave us more than 100 pages of testimony given by Lentchner, filled with innuendos, insinuations and outright lies.

I confronted Dr. Lentchner on the evening of May 2. When he admitted his involvement, my anger raged. His ambition to take over the Institute was horrible, but his collaboration with the Prosecutor's office was disastrous for me. Realizing this, in blind anger I shouted, "I'd like to kill you for all that you've done to me!" This, of course, was not meant literally, but as an expression of my rage.

On May 3, Lentchner added the finishing touch. It was my first day back at the Institute following my "vacation." I saw six or seven patients that day while the Lentchners were conspicuously absent. All of Dr. Lentchner's patients had been canceled for the day, but I did not know why. I had finished with my last patient and sat back to reflect upon the day. I had postponed the meeting that Lentchner had called with the Board. Now I intended to write a letter informing Lentchner that I was removing him from his position of Clinical Director.

Suddenly with no warning, police officers and members of the Prosecutor's office burst into the building with guns drawn. Two of them broke into my office, told me to face the wall and spread my arms and legs. One of them held a gun to my head and demanded I give him the keys to Janeen's parents' camper which was parked outside. I was patted down. I heard the sounds of police officers throwing open office doors and bringing out terrified therapists and patients at gunpoint.

When they had finished searching me, I was ordered to sit on the couch in my office. One officer stood with his gun pointed at me. Another took the keys to the camper and led an expedition of four or five police to the parking lot. They searched the vehicle. From my vantage point, I could hear and see other police herding therapists and patients alike out of consultation rooms and seating them in the waiting room. I, along with other therapists, attempted to question the police, only to be told to "Shut up!" We were held at gunpoint until the search party finally returned.

Detective Robert Muccigrossi informed me I was under arrest for allegedly threatening the life of Dr. Lentchner. His manner was obtrusive and arrogant. Janeen, along with the office staff, therapists and patients, watched in disbelief as I was led in handcuffs from my office. I was taken to the Randolph Township Police Station for the second time in six months.

Janeen called Herb and Steven to tell them of my arrest. I had to borrow another thousand dollars from some of my friends to pay my bail. The camper, which had been torn apart in the search, had to be driven to Pennsylvania to avoid the possibility of it being impounded by the police. Janeen and I had to hide out in the camper in Pennsylvania for several days until Herb and Steven were sure no other charges were pending.

When the dust finally settled, it did not help to have Herb tell me these charges were nothing to worry about. He said they would ultimately be dismissed since they had no merit. It did little for my emotional state to hear that the Prosecutor had been only too willing to cooperate with Lentchner and add another arrest to the charges already pending. Such things, I was told, were not out of the ordinary for prosecutors. As Herb had predicted, the charges were administratively dismissed by the Prosecutor about nine months later.

The Board of Directors was as shocked as I at Lentchner's actions. I spoke to the chairman of the Board from my hideout in Pennsylvania the morning after my arrest. I told him what had happened, and that I wanted to issue an Executive Order removing Lentchner from his position at the Institute. After the chairman made several phone calls, seemingly to verify the facts, he called me back and said he would support my Executive Order and would send a telegram to the Institute to that effect. He did and Lentchner was fired.

In addition to losing his job, Lentchner also lost most of his friends and whatever was left of his personal honor and integrity, once all the facts were known. A few months later, the Lentchners moved lock, stock and barrel to Florida. I was glad it was they, not I, who had turned tail and run.

The Institute could not withstand this blow, however, and closed its doors two days later. Now I had lost both my teaching position and private practice income. I was devastated, emotionally, and broke, financially. I fell into deep despair and depression. I had reached my lowest point of the entire ordeal. The situation now seemed utterly hopeless.

June and July 1984

By early June, I felt that I had been living this nightmare long enough. Each day I grew increasingly more impatient and pressed my attorneys for movement of some kind. But Herb and Steven knew the legal ropes and told me the judicial system moved slowly. This fact often works against the accused; it wears an individual down, nerves an individual up — in a sense, primes the accused to play into the Prosecutor's hands. Still, I had had enough delays. I wanted to have either a trial date set or the charges dismissed. Herb entered a motion in court to force one of these two issues.

Our motion succeeded. On the morning of June 18, the trial began. It was not an overstatement to say I was completely debilitated. The morning the trial began, Janeen helped me get ready and Nancy drove us to the courthouse in Morristown. It was still difficult to believe this case was being tried on the evidence thus far gathered, but indeed it was.

The courtroom was packed. Many of my friends, former patients and students had come to lend their support. What surprised me most was the overwhelming presence of the press. Although local newspapers had followed this case from the beginning, reporters from statewide newspapers came to cover the proceedings. Judge Egan was involved in another case at the time, so my trial was held before Judge Arnold Stein. The courtroom buzzed as I walked in and sat down. I felt ashamed to even be there, like a freak in a sideshow that everyone had come to watch.

This feeling intensified a few moments later when Valori entered, carrying my frightened and bewildered little daughter in her arms. Valori shielded Jessie from seeing me. Almost seven months had passed since I last saw her and for us to finally be together in this way was beyond comprehension. Jessie was too upset to realize I was in the room.

The State based their case around two principal witnesses, Valori and Jessica. But before the judge began jury selection, Jessica had to be declared competent to testify. If it turned out that Jessica was not competent and the State had no other witnesses to call, there would simply be no case.

The proceedings began. Soon my little child sat crying, hardly visible behind the witness box. I sat and watched as the Prosecutor attempted to qualify her as a witness for the State. I never felt such outrage, indignation and sorrow in my entire life.

I listened to the sobs of my little girl as the Prosecutor repeated questions like, "Did your Daddy hurt you?" "Tell us how your Daddy hurt you." It seemed to go on forever. The judge finally put a stop to it. The issue of Jessica's competence was settled quickly by Judge Stein, as seen in an excerpt from the court transcript labeled here as Exhibit E.

EXHIBIT E

```
                                                          144

  1            THE COURT:  Yes.  I saw enough here

  2       today as to the age of that child and her

  3       demeanor to make it totally inappropriate to

  4       even attempt to qualify her.

  5            The record may not have reflected that,
```

but this child would not leave the arms of her

mother, even though she was being soothed and

comforted by the mother. And apparently had --

knew you to some extent, and that still wasn't

satisfactory.

MR. RUBBINACCIO: Yes.

THE COURT: So that would -- well, first

of all, I'm satisfied that there is no way that

this child can be competent enough to take an

oath; and second of all, the prejudice inherent

in that kind of -- those kind of proofs in this

sensitive a case would far outweigh any

probative value which can come from getting a

person to testify. The bottom line ruling on

that is, there is no way that this child is

competent to testify.

is there anyt...

Prosecutor Rubbinaccio, seeming to know that his attempt to qualify Jessie as a witness had failed, sought another way to have her testify. He wanted Jessie to testify from Valori's lap to ease the child's fear. Judge Stein denied the Prosecutor's request that Valori be permitted to sit on the stand with Jessica. He told the Prosecutor to either drop the charges or appeal his ruling. Jessie was not, in his opinion, competent to testify.

The Prosecutor chose to appeal Judge Stein's ruling. Before the court adjourned, Herb again asked that the condition of bail which prohibited me from seeing Jessie be modified. It was denied while the Prosecutor made his appeal. The hearing ended ninety minutes after it had begun. We now had to wait to hear from the Appellate Court. Would it agree with Judge Stein's finding that

Jessica was incompetent to be a witness?

We waited and waited as the judicial wheel turned slowly. Eventually, the Appellate Court responded to the Prosecutor's appeal. It was quite a strange response when it finally came. They ruled Judge Stein should allow Jessie to sit on her mother's lap and make statements to the court. He was to evaluate Jessica's competency based again on this kind of testimony. Then the Judge would send his decision directly to the Appellate Court. It would review Judge Stein's decision and then issue their decision as to whether or not Jessie could testify and, if so, under what conditions.

So on June 26, we were once again back in court to hear Jessie's testimony. It was not what I expected. I had anguished over the fact that I would again see my child crying as she was asked the same questions. I was wrong. Valori sat with her on the witness stand and this time Jessie did not seem upset at all. To the contrary, she spotted me sitting in the courtroom and said, "Daddy, Daddy, there's my Daddy! Hi Daddy." She spent most of the time giggling, waving and smiling at me. When a recess was called and Valori carried her from the courtroom, Jessie called to me, "Bye, Daddy. We'll wait in the hall for you." My eyes clouded with tears. The condition of bail still prohibited me from talking to her.

After the recess, there was another period of questioning with Jessie sitting on Valori's lap. Again, Jessie spent much of the time waving and smiling at me, which Herb made certain was reflected in the court record. The judge soon decided that he had gathered enough information to form his decision and declared the hearing over. He stated he would move quickly to write his decision on Jessica's competency and send it to the Appellate Court for review. Once again, we were sent home to wait.

Even with all that was happening, strangely, there was nothing to do. I had no office, no patients, no money. We depended on friends and relatives for rent and food. I was quite suicidal at the time and Janeen was afraid to leave me alone. But suicide would have been seen as an admission of guilt. The impact it would ultimately have on Jessie and Janeen was unthinkable.

The days passed slowly and turned into weeks. We waited for Judge Stein's decision on Jessie's competency, but no word came. Herb was sensitive to the fact that I still could not see my daughter and now he appealed the condition of bail to the Appellate Court. So we were now waiting for two decisions: one, a determination on competency; the other, on a change in the bail condition. Each day I would call Herb's office, only to be told there was no news on either point.

I continued to try to channel my efforts toward constructive activities. I began an ambitious campaign of letter-writing. I wrote letters to the Governor, the Administrative Officer of the Courts, the Public Advocate, the Attorney General, my Senators, Congressmen and many others. I wrote to those in public office who might have an interest in or responsibility for my case. But my letters only served to increase my frustration and despair. I received one bureaucratic response after another, all leading nowhere. The government "of the people, by the people and for the people" kept advising me who I should contact instead of them.

August 1984

Finally on August 3, Judge Arnold Stein issued his complicated decision to the Appellate Court. On the primary issue, the competency of Jessica, the judge qualified Jessica "only if she testified under the same conditions in which the hearing was conducted," namely sitting on the lap of her mother. This was something unheard of in a courtroom according to my attorneys. Herb and Steven had mixed feelings about this decision. They felt the Appellate Court would not try to establish a new legal precedent by permitting such testimony. However, we would not know for sure until the Appellate Court issued their ruling, which would be derived from reviewing Stein's decision.

September and October 1984

The dog days of August slipped into September. Janeen and I continued our semi-seclusion. We stayed in the apartment, trying to comfort each other as the politicians' letters arrived in one bureaucratic response after another. The door to Jessie's room remained closed, like a monument to my missing child.

On September 11, the State Court of Appeals denied my

appeal for change in the condition of bail. Despite Herb's fervent pleas for compassion and humanity in this case, the cold response from the Appellate Court can be seen in Exhibit F. The court gave no reason for the denial.

EXHIBIT F

AM -1238-83T5

	ORDER ON MOTIONS/PETITIONS	
		SUPERIOR COURT OF NEW JERSEY APPELLATE DIVISION
	REC'D. APPELLATE DIVISION	DOCKET NO. AM-1238-83T5
		MOTION NO. M-5586-83
STATE OF NEW JERSEY		BEFORE PART E
VS	SEP 13 1984	JUDGES: PRESSLER BRODY HAVEY
LAWRENCE D. SPIEGEL	*Elizabeth McLaughlin* Clerk	FILED APPELLATE DIVISION SEP 13 1984 *Elizabeth McLaughlin* Clerk

MOVING PAPERS FILED _____ AUGUST 17, 1984
ANSWERING PAPERS FILED _____ AUGUST 31, 1984
DATE SUBMITTED TO COURT _____ SEPTEMBER 10, 1984
DATE ARGUED _____
DATE DECIDED _____ SEPTEMBER 11, 1984

ORDER

THIS MATTER HAVING BEEN DULY PRESENTED TO THE COURT, IT IS

HEREBY ORDERED AS FOLLOWS:

	GRANTED	DENIED	OTHER
MOTION/PETITION FOR LEAVE TO APPEAL		X	

SUPPLEMENTAL:

I hereby certify that the foregoing is a true copy of the original on file in my office.

Elizabeth McLaughlin
Clerk

FOR THE COURT:

[signature]
SYLVIA B. PRESSLER   P.J.A.D.

WITNESS, THE HONORABLE   SYLVIA B. PRESSLER   , PRESIDING
JUDGE OF PART E , SUPERIOR COURT OF NEW JERSEY, APPELLATE DIVISION,
THIS 11th DAY OF SEPTEMBER 19 84.

MM(nmr)

Elizabeth McLaughlin
CLERK OF THE APPELLATE DIVISION

Herb, outraged that the Appellate Court had denied to change my condition of bail, filed an appeal to the State Supreme Court, hoping against hope that they would ultimately come to our aid. For me, the denial of the Appellate Court was a crushing blow. Yet, it was also a turning point. It, more than any other single event, began the slow process of the transformation from pain into anger. The first sparks of outrage were evident in the editorial I wrote as an open letter to the Supreme Court, Exhibit G.

EXHIBIT G

Letters to the Editor

Judicial System's Inaction Decried

While the judges and justices of New Jersey's highest courts are enjoying the holiday season with their children, grandchildren and the rest of their families, I wish to make them aware of a small segment of New Jerseyans who, due to the inaction of these guardians of justice, will not have an equal opportunity for holiday cheer.

Two of those New Jerseyans are myself and my little girl, ages 39 and 3, respectively, who, despite their ages and their presumed innocence until proven guilty, are being punished as if they were criminals through the lack of action and attention by the aforementioned judicial bodies.

On Dec. 9, 1983, I was charged with sexually molesting my two-and-a-half-year-old daughter. Since then, there has been a "temporary" condition of bail in effect that I was to have "no contact with the alleged victim," my little girl.

Now, over one year later, that "temporary" condition of bail remains in effect, as a consequence of judicial bureaucracy and legal technicalities. Despite all our efforts, my attorney and I have not been able to get the courts to hold a hearing on this matter, even though such a hearing is clearly required by law.

Time after time in the Superior Courts of Morris County, I have listened to judges express their personal concern and disgust at the events of this case, only to have them declare that for one bureaucratic reason or another, it was not within their purview to order that a hearing be held to determine the efficacy of this condition of bail.

The last time we were in court, the judge stated that since this motion had come before the Appellate Court in November, it was no longer within his jurisdiction. He may not have known, however, that when this motion was brought to the Appellate Court, nearly eleven months after my arrest, they declined to hear it. No reason given. It had first been brought to the Appellate

Court in June of 1984, and it took them until November to decide that they would not hear it. It was immediately appealed to the Supreme Court. They seem to be too busy, however, or did not deem the destruction of a parent/child relationship an important enough matter to have considered as yet. We have had no word from them.

Now, there is no place left to turn. One cannot go to the federal courts until the state remedies have been exhausted. The Appellate Court has refused to hear my plea, the Supreme Court hasn't found time to consider it yet, and the Superior Court feels it no longer has jurisdiction. Meanwhile, the Cabbage Patch doll I bought for my little girl last Christmas, still sits unopened in her room, along with her untouched Easter Basket. Her second Christmas with no Daddy.

The question raised here is not one of guilt or innocence, though I have maintained my innocence throughout. Ultimately the courts will determine that. The issue here is a blatant violation of constitutional and parental rights by the state of New Jersey, and the fact that such an issue can fall through the cracks in the bureaucratic structure of the courts. The issue is the callous destruction of an intimate parent/child relationship, without so much as a hearing for the accused or the child.

I am not alone. In the current climate of hysteria which surrounds the issue of the sexual abuse of children, there are tragedies like these occuring all over the country. How many more families must be disrupted by a legal system which was never designed to handle family matters? When will the judges stop the legal arguments about jurisdiction and have the courage to act and put an end to these outrages? Why can't I have a hearing on this issue? Why am I being treated as guilty before ever being convicted? Why does it seem as if no one cares?

These questions I ask of the members of New Jersey's courts as they enjoy the holiday season, and invite them to respond.

DR. LAWRENCE D. SPIEGEL
Clinical psychologist
151 Route 206 B-33 A-3
Flanders

(Editor's Note: The sexual assault charge against Spiegel is still pending an appellate court decision on whether the child is competent to stand trial. Earlier this year, a Superior Court judge, sitting in Morristown, ruled she was not competent to stand trial but the Prosecutor's Office appealed that ruling.)

December 1984

On December 12, the State Supreme Court denied our appeal to overturn the lower court's ruling on my condition of bail. Their brief statement appears as Exhibit H. This meant no court in the State would allow me to see my daughter.

EXHIBIT H

SUPREME COURT OF NEW JERSEY
M-326 SEPTEMBER TERM 1984

```
                                    :

                                    :

STATE OF NEW JERSEY,                :              23,260

    Plaintiff-Respondent,           :

        vs.                         :

LAWRENCE D. SPIEGEL,                :          O R D E R

    Defendant-Movant.               :

                                    :

                                    :

                                    :
```

FILED

DEC 13 1984

Stephen W. Townsend
CLERK

This matter having been duly presented to the Court, it is ORDERED that the motion for leave to appeal is denied.

WITNESS, the Honorable Robert N. Wilentz, Chief Justice, at Trenton, this 11th day of December, 1984.

A TRUE COPY

Stephen W. Townsend

Stephen W. Townsend
CLERK

n

This ruling, according to Herb and Steven, was a direct violation of federal law which clearly stated that natural parents cannot be barred access to their children without a full court hearing. This law offered me some hope for a legal basis to fight for my right to see Jessica. The false abuse charge was one thing; seeing Jessica until I was cleared of that charge was another. Both situations needed my energy and efforts. Steven, Herb and I began to discuss taking the condition of bail issue to Federal Court. Making constructive efforts gave me more energy to fight back and less time to feel depressed.

Before taking on the Federal Courts, we decided to file one last motion in Morris County, requesting one simple modification in the condition of bail. This was a desperate long shot on our part — a hope that we could convince Judge Egan to grant just one supervised holiday visit with Jessie. We succeeded in having this motion heard. I listened to the impassioned plea as Herb brilliantly depicted the insensitivity of my bail restriction. He asked the judge to allow our one modification, a brief supervised Christmas visit with Jessie, whom I had not seen in more than a year. Judge Egan's comments, appearing in Exhibit I, leave little doubt as to his feelings. He spoke strongly about the case.

EXHIBIT I

24	THE COURT: Okay. What if it turns out
25	that this is a totally fraudulent charge trumped
1	up by an angry wife using this deprivation of
2	visitation as some form of leverage?" What if it
3	as a phony as a three dollar bill? Let's
4	assume, just for the sake of discussion, that
5	you have an evil, venal woman who has put up her

child to make scurrilous, unfounded, totally

untrue charges against her husband or ex-

husband, and because of the law's delay he

becomes, in effect, a stranger to his child?

I've always heard that in the law that

there's a remedy for every wrong. But what's

the remedy to this kind of separation; if, if

Mr. Speigel is totally innocent and is more the

victim than the criminal? Doesn't that bother

you just a little?

MR. SCHONWALD: Your Honor, it does, and

I don't have an answer for that. To the best of

my knowledge, this is not a frivolous charge, we

take it rather seriously. But also, to the best

of my knowledge, I don't think that anybody has

been dragging their heels on this case. We've

been trying to move it, and because it's on

appeal --

THE COURT: I'm not suggesting that. I'm

just saying, what if it is a false charge, a

pack of lies in which the mother has swayed her

child the way you're suggesting, that the father

might sway his child if he had her. The mother

has had her for, I guess, over a year now. And

if there's any possibility of influencing the

```
6    witness, certainly the mother has had the

7    opportunity to do it.  Does that strike you as

8    justice?

9         MR. SCHONWALD:  Well, if this witness is

10   being influenced in that way, certainly it's not

11   -- it's not fair, and it's not justice.  But we

12   have no evidence of that, your Honor.  We've

13   been in contact with the mother and the child,

14   and it's never been brought to my attention that

15   that's been happening.

16        THE COURT:  Well, I'm sure the mother

17   isn't going to say, I'm swaying my child.  So

18   how do you know it's not happening?
```

Judge Egan concluded by saying if the charges were false, then those responsible for making false charges were guilty of a crime. That was the first time I had heard anyone take a direct and clear position against those who falsely accuse. That comment, in itself, added to my strength and hope. Then came his decision on the motion. Since the higher courts, the Appellate and State Supreme Court had decided to maintain the condition of bail, it was beyond his jurisdiction to grant our motion. There was nothing he could do for us.

Herb and I walked dejected from the courtroom. Once outside, he told me not to give up, that better days were ahead. I thanked him for his efforts and words of encouragement. But after all was said and done, I was still not able to see my daughter; no court in the State would allow me to do that. I was still faced with serious criminal charges, still broke, still waiting for the next round of madness and above all, still innocent. I headed home to face the dreaded Christmas of 1984, the second one without Jessie.

5

THE END OF THE BEGINNING

Stage 5: The Transformation

The New Year 1985 came, bringing with it the continued frustrations of the old year. Even Janeen was consumed by depression. She was losing weight and looked worn and t red. Seeing this sparked my anger and made me realize we needed professional help. Although I had previously thought about counseling, I hadn't the energy or money to do anything about it. Now it was clear we needed help, so I decided to act. This decision became a major step in transforming my depression into anger and indignation.

One name immediately jumped into my mind. Stanley Machlin. If anyone was capable of helping, he was. As a psychiatrist, he had treated me many years ago, when I was struggling with my own identity issues. Janeen and I discussed Machl n and decided to give him a call. I had no idea if he was still in practice or even alive for that matter. I went through old files and found his phone number.

As I dialed, my mind filled with questions. Would he still be there? Would he remember me? Back then, I was an undergraduate theater arts major and now I was a doctor of psychology, due in part to his influence. Yet he knew none of this. On the third ring, the phone was answered in a strangely familiar voice.

"Dr. Machlin," the voice said.

"Dr. Machlin, this is Larry Spiegel, well it's Dr. Spiegel now. I don't know if you remember me, but ... "

"Of course, I remember you," he said. "What can I help you with?"

I explained the situation. He immediately set up an appointment for Janeen and me. Just hearing his voice made me feel better. That initial visit and the many that followed brought strength and hope back into our lives. Dr. Machlin helped us cope with the situation and deal effectively with the grief which often consumed me. He provided the reassurance we needed to deal with the crisis. More importantly, he helped me develop my newfound need to fight back. Janeen and I learned to channel our outrage into constructive efforts.

Encouraged by Dr. Machlin, we also sought medical help for the physical symptoms of stress which were taking their toll on Janeen and me. Fortunately, I had a physician and friend, Dr. Gary Safier, who had real compassion for his patients. His medical practice treated my mind as well as my body. Time after time, Janeen and I would confront him with a host of medical problems caused by external events. We came with depression, headaches, chronic stomach troubles, etc. He would treat the body and, more importantly, renew our hope that this trauma would end. He really cared. Drs. Safier and Machlin became an integral part of our support system.

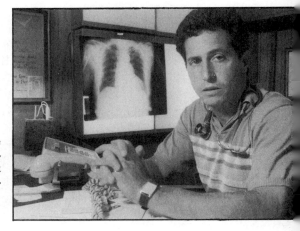

Dr. Gary Safier did more than treat my physical symptoms. His encouragement was a cornerstone of my support system.

Another event which solidified my willingness to fight happened in January. There was a national news story of twenty-five adults in Minnesota who were accused of sexually abusing children. Following that were stories of day-care center abuse scandals in California and New York, and other cases which seemed similar to my own. Suddenly, sexual abuse of children was national news. I found out I was not alone.

When the "Phil Donahue Show" featured the Minnesota abuse story, the panel was composed of those people accused. They announced the formation of VOCAL (Victims Of Child Abuse Laws), an organization designed to fight for the rights of those unjustly accused. Phil Donahue opened the show with the commentary in Exhibit A.

EXHIBIT A

DONAHUE TRANSCRIPT #01155

APPEARANCES: Mr. Phil Donahue

Lois Bentz	Atty. Will Outlaw
Robert Bentz	Michael Ruwe
Jon Conte, Ph.D.	Ralph Underwager, Ph.D.
Peg Doe	Barry Voss

Phil Donahue: Here's the story. Increasing numbers of sexual child abuse cases have come to the attention of authorities. Who is to decide who's guilty and who can accuse you of child abuse. Because if somebody does you'll probably wind up on the evening news and you are going to look very, very guilty. And what is child abuse? What's the difference between changing a diaper and child abuse? And who is watching your children in a culture that is increasingly finding numbers of its own children without parental supervision. And who is your babysitter and if it's a girl, who is her boyfriend, and is she visiting at night? And is he visiting her while she is working for your children? And what do we know about him? And what about the blended family? How about the mother who marries for the second time, has a teenage daughter? What is child abuse and should children be able to accuse you, and is that information enough to convict you? And how do you feel about children testifying in the impersonal atmosphere of a courtroom? And who's watching the prosecutors? We are scared to death of child abusers in this country, and it appears that we on more than one occasion have perhaps gone too far and railroaded innocent people. And once you're accused, can the officials of the county prosecutor's office interview your neighbors? And if they interview your neighbors and it's revealed that there's a charge against you, you've probably gone to your last block party. And can you ever get rid of this fly paper? And perhaps the most important question of all, how do we most effectively take out of society those who abuse our children? Lois and Robert Bentz have lived this nightmare. They are from Jordon, Minnesota. This is a town that did not want to be on your front page but it has been. You have three children, all boys, aged seven to thirteen.

A Question of Innocence

I called Minnesota and spoke with Mary Lou Bauer, a co-founder of VOCAL. She told me VOCAL had received thousands of calls from people caught in the same trap. She said they were encouraging each state to form its own chapter of VOCAL. She gave me the name and phone number of another man, Chris Clauss, who had called from Burlington, New Jersey. Naturally I called him.

There was a remarkable similarity in our cases. Just after his divorce, his ex-wife accused him of molesting their little girl, who was the same age as Jessie. He said he had spoken to others in New Jersey who were falsely accused. They planned to meet at his home early in February. I assured him I would be there.

These events jarred my memory. In September or October, 1983, Nancy had given me an article from the *Newark Star Ledger* about a male nurse who had had similar troubles. Back then, I was so depressed that I barely looked at the article. Now I searched the house and found it. I contacted the accused man, Nick Andrian, and we spoke about our situations. He lived just fifteen minutes away. Nick was an extremely articulate, intelligent and compassionate individual. He, too, had landed in the trap of the falsely accused. He had formed an organization, the Coalition for the Unjustly Accused, before hearing about VOCAL. I told him of the meeting in South Jersey. He said he would attend. That conversation marked the beginning of our friendship. We would become allies and confidants.

February and March 1985

In February, Janeen and I drove to Burlington to what became the start of the New Jersey chapter of VOCAL. It was a strange meeting with an incredible diversity in the group of people. Yet all of us had the same problem. Exhibit B, an article from the *Philadelphia Inquirer*, tells about that meeting.

EXHIBIT B

In defense

Burlco group forms to fight false sexual child-abuse cases

By Dwight Ott
Inquirer Staff Writer

Six people gathered in Chris Clauss' living room in Burlington City yesterday to become part of a national organization established to fight for the rights of those falsely accused of sexually abusing children.

Three of the six have been charged with sexually assaulting their own children. One was the wife of a minister who said her husband was charged with child molestation by a vengeful member of his congregation. Another was a substitute teacher, who said "politics" was involved in charges that he sexually abused children in his care, and another was a social worker, who declined to reveal the details of his case.

Four asked that their names not be used. All say the charges — still pending — are false. Nonetheless, they say, because of the charges, plans for remarriages have been dashed, jobs lost and, in some cases, child visitation prohibited.

"We're guilty until proven innocent," said Clauss, 26, who was charged in a case in April.

The group is patterned after an organization called VOCAL (Victims Of Child Abuse Laws), formed in Hampton, Minn., in October after 25 people in nearby Jordan, many of them parents, were charged with

sexually abusing children. Charges later were dropped against 22 of the defendants. One person pleaded guilty, and two were acquitted.

Mary Lou Bauer, a spokeswoman for the organization in Hampton, said in a telephone interview yesterday that the organization had about 27 chapters in 18 states and was receiving more applications for membership than it can handle. She said the group had one chapter in Pennsylvania. If it becomes a chapter, the Burlington group would be the first in New Jersey.

Bauer said the organization's goals were to publicize the plight of those falsely accused of sexually abusing children and to monitor public officials, the media and legislation regarding child sex abuse.

"We [the members] were all people personally involved [in the Minnesota case] who were angered because we were becoming victims of a kind of national hysteria caused by the media, the federal government and social workers who want to make their jobs look important," Bauer said.

She said that in most sexual abuse cases there was no jury, and the judge was fed information from an array of attorneys representing the child and social service agencies — all pitted against the defendant.

One of the members of the newly

formed Burlington group, Lawrence Spiegel of Morris County, said sexual-abuse charges can be made for revenge, and agencies investigating such charges can become unwitting tools of the accusers.

Several members of the group were especially critical of the state Division of Youth and Family Services (DYFS), which is responsible for conducting preliminary investigations of sexual-abuse charges.

"DYFS is not doing its job," said the 39-year-old Spiegel, adding that his clinical psychology practice and re-marriage plans were wrecked as a result of charges still pending against him from December 1983.

"If DYFS were doing a thorough investigation, most of these cases would not get to the prosecutor's office. They're essentially using the prosecutor's office to sweep the clutter off their desk. Meanwhile, we're the victims."

Charlene Brown, a spokeswoman for DYFS, said yesterday that "generally, in any child abuse case, DYFS is called in by law. People, by law, are required to report any incident of child abuse. Then DYFS — depend-ing on the seriousness of the charge, and whether DYFS believes the charges are substantiated — reports it to the prosecutor. At that point, it is the prosecutor's responsibility to investigate the case more thoroughly.

"If they [VOCAL] have a problem with the way the cases are investigated, they should take their complaint to the prosecutor in their county. DYFS has a role in the initial preliminary investigation, but once they substantiate that there is reason to believe the child may have been abused, it is the prosecutor's office who then does a full investigation."

Spiegel said DYFS was not the group's only target. He said the group believed that the courts were ill-equipped to handle family matters — especially child sexual-abuse cases that might involve marital revenge.

"We want to make people aware that this can happen to anyone," said Clauss. "I would like DYFS [and other agencies] to do as much investigation as possible, but they should do it thoroughly. ... This is a serious charge."

One of several results of that first VOCAL meeting was the drafting of a letter to the Attorney General of New Jersey. We notified him of VOCAL's formation and outlined our purposes and intended actions. We advised the Attorney General that VOCAL would monitor the activities of his office, DYFS and any other agency concerned with child abuse. In addition, VOCAL intended to hold DYFS workers, prosecutors and state agency officials legally liable and accountable for their actions. VOCAL was here. We weren't fooling around.

Steven and Herb questioned my involvement in VOCAL and were concerned about my statements to the media. I realized they spoke with my best interests in mind. However, they had to understand I needed to work with VOCAL for my own sanity. We argued the pros and cons of continued press coverage, but that discussion was resolved for us. A precedent-setting decision, emanating from the Appellate Court, hurled my story nationwide.

On March 25, the Appellate Court released their decision. The court ruled that Jessica was competent as a witness and she would be permitted to sit on her mother's lap and testify. Suddenly, my story was in the headlines and caught the eye of Associated Press and United Press International. The Court's decision, as well as my story, became national news. Exhibit C exemplifies one of those news stories.

EXHIBIT C

3-year-old may testify on mother's lap

TRENTON (AP) — A 3-year-old girl may sit on her mother's lap and testify at her father's trial on charges of sexually abusing her more than a year ago, a state appeals court ruled in a plit decision yesterday.

Ruling on the issue for the first time, the Appellate Division of Superior Court said a mother could sit with a child on the witness stand or hold the child on her lap in order to put the child at ease.

The case has no precedent in a state court in the nation, said Herbert Korn, the defendant's lawyer. A 1948 federal court ruling allowed a 9-year-old rape victim to testify while seated on her mother's lap, the Appellate Division said.

"No 3-year-old child should be compelled to approach this task in a state of childish fright," said Judge William T. McElroy.

The girl, who was ruled competent to testify by a Superior Court judge in Morristown last June, may be the youngest person ever qualified as a witness, said Catherine S. Arnone, spokeswoman for the state's judiciary.

THE APPEALS court majority said she met the state Supreme Court's standards — that she understands the difference between right and wrong; that to tell the truth is right; and that she will be punished in some way if she lies.

The ruling came in the case of a Mount Olive man awaiting trial in Superior Court in Morris County on charges of aggravated criminal sexual contact with his daughter, who was 2 years and 8 months old at the time of the alleged offenses during visits with him in the fall of 1983.

The defendant, who is divorced from the girl's mother, was identified in court documents by his initials, L.S. The girl, who will turn 4 on April 6, lives with her mother in Georgia and Florida.

The father contended that to permit the girl, identified as J.S., to sit on her mother's lap in front of a jury would be prejudicial and deny him a fair trial.

Korn said his client maintains he is innocent and that the charges were prompted by his "vindictive" former wife.

THE APPEALS court said that if the child testifies out of the presence of the jury and cannot sit alone, the judge should explain the mother's presence. Recently, the courts have allowed the testimony of alleged sexual assault victims to be shown by television to jurors.

At a pretrial hering last June, the child was not allowed to sit on her mother's lap and was unresponsive to questions. After a state appeals court said she could sit on or with her mother at the counsel table or witness stand, she sat on her mother's lap and answered questions. The judge said she qualified as a witness.

Judge Thomas Shebell dissented in the 2-1 appeals decision, saying, "This child had no comprehension whatsoever that 'to tell the truth is 'right.'"

The day my story was picked up by the press wire services, the phone in my apartment rang continuously. Herb finally got through and asked me to come to the office. He needed to review with me the actual decisions and discuss their impact. I went right over.

Herb showed me three documents, one from each of the three Appellate Court Justices who issued this landmark decision. One document was forty-six pages in length, the second was eleven pages, and the third was eight pages. It was obvious from the summary cover page of the documents, that each judge's decision contradicted in part, the decisions of the other two. The decision was quite complicated.

This legal development and the national attention it brought, forced us to reexamine our legal strategy. For several reasons, Herb and Steven wanted to appeal this decision to the State Supreme Court. They did not want a jury to hear the practiced phrases of Jessica. Herb had had no experience with cross-examining such a young child. Having Jessica testify would establish a dangerous precedent — allowing infants to testify, especially while sitting on the accuser's lap. Floodgates would open to release streams of false accusations. Children would be programmed to say what an accusing parent wanted them to say. Divorce and custody disputes would resort more and more to this tactic.

I wanted to appeal the Appellate Court decision because I did not want the trial to focus on Jessie. I knew Valori had created this disaster and the heat belonged on her, not on my little girl. We agreed to appeal the competency ruling on Jessica to the State Supreme Court.

As these events were unfolding, Steven allowed me to use an office in his suite. I can imagine the difficulty he had getting permission from his partners to share space with an accused child molester. Somehow he managed it. As part of my psychology at making a comeback, I began to see a few patients again.

It was still very difficult. The transformation stage is a constant vacillation between depression and anger. My work did help to boost my spirits. At the same time, Steven needed a receptionist. Janeen took the job and was able to assist me as well.

April 1985

In that office in early April, I held my first press conference. In addition to the wire services, several reporters from local papers came. I read from a prepared statement. The reporters were eager to know more about the Appellate Court decision, my appeal of it to the State Supreme Court and my immediate legal plans. Although my statement was carefully worded to avoid problems once I was in court, the reporters dug for information beyond my press release. It was my first taste at how cleverly phrased reporters' questions can be when they want the facts. Exhibit D is an example of one of the newspaper stories.

EXHIBIT D

Flanders psychologist to appeal judges' child -testimony decision

TRENTON (UPI) —

Claiming that those accused of sexual abuse of children are "being treated as guilty until proven innocent," a Flanders psychologist said Thursday he will appeal an appellate court's decision allowing his 3½-year-old daughter to sit on her mother's lap and testify against him.

Dr. Lawrence Spiegel, 39, made the announcement in a four-page prepared statement he read at a press conference at his Parsippany office. Spiegel's attorney, Herbert Korn, said a motion for leave to appeal had been filed with the state Supreme Court Tuesday.

Korn said he feels the court will grant argument on the appeal because of the dissent in the 2-1 March appellate court decision and because of the "many questions" now surrounding the issue of how child witnesses in such cases may be questioned.

Spiegel is charged with aggravated sexual assault for the alleged Dec. 3, 1983 molestation of the girl in Budd Lake when she was 2½ years old. The charge was brought by Spiegel's ex-wife one month after a divorce ended with the two being given joint custody of the child. The March appellate court decision allowing the child to testify came as a result of Spiegel's appeal of a decision last summer by Superior Court Judge Arnold M. Stein that the girl was competent to testify.

Stein made his decison after hearing the girl testify on her mother's lap at a hearing. Prosecutors have said they have no case with the girl's testimony.

Spiegel said Thursday "there is indisputable scientific evidence that children do not have the capacity for long term memory recall until at least the age of 7."

"My point here is not to discuss ... my case at all. The issue now is to discuss the ludicrousness" of putting judges in a position of making decisions on what young children can remember, Spiegel said, adding that many cases involving allegations of sexual abuse are arising in "bitter" divorce settings.

"The courts are being used by parents as a means of obtaining instant custody by simply alleging abuse and punishing their former spouse," he said. He claimed statistics have indicated that about

80 percent of sexual abuse allegations which arise out of matrimonial or custody disputes turn out to be false.

Spiegel said he and a national organization called Victims of Child Abuse Laws (VOCAL) will try to convince Gov. Thomas Kean to restructure procedures of the state Division of Youth and Family Services (DYFS), which investigates many sexual abuse allegations.

The psychologist said he has not been allowed to see or even talk to his daughter in almost two years, and the accusations against him have "completely ruined my life." His daughter and former wife now live in Georgia, he added.

As a result of the press conference, my lawyers and I were inundated with letters, phone calls and telegrams from additional reporters, lawyers, mental health practitioners and victims. We could not respond to all of them. I received a call from the VOCAL national office in Minnesota, congratulating me on my decision to fight. For months, letters and inquiries arrived from all over the country. Someone from California sent an article by Jay Mathews, a writer assigned to the Los Angeles bureau of the *Washington Post*. The article featured the case of an assistant Attorney General in California, who had been charged with sexual abuse and eventually cleared of the charges.

I, along with the members of the New Jersey VOCAL chapter, soon realized we were dealing with more than some isolated instances of false allegations. There was a phenomenon sweeping the country. Although it pointed to a serious social problem, it also revealed numerous instances of wrongdoing by Prosecutors and a blatant abuse of power by various state child protection agencies. The more we delved into matters, the more we learned about the problems within our child protection system.

With the New Jersey chapter of VOCAL organized, politicians and government officials who had responded to our individual letters with bureaucratic replies, seemed to take us more seriously collectively. Members of VOCAL's executive committee were given appointments with the Attorney General's office, the Commissioner of Human Services, the Director of the Division of Youth and Family Services and other agencies. We hoped our problems would be heard and investigated. Our hope was not realistic.

My first meeting was with the Attorney General. Janeen and I fought our way through downtown Trenton and arrived at the Hughes Justice Complex. We were asked to sign in, told we were expected, given official identification badges and immediately ushered upstairs through glass doors which read:

Attorney General
State of New Jersey
Irwin I. Kimmelman

We were led down a long office corridor into an enormous conference room. Three sides of the room were glass. Looking down at the city of Trenton, we felt as though we were in an ivory tower. It soon became apparent to us that those who occupied the Attorney General's office certainly were.

After we waited five minutes, the door at the opposite end of the room opened. Two women walked in. One woman introduced herself as Charlotte Kittler, the First Deputy Attorney General. The other woman was a representative of the Department of Human Services. We were informed that the Attorney General was unavoidably detained and that he extended his regrets for not being present. This was the first indication that the meeting was intended to merely pacify VOCAL. This feeling was soon confirmed by our conversation. I outlined the problem of the falsely accused, giving specifics as they were needed. Both women seemed genuinely surprised by the scope of the problem as we presented it.

We gave the First Deputy Attorney General some professional studies issued by the national VOCAL office. These clearly illustrated the problem of false accusations. We presented a written appeal which requested that the Attorney General appoint a special task force to investigate and monitor the activities of DYFS and the offices of the county prosecutors, as had been done in Minnesota.

The First Deputy Attorney General gave a bureaucratic response clearly designed to placate us. "I will certainly discuss this matter with Mr. Kimmelman and determine if there is anything..."

I said VOCAL wanted a reply from the Attorney General's office by week's end or we would demonstrate in Trenton prior to the upcoming elections in which the Governor was seeking another term.

Ms. Kittler doubted that the Attorney General had the power to initiate such measures and said she would call me by the end of the week. I told her the Attorney General of Minnesota was able to do so. She responded by saying this was New Jersey, not Minnesota. I was glad we clarified something at this meeting.

The executive committee updated VOCAL members on their meetings with various government officials. Each meeting had gone in a basic bureaucratic way. This approach produced few results for us. The only interesting and unusual event came with the sudden announcement from the office of the Commissioner of Human Services, the office which oversees DYFS. "Mr. George Albanese, Commissioner of Human Services, has suddenly announced his resignation, giving no official reason for it." The report indicated the Governor had asked Mr. Albanese to remain until after the elections in November, but Albanese refused.

The Commissioner's resignation occurred a few days after VOCAL requested a meeting with him. The timing of his resignation raised many questions. Did he resign to avoid some impending conflict? Was VOCAL poking into matters that could bring this government agency embarrassment or something even worse? What about issues like black market babies, missing children, private adoption services? Were we stumbling into something above our heads, beyond our own individual problem of false accusations? I seriously wondered.

We decided that VOCAL would retain an attorney, Robert Cherry. He, along with my friend and fellow officer Nick, the secretary, Sharon and I would attempt to meet with the Governor. After several phone calls to the Governor's Office, I spoke with a top aide. I informed him that VOCAL had retained an attorney and we scheduled a meeting with the counsel to the Governor, Ollie Hawkins, and the Director of DYFS, Thomas Blatner.

May 1985

On May 8, Bob Cherry, Nick, Sharon, Janeen and I departed for the meeting in Trenton. Though Nick and I still had hopes that something could be accomplished, our counsel, Mr. Cherry, was

Nick Andrian was always at the center of VOCAL's critical issues. We had countless questions. Often, the answers were not easy to find.

not as optimistic. He was prepared to inform the Governor's counsel that VOCAL would institute a class action lawsuit if we did not get an adequate response from our eleven-point proposal.

The Governor's counsel, Ollie Hawkins, made a strained effort to be diplomatic, but he answered every question with political platitudes. Nothing we said changed his posture. On the other hand, the Director of DYFS, Thomas Blatner, seemed concerned with our matters. Yet he had just become the Director; he could offer little advice or assistance at the time. Forty-five minutes after the meeting began, Bob Cherry stood up, opened his briefcase and put his papers away.

"I think we have heard enough," he said. Turning to Mr. Hawkins, he commented, "You can inform the Governor that the New Jersey chapter of VOCAL intends to file a federal multiple plaintiff lawsuit, naming the Governor as the primary defendant."

"Now wait a minute," said Hawkins, standing up in his most animated expression of the day. "Surely we can work something out here." He then agreed to "look into" the possible development of a special task force and contact us within ten days.

"Maybe he will do something," I said to Bob Cherry as we walked out of the Statehouse, trying to maintain some sense of optimism.

"Don't hold your breath," came the reply.

We were a sorry-looking group as we exited onto the busy street outside the Statehouse. Nick and Sharon were fuming, Janeen and I were disappointed and Bob Cherry continued to walk purposefully toward the parking lot.

Before getting into our respective cars, we briefly discussed our situation. We agreed to take no further action until the next VOCAL meeting. That would provide the Governor with time to react to Mr. Hawkins' report. It also gave us an opportunity to clear our heads. Bob Cherry, with his sharp legal wit, said Hawkins had unwittingly given us what could be an important piece of information. He reminded us that Hawkins had said a special task force to review the activities of DYFS had been created by the Governor when he first took office.

"Doesn't that make you a little curious?" he stated in his typically blunt manner. "I suggest that you get some people to research the findings of that task force. This may not be the first time DYFS has come under close scrutiny. It may help us to know some of that history. Meanwhile, I have a lawsuit to file."

With that he got into his car and drove away, leaving the four of us standing in the parking lot. We agreed that Nick would research the past activities of DYFS, Sharon would write up notes of the meeting and I would maintain contact with the Governor's office. We got into our vehicles and left for our homes.

Within ten days Mr. Hawkins called me. He said there was nothing the Governor could do about our problems. I responded by telling him we were left with no option but to file the federal lawsuit. He responded with an arrogant, "Go ahead." I told him VOCAL would telegram the Governor, informing him that we took the advice of Mr. Hawkins and filed suit. That took him aback, but he responded with, "That's fine," and hung up.

I immediately sent this telegram, seen in Exhibit E. Coincidently, Mr. Hawkins resigned his position some weeks later.

EXHIBIT E

```
MAILGRAM SERVICE CENTER
MIDDLETOWN, VA. 22645
22PM
```

Western Union Mailgram

```
4-045450S142002 05/22/85 ICS IPMMTZZ CSP NWKB
1 2019271547 MGM TDMT FLANDERS NJ 05-22 0941P EST


DR L SPIEGEL
151 RT 206 BLDG 33 APT 3
FLANDERS NJ 07836



THIS IS A CONFIRMATION COPY OF THE FOLLOWING MESSAGE:
```

```
2019271547 MGMB TDMT FLANDERS NJ 135 05-22 0941P EST
ZIP
GOVERNOR THOMAS KEAN
STATE HOUSE
TRENTON NJ 08625
AFTER NUMEROUS FUTILE CONVERSATIONS WITH VARIOUS STATE OFFICIALS AS
WELL AS YOUR OWN COUNSEL THE MEMBERS OF THE NEW JERSEY CHAPTER OF
VOCALS HAVE DECIDED TO FOLLOW THE ADVICE OF YOUR OWN COUNSEL MR
HAWKINS AND MR EDWARDS WHO SUGGESTED TO ME TODAY ON THE PHONE THAT WE
INSTITUTE A FEDERAL CLASS ACTION SUIT AGAINST THE STATE OF NEW JERSEY
NAMING YOU AS CHIEF EXECUTIVE RESPONSIBLE FOR THE VIOLATION OF
PARENTAL AND CONSTITUTIONAL RIGHTS.

IN ADDITION NEW JERSEY VOCAL SUPPORTED BY THE NATIONAL ORGANIZATION
INTENDS TO BE A DECISIVE FORCE IN THE UPCOMING NEW JERSEY ELECTIONS.
SHOULD YOU WISH TO AVOID THIS ACTION YOU MAY PERSONALLY CALL ME AT
(201)334-2420 AFTER 1PM ON THURSDAY THE 23RD OR FRIDAY THE 24TH.
   DR L SPIEGEL EXECUTIVE COMMITTEE
   NEW JERSEY VOCAL

IN THE EVENT OF ANY SERVICE INQUIRIES, PLEASE DIRECT CORRESPON-
DENCE TO:

             NATIONAL CONSUMER SERVICE CENTER
             C/O WESTERN UNION TELEGRAPH COMPANY
             308 WEST ROUTE 38
             MOORESTOWN, NJ    08057

21:41 EST

MGMCOMP
```

TO REPLY BY MAILGRAM MESSAGE, SEE REVERSE SIDE FOR WESTERN UNION'S TOLL - FREE PHONE NUMBERS

June and July 1985

Disappointment and frustration lined the faces of those at the conference table in the Hilton Inn at Tinton Falls, New Jersey. The VOCAL membership was being informed of our lack of progress with the Governor's Office. By now the membership was numbering near fifty. A heated discussion erupted, punctuated by outbursts of anger. The president, Chris Clauss, attempted to maintain order.

This behavior was the affect of long-term futility exerted on normal people. To listen to law-abiding people talk about civil disobedience was indeed an education. We needed an outlet for our frustration and desired to make something happen. We were tired of waiting for the system to deal with us. We wanted to move the system.

State officials had never seen this volatile side of the accused.

Yet when the government prohibits a parent-child relationship without clear and positive proof of wrongdoing, it has clearly gone beyond protection and justice to a dangerous and damaging point. The heated meeting finally ended with two resolutions. First, we would proceed with a federal lawsuit, which at this time is still pending. Secondly, we would bring this issue to the media to increase awareness and generate public pressure. We hoped media coverage would effect attitudes in the judicial system, as well as policies in governmental agencies like DYFS.

Since Father's Day was a few weeks away, VOCAL decided to demonstrate on June 16 at the Governor's home in Livingston, New Jersey. Because my case had already attracted some national publicity, I would be in charge of notifying the press. Other members assumed various tasks necessary to organize the demonstration.

I went to work on strategies for press coverage. I thought the local press and wire services would be interested, yet I knew we needed something more — a national publication which would make this Father's Day demonstration a headline not to be ignored. My own ability to fight back was reaching its highest peak. I pondered who I could call to achieve maximum exposure.

I sat in my office one afternoon, contemplating the problem of national exposure for VOCAL's efforts. I kept running into brick walls attempting to get through to *Time*, *Life*, and even *New Jersey Monthly*. I inevitably got a polite, "don't call us, we'll call you." Throughout my calls I had the nagging feeling that I was overlooking something. Try as I might, I could not remember what it was.

That evening as Janeen and I were eating dinner at home, it finally came to me. I jumped up from the table, ran over to my desk and began shuffling through the mounds of paper, newspaper clippings, and court documents.

"What in the world are you looking for?" Janeen asked, as she followed me into the living room.

"Remember that article I received months ago, the one from the *Washington Post*? That writer, I can't remember his name, seemed to have insight into this kind of injustice. He wrote that article about the Assistant Attorney General out in California who was falsely accused."

The End Of The Beginning

Janeen had only a vague memory of it, but began to help me sort through the papers. After a half-hour of frustration, she finally stood up with an article in her hand. "Is this it?" she asked.

I grabbed the paper. Sure enough, there it was. It had been written by Jay Mathews, senior staff writer in the Los Angeles bureau. I had a very strong intuition he would help. I glanced at the clock; it read 7:45 p.m. "Damn, it's too late to call him," I said. Then I remembered, "Wait a minute, he's in California. Maybe I could catch him."

"Go ahead and call, it's worth a try," Janeen said.

As I got the number for the Los Angeles bureau of the *Washington Post*, I had no idea what I was going to say. I simply dialed, believing I could convey the circumstances clearly. A female voice answered the phone, "*Washington Post*."

"Is Jay Mathews there?" I asked.

"Whom shall I say is calling?" the voice responded.

"Tell him it's Dr. Spiegel calling from New Jersey," I said, as though that would mean something.

"Just a moment, please." I was put on hold. This is ridiculous I thought as I waited. He's not going to speak to me. I fully expected the same female voice to come back on the phone to inquire, "May I ask what this is in reference to?"

In the midst of this thought, I heard the phone click and a voice say, "Yes, this is Jay Mathews."

He took me totally by surprise and for a second I couldn't say a word. Then I began blurting out a series of disjointed statements about having read his article and the nature of our own plight. I was barely comprehensible.

When I had finished, he said, "I'll tell you what. I'm not sure there is anything I can do for you, but if you can send me some written information by Friday, I'll look at it over the weekend. I'll give you my home address."

I found this hard to believe. As I wrote down his address, my mind was racing. "This is Wednesday night. If I can collect everything he needs by tomorrow, I could send it in the overnight mail." Between these thoughts I thanked him and said I would get the material to him.

"Fine," he said. "Call me collect on Monday and we'll discuss it. Make sure you include documentation, legal papers, and news articles. Don't leave anything out."

Janeen and I began working that night. By Thursday afternoon, we had compiled and copied the necessary information on my case and the plight of VOCAL. The package weighed two pounds. We rushed to the post office and sent it. Now we had to wait until Monday.

About 4:00 p.m. on Monday, I called Jay Mathews. I thought to myself, "he has had enough time to digest the material." But I actually feared he had not even looked at the package. Perhaps my call would push him into reading it.

I picked up the phone and dialed the number, calling collect as he had instructed. My fears could not have been more unfounded. He told me he was aghast at the situation, outraged at the injustices which it pointed out. He felt the *Washington Post* had an obligation to bring such news to national attention. He asked for more and more details, especially on my case. When I told him about DYFS releasing a three-year-old into my custody after being accused of molesting my own daughter, he said, "This is crying out for a story."

On June 14, he called to say he was writing the story and wanted to headline it in Sunday's paper, Father's Day. He needed a picture of me and was sending out an Associated Press photographer from New York. Jay Mathews wrote a section of the article, then called me. After gathering more information, he wrote the next section. This went on for several hours. By midnight, the photographer had not arrived, but Jay had finished the story.

In my final conversation with him, I asked if his story would definitely appear on Sunday. He responded, "Unless the hijackers blow up the plane in Lebanon and barring a major earthquake, it will be in Sunday's edition."

On Father's Day, Sunday, June 16, 1985, I was up at 6:00 a.m. The demonstration at the Governor's home was scheduled to start at 11:00 a.m., but first I had to get a copy of the *Washington Post*. I headed for New York City to buy the paper, listening to the radio while driving on the deserted roads. I heard a CBS radio announcer say, "And the *Washington Post* reports this morning that a clinical psychologist from Flanders, New Jersey, will spend Father's Day demonstrating in front of the home of Governor Thomas Kean. Dr. Lawrence Spiegel, who has been charged by the State Division of Youth and Family Services with molesting his two and a half-year-old daughter, says he has been denied due process and is innocent of the charge. He is trying to get the Governor to intercede on his behalf so that he can see his little girl. He has been barred from having any contact with her since the charges were filed in December of 1983."

I was so astounded to hear my name on the radio, I actually went through a red light, almost causing an accident. The realization that my situation had gotten national attention was certainly a hopeful sign for me and the thousands of others like me.

At the bus terminal newsstand in New York, I bought two copies of the paper. I turned the pages and the headline jumped out at me, "Child, 4, to Testify of Alleged Sex Abuse." There was a full half-page article which appears here as Exhibit F.

EXHIBIT F

Child, 4, to Testify of Alleged Sex Abuse

Legal Dispute Stirred Over Case's Reliance on Memory of Long-Past Events

By Jay Mathews
Washington Post Staff Writer

Sometime this fall, bouncy, blue-eyed Jessica Spiegel, age 4, is expected to sit on her mother's lap in a New Jersey courtroom and testify to alleged sexual abuse by her father when she was 2½.

Legal experts say this apparently will be the first time a child so young is allowed to testify in such circumstances about events so far in the past. Word of the case, the result of a novel court decision in the wake of a messy divorce, has put a growing number of fathers' rights groups around the country in an uproar and added to a bitter national debate over child-abuse prosecutions.

Jessica first was asked to testify when she was 3½. She spent most of the time crying or waving at her father across the courtroom.

Examinations by three doctors have failed to uncover physical evidence of abuse, Jessica's father said, but this is not necessary for a molestation arrest in New Jersey. So the father, Lawrence Spiegel, 39, stands accused of aggravated sexual assault, carrying a maximum penalty of 20 years in prison.

For Spiegel, a clinical psychologist, this Father's Day will be spent demonstrating in front of the home of New Jersey Gov. Thomas H. Kean, demanding a new look at molestation laws, and pondering the 18 months he has been denied contact with his only child.

Valori Mulvey, 26, Spiegel's ex-wife and Jessica's mother, could not be reached for comment. A woman who answered her telephone and identified herself as Mulvey's mother said she had been advised to say nothing until after the trial. Mulvey's attorney did not return a call.

Morris County assistant prosecutor Michael Rubbinaccio said he is barred from commenting on pending cases but that he carefully considers the age of a child witness and the complications of a bitter divorce before proceeding with a molestation case.

Spiegel's clinical practice is a shambles, although the same state agency that brought the charges recently let him escort a ward of the court, a 3½ girl, to her relatives in Detroit. Unopened Christmas presents for Jessica sit in her empty room at his home in Flanders, N.J. Spiegel said during a telephone interview that his morning depressions are sometimes so great "I can hardly find the strength to pull myself from the bed."

"Much has been said and written lately about the possible trauma to a child who may have been sexually abused, if they are asked to testify," he said. "Yet nothing has been said about the trauma of a child who very possibly has *not* been sexually abused, who is not only made to testify against a parent, but who also must suffer the absence of that parent with no explanation."

Although no statistics are available, attorneys familiar with child-abuse cases say that molestation charges are becoming much more frequent in child-custody disputes. Fathers usually are the targets, but new civil rights groups concerned with the trend, such as Victims of Child Abuse Laws (VOCAL), have many female members.

VOCAL, founded following a celebrated Minnesota child-abuse case, has 52 chapters around the country and is leading the New Jersey effort to publicize Spiegel's story. It has called for laws that would allow prosecution of persons who make false child-abuse reports.

According to Spiegel, "my work, my dreams, my life and everything I had struggled for were shattered" the afternoon of Dec. 9, 1983 when county investigators arrested and handcuffed him in the parking lot of his Randolph, N.J., office.

He married Mulvey in March 1981, when she was pregnant with Jessica, a year after they met in a class he taught at a local college. The child was born April 6. His first marriage had ended in divorce after 13 years with no children.

After a year, his new marriage was in trouble. He and his wife 'sought counseling. But in January 1983 she left, unannounced, with their baby. When he tracked her down after three months and presented a court order giving him the right to see the child, she refused to honor it.

Under their October 1983 divorce agreement, he provided her with an apartment, nursery school fees and tuition to complete her college degree—total support of about $16,000 a year. He retained rights to see Jessica two days a week and every other weekend.

Two weeks after the divorce, Mulvey took Jessica to Cincinnati. Court action by Spiegel brought her back, only to charge that she was trying to save her child from being sexually abused by him. With no evidence to support the accusation, the judge ignored Mulvey and gave Spiegel joint custody of Jessica.

Spiegel's attorney warned him to document carefully any time he might spend alone with his daughter. During one visit, Spiegel said, Jessica cheerfully told him for no apparent reason, "Daddy, don't put your face in my pagina [sic]." Spiegel said he believed her mother had taught her to say that.

When Mulvey complained to the state youth and family services division about an alleged molestation one weekend in December 1983, Spiegel thought he was well prepared. A babysitter, his fiance and his first wife, who remained a good friend, had been with him and Jessica all weekend. Father and daughter had never been alone, he said.

Nevertheless, Jessica apparently answered affirmatively when asked by investigators if her father had touched her near her genitals. Spiegel was arrested and released on bail. The case went to court.

Her first time on the stand, Jessica simply cried. The prosecutors asked if the mother could sit with her, and an appellate court agreed to allow it just to see if her answers indicated she could qualify as a witness. At first, she simply responded to questions by waving, smiling and calling to Spiegel, "Daddy, Daddy."

After a recess, she said "yes" when asked if her father had touched her, and indicated the area of her buttocks. She also indicated that her memory was part of a "dream" and said "no" when asked if her father had hurt her.

The prosecution asked that her testimony continue on her mother's lap. Spiegel's attorney called this "akin to having Charlie McCarthy testify on Edgar Bergen's lap." Asked what would happen if she didn't tell the truth, Jessica testified, "My mommy will slap me."

But the appellate division of the superior court voted, 2 to 1, to allow the testimony. Two weeks ago, the state Supreme Court refused to review the case.

University of Nebraska psychologist Gary Melton, an expert on child-abuse law, said that some judges in the growing number of abuse cases are beginning to allow parents on the stand with child witnesses. But he said he had never heard of a child as young as Jessica being asked to recall events nearly two years in the past.

He said studies indicate that "recognition" memory, the ability to identify faces in a line-up, is well developed by age 4 but "free recall," the ability to recite past events, is far less certain, particularly if it concerns events on which the child was not focusing at the time.

Jessica qualified as a child witness when the court ruled that she met New Jersey's three-point standard: knowing the difference between truth and lies, showing a commitment to telling the truth and understanding that there is a penalty for not telling the truth.

Spiegel said he remains confident a judge eventually will dismiss the charges. He said the threat of jail bothers him far less than the time he has missed with Jessica.

"Unless the laws are revamped," he said, "any family in the country is vulnerable to the government coming in and taking their children."

Last Christmas Spiegel asked Superior Court Judge Charles Egan to let him see Jessica once during the holidays. Egan said that it was out of his jurisdiction because a similar request was before the appellate court. But Egan commented to the prosecutors opposing the visit:

"Let's assume, just for the sake of discussion, that you have an evil, venal woman who has put up her child to make scurrilous, unfounded, totally untrue charges against her husband or ex-husband, and because of the law's delay he becomes, in effect, a stranger to his child.

"I've always heard that in the law that there's a remedy for every wrong. But what's the remedy to this kind of separation? If Mr. Spiegel is totally innocent and is more the victim than the criminal? Doesn't that bother you just a little?"

I read it again and again, amazed at how well-written it was. Every detail was there. Next to seeing Jessie, this was the best Father's Day gift I could have had. Not only did it open other media avenues, it consolidated and reinforced my will to fight back. Reading that article over and over fueled my fire. Now I would not stop fighting until the injustice had ended and I could see my little girl. Jay Mathews helped me that Father's Day and many days afterwards.

From New York City, I drove to New Jersey to the demonstration at Governor Kean's home. That rally achieved our goal. Many people throughout the State were made aware of our situation. Child abuse, hideous crime that it is, was not always a simple black and white issue. Some who were falsely accused had come out of their closet and were publicly making their statement, "I am innocent." Now even the Governor knew firsthand of our serious and desperate situation.

The members of New Jersey VOCAL were extremely encouraged by the *Washington Post* story and the media coverage of the demonstration as seen in Exhibit G. Perhaps the shell which had concealed this crisis from public eye was cracking open. Maybe we could move closer to resolving our personal cases and the problems of the falsely accused everywhere. Maybe we could generate some influence on the legal system and social agencies who were completely unable to deal effectively with the falsely accused. Maybe better days were ahead for all of us.

Most importantly, I had moved successfully through the transformation stage of The False Accusation Syndrome. Now I was clearly being guided by my need to fight back. Exhibit G told my story and for me, Round One was just beginning.

EXHIBIT G

Photo by Joe Gigli

Protesting child-abuse laws they say found them wrongly accused of child abuse are Ted Piperno of Burlington; Chuck Walker and Nancy Rosa, both of Lindenwold; and Chris Clauss of Burlington. The action took place yesterday in front of Gov. Thomas H. Kean's Livingston home.

Laws that abuse some parents

By NANCY HASS
Staff Writer

For Chris Clauss, yesterday's clouds made Father's Day especially bleak.

The Burlington County construction worker has not been allowed to see his daughter, who is now almost four, for nearly a year.

Clauss says he considers himself a victim of a blacklist more damaging than the "Red Scare" of the 1950s.

In May 1984, his estranged wife accused him of sexually abusing his daughter, and his visitation rights were terminated by the court.

Clauss says he has maintained his innocence since the spring afternoon when four police officers, guns drawn, interrupted his backyard barbecue and presented a warrant for his arrest.

During the ensuing year, he says, he has lost weight, sleep, construction jobs, and nearly $50,000 in legal fees. His girlfriend, Margaret Allen, says the past year has been "devastating."

Paul Patnode, an electrical engineering professor from Connecticut, also was arrested last June on molestation charges.

He says the arrest stemmed from a forest ranger's report in a park where Patnode had taken his son camping. The ranger filed a vague report, says Patnode, that she had seen him — from a distance of 300 feet — "touch someone, probably a woman," in a pond.

Patnode says he merely had been bathing the child in the pond.

In any event, he continues, police trailed him to his brother's New Jersey home, where they brutally arrested him, beating him and handcuffing him roughly.

The only evidence the department had against him, he says, was a doctor's examination made by inserting a "dangerously too-large test tube" into his 2-year-old's rectum.

"The only damage to my son was the damage that doctor caused when he 'raped' the child with that instrument," the father alleges.

Nonetheless, the somber, bearded educator spent 11 months in New Jersey jails before being acquitted last month.

"I couldn't raise $35,000 in cash for the bail," he says. "I lost my job at the college. My wife is trying to sue me for not making support payments while I was in jail."

The "everyday nightmare" of these accusations has turned Clauss, Patnode, and a growing group of people accused of child molestation nationwide into overnight activists.

Increased media attention to the problem of child abuse and sexual molestation in the United States has created a threatening backlash, they say. As the number of reported abuses has skyrocketed, the tally of false charges also has soared.

6

THE BEGINNING OF THE END

Stage 6: The Anger

The Father's Day demonstration and the *Washington Post* article were behind me and piles of mail were before me. Some of the mail came from people in jail who spoke of being falsely accused and convicted. Other letters came from people in all walks of life throughout the country. The media became extremely interested in VOCAL and the issue of false charges of sexual abuse. Network shows, local TV, news specials, major newspapers and many magazines published stories on false accusations of abuse. Public awareness of the issue quickly mushroomed.

I channeled my energies into working with VOCAL. We planned more demonstrations and the media did more coverage. The Trenton, New Jersey, protest resulted in ABC's affiliate in Philadelphia doing a special investigative report on VOCAL and the problem of false accusations of abuse. A news team, complete with camera crew and investigative reporter, Dave Frankel, came to my apartment. Janeen and I were interviewed for three hours. They asked to film in Jessie's room. It was the first time I had opened her door in months. The Christmas presents I had bought for her still lay about, a reminder of this ongoing tragedy.

June and July 1985

Throughout the summer months, I, along with the VOCAL organization, began to see the broader picture of the false accusation problem. The mail and the media profiled the problem in headline stories. The *Los Angeles Times*, *Philadelphia Inquirer*, *Miami Herald*, *New York Times*, *Boston Globe* and numerous other newspapers carried stories of the increasing number of people falsely accused in child abuse cases. Through them, we gained additional insight into how state agencies compounded the problem. We began to understand more clearly our own cases. Besides being falsely accused, we were also victimized by the governmental agencies handling our cases. Now we needed to know how those agencies really worked and we began to poke around. We became the investigators, not just the investigated. What we found was frightening.

We had made contact with people in various state agencies who were willing to talk. More than once, we were warned that our investigation could be dangerous to us. One government official even said the problems involving the child protection agency were "bigger than the Governor." We began looking deeper into the problems.

Meanwhile, our VOCAL chapter received a letter from the Acting Commissioner of Human Services. He acknowledged receipt of our VOCAL letter concerning the Review and Operating Procedures in the Division of Youth and Family Services. He actually assured us that the Governor was looking into the matter. We would be hearing from the Governor. That sounded encouraging, but then "strange things" began to happen.

Chris called and said VOCAL mail was arriving opened. Other members indicated their phones may be tapped. Threatening anonymous calls were made to me and others. One member's home was placed under surveillance. Nick received a phone call from Peter Shapiro's campaign manager. Shapiro was Governor Kean's opponent in the upcoming election, so we thought it a good idea to enlist his support. Nick was told in no uncertain terms that Mr. Shapiro was "not interested" in this issue and would not "touch it" during the campaign. Was there significance in this or was it just safe political strategy?

Then came information about that special task force the Governor had established after his election — the one Mr. Hawkins mentioned and VOCAL attorney, Bob Cherry, suggested we research. Suddenly, the DYFS issue became more complex, more alarming. In 1982, the Governor's Task Force investigated a variety of severe problems which clearly indicated mismanagement and organizational shortcomings within the agency. Although these problems were different in nature than the kind was now experiencing, they revealed that DYFS had had serious internal problems.

As a result of this mismanagement, the agency became so overly concerned about abuse that they began overreacting in cases like mine. Apparently these atrocities, which are headlined in Exhibit A, were still under investigation. Were they the result of gross incompetence or organized corruption? Was my own case and many like mine part of the price tag for previous mistakes made by this agency?

EXHIBIT A

SHAKE-UP
DYFS in store
for revamping

By ROBERT JOFFEE
Staff Writer

The Kean administration is about to unveil plans for a shake-up of New Jersey's child-welfare agency, but no one expects sudden improvement in the prognosis for the agency's clients.

The agency is the ever-controversial DYFS, the state Division of Youth and Family Services. It has not enjoyed a good reputation for years. Its staff is said to be undertrained, overburdened and top-heavy with management. Its finances are said to be handled sloppily and its programs ill-conceived and inefficient.

The agency's clients include more than 30,000 children living in extremely troubled families, 7,000 children living with state-subsidized foster parents and 1,400 living in state-supported institutions.

ANALYSIS

Commissioner George J. Albanese, the man chosen by Gov. Thomas H. Kean to reform DYFS and other agencies in the sprawling Department of Human Services, has formed a task force to produce plans for revamping the child-welfare agency. He says the plans will deal with "policy, practice, procedures, training, finances ... everything."

A SPOKESMAN for Kean says the governor expects "a reshuffling and restructuring of the entire DYFS operation."

But, since no bureaucratic shake-up can revolutionize human society, many of the DYFS children are likely to continue to suffer.

Only a few will die from abuse or neglect by their parents. But many will undergo slow destruction in homes troubled by mental illness, alcoholism, drug abuse and extreme poverty. And many others will be crippled by the "emotional limbo" associated with foster and institutional care.

So, even if Albanese can work his will on DYFS, he cannot expect to eliminate the suffering of its clients, only to reduce it.

The history of DYFS shows that often even the best-intentioned intervention by state caseworkers can do more harm than good.

Nick and I continued our investigations. A number of lawyers contacted me or my attorneys for help with their cases. Some were prominent attorneys and former government officials. A few even offered the services of on-staff private detectives to help Nick and me uncover what was behind this new epidemic of false accusations and why DYFS was frequently a hindrance rather than a help.

We met in "secret" meetings. Those most knowledgeable about this problem were the most cautious about where we met and who attended. We were equally wary about telephone conversations, especially those concerning information we might bring to the State Commission of Investigation. Some of the group felt we could not trust that body either. To whom could we take our information once we were ready?

The mail continued to arrive at VOCAL. Chris and another VOCAL officer, Margaret, compiled the different cases. An excerpt of Margaret's lengthy letter to me, Exhibit B, provides an insight into some typical cases. The name and address have been omitted from this document to protect the privacy of those mentioned. But there were literally dozens like this coming to our attention.

EXHIBIT B

Larry,
    These are cases where the children were taken away by DFYS,
some in NJ & PA. Also a list of the people already incarcerated.

CASE: Started in 1981, going through a divorce, father made a
        complaint that the daughter had been physcially abused.
        no, medical exam done- later a charge of burning the child
        with cigerettes, mother has a boyfriend now neither one
        smoke. DYFS stepped in and gave the father temporary
        custody 1 day a week, mother every other weekend, the rest
        of the time a foster home. Father remarries gets control
        of the daughter not custody, mother gets one day a week,
        not long after that mother &now husband get charged with
        sexual abuse. No visitation for 2 yrs. with daughter.
        New Husband Gerorge gets scared with the threat of 20 yrs.
        takes the plea bargining of 6 months in jail. Mother will
        not givein. There is a trial..daughter sees mother for the
        first time in 2 yrs. Daughter is now 6 or 7 yrs. old.
        Child waves to the mother and is very responsive. Prosecu-
        or is a female, questions the child for 30 min or so asking
        the samequestion over and over,did your mother or George
        do anything to you and if so what.... Child said no three
        times. Prosecutor ask the judge for a short dismissal , the
        child is tired, the prosecutor takes the child out into the
        hall for 30 min. then they return. Questioning starts all
        over again then the same question again about three more
        times. Did your mother help George do anything to you?
        Child still answers the same nothing happened. Prosecutor
        ask the child if she likes McDonald's she must be hungry.
        Court is dismissed for one hr. lunch. Prosecutor takes the
        child to lunch. Return from lunch child on stand again same
        questioning...Child stands up puts her hands on her hips and
        says I told you nothing happened. Mother found innocent of
        charges. This 1983. close to 1984. Right now as it stands
        the mother has visitation with the daughter for 2 hrs. every
        week in Vincentown,NJ with a supervisor and the step-father
        is not allowed near the child and the child is not allowed
        at the mothers home. Last conversation which was on July 11th
        she was trying to normal visitation. Gerorge served his 6
        months.

Accused by wifes x-husband of touching wife's 12 yr. old. 1983 one
week befor e Christmas or around that time. He was threatened so
badly by the prosecutor that he took the plea barging which was a
charge of lewd behavior which consisted of walking from the bathroom
to the bedroom with a towel on his shoulder. He gets off probation
July 28th

Mother was going through a nervous breakdown and made a statement that
the father was sleeping with the child 12 yrs. old, something to
that effect. Later after she was better tried to retract the
comment but DYFS was already on the war path. Child already
had 3 medical exams by thefather and none of them showed that
she had been raped. The child even said that nothing had
happened. the son said nothin g h" pened. They put the children
in a foster home for 6 months and will not allow the father
back in the hime again.

  Larry, the stories go on and on the same garbage
  They are GOD the law and jury.

August 1985

Soon, what we learned through VOCAL began to help us with
my case. When the State Supreme Court had denied our appeal of
Jessie's competency, a new court date was set for August 1985.
Almost two years after my arrest, we were right back where we
started. We were determined to make them prove the charges
without putting my little girl on the stand to have her repeat the
"catch" phrases Valori had apparently taught her.

Bob Cherry, the VOCAL legal consultant, worked with my
attorneys, Steven and Herb. It was decided that Herb would file a

motion requesting an independent psychiatric examination of Jessie. The Appellate Court had established her competent to testify under New Jersey evidence rule 17. To satisfy this rule, an individual had to pass a three-pronged test: 1) be able to know the difference between truth and lying, 2) know that one will be punished for lying and 3) understand that one has a moral duty to tell the truth. Understanding of these three principles demonstrates a person's competency to testify.

Evidence rule 19 refers to the "capacity" of a witness to have individual and firsthand recollection of the alleged events. Based upon rules 17 and 19, Herb asked for the psychiatric examination. Although this type of motion had never been granted in New Jersey, there had been a recently published decision from the Appellate Court which paved the way for our motion. In that case, the Appellate Court reversed a lower court's ruling which did not allow a psychiatric examination of the defendant.

Our motion was heard on August 2. It was carefully framed to either permit the examination or allow us to appeal. I knew from my training in cognitive psychology it was impossible for Jessie, now four and a half years old, to independently recall an alleged event from two years before.

By now, the press watched every move we made. A flurry of newspaper articles appeared when the motion was filed. Exhibit C, an example of that coverage, was published the day after the motion was filed.

A few days later, the Prosecutor countered our move by objecting to the examination. Assistant Prosecutor Rubbinaccio wrote in a brief submitted to the court, "The infant witness has no indication of any mental derangement or any psychiatric problem." He went on to say, "The New Jersey Supreme Court has consistently held that the granting of a psychiatric examination of a witness must be engaged in with great care and only upon a substantial showing of need and justification." He concluded by saying, "The witness can recall and relate events that happened to her."

Apparently, Rubbinaccio was not interested in determining what Jessica remembered, if anything, independent of Valori's coaching. I believed the examination would clarify the alleged sex-

EXHIBIT C

Psychiatric review of young girl sought in molestation case

By BRIAN MURRAY
Daily Record Courthouse Writer

A psychologist charged with sexually molesting an infant girl in 1983 is demanding the alleged victim, now age 4, undergo a psychiatric review to determine whether she has any independent recollection of the alleged incident.

Legal papers filed yesterday on behalf of Dr. Lawrence Spiegel, 39, of Flanders contends the child may have no recollection of the day Spiegel allegedly molested her except for what has been told to her by her mother — the person who filed the charges against Spiegel.

Spiegel, who maintains his innocence, was charged with sexual assault in a January 1984 indictment that contends he molested the child when she was 18 months old in December 1983.

Review's importance

The importance of the psychiatric review, contends his attorney, Herbert Korn, "lies not only in the fact that the witness is only 4 years old, but also in the fact that the conduct that the state will attempt to have the witness testify about allegedly occurred in the fall of 1983."

Spiegel is scheduled to go to trial this fall, almost two years after the alleged assault.

Korn said it must be determined whether the child remembers anything about the day she was with Spiegel if she is to be considered a competent witness.

"To aid the trial court or a jury in determining whether the infant truly has a capacity to recollect the events and not simply repeat her mother's own interpretations and opinions about the alleged events, a psychiatric examination is vital to the defense of this case," Korn added in the documents filed with the Morris County clerk's office yesterday.

Plan upheld

An unprecedented appellate court ruling recently upheld plans by the Morris County prosecutor's office to have the girl testify against Spiegel while sitting on her mother's lap.

Korn unsuccessfully opposed having the girl testify in that manner, contending she was too young to determine fact from fantasy and that she could be easily coached by her mother.

The state Supreme Court has refused to review the appellate court decision, but should Spiegel be convicted after a trial, the appeal could be taken up again.

ual abuse for what it was — a false accusation. Perhaps the Prosecutor's office thought the same thing.

Oral arguments were heard on August 9. Herb argued that the court needed to determine if Jessica, especially if she was to be a witness in the case, even remembered the day of the alleged abuse or was only retelling what may have been related to her by her mother. Judge Egan listened intently to both sides of the argument and came to the conclusion that an examination was indeed necessary.

Judge Egan stated, "Fundamental fairness clearly indicates an examination should be allowed." But the judge foresaw the problems of the prosecution or the defense selecting the psychiatrist. He stated, "I have to take into consideration that the defendant is a psychologist. He is in a position to find one of the boys. He has many friends in the field of psychology. I want to purify it ... and not have the appearance that the State has a state-oriented psychologist or the defense a defense-oriented psychologist." Judge Egan ruled that he would select the doctor that would examine Jessie. His decision finally gave us reason to rejoice.

After Judge Egan announced his decision to grant the examination, the Prosecutor produced a document. He explained that Valori, on the advice of her counsel, Mr. Wahl, had had a psychological examination of Jessie done on June 30 by Psychology Associates in Tallahassee, Florida. The Prosecutor wanted the judge to accept the findings of this examination and not conduct the one we had requested. Judge Egan held to his decision and ordered another examination. The psychological examination presented by the Prosecutor would later prove to be one of his greatest mistakes.

When I read the psychological report by Dr. Kennedy which the Prosecutor had submitted, I couldn't believe my eyes. It was the most unprofessional evaluation I had ever seen. In addition to misspelling both Valori and Jessie's names, Dr. Kennedy put Jessie's age at the time of the alleged trauma at 18 months when it was actually two and a half years. Although he had been provided with the names of Drs. Lapkin, Rogers and Frankel, he never bothered to consult with any of them about Jessie.

The report was custom-made for Valori's needs. It seemed to

simply accept Valori's statements as true. It included statements
like, "Jessica displays clear eidetic (picture) memory from 'that'
period, and no evidence of these memories having been tampered
with by an adult." The report, as seen in Exhibit D, stated that, "She
would make a competent State witness," as though Dr. Kennedy
had a degree in law as well as psychology. The report was as subtle
as an atom bomb.

EXHIBIT D

P S Y C H O L O G Y   A S S O C I A T E S
of Tallahassee

Clinical Psychology Consultants

904-878-3571
130 Salem Court
Tallahassee, Florida 32301-2810

PSYCHOLOGICAL REPORT
June 13, 1985

I.D. #:

NAME:	Jessica Spiegle
PARENTS:	Valerie Malvey
ADDRESS:	

EXAM DATE: 6-10-85
EXAMINER: Robin McCallister, Ph.D.
EXAM PLACE: Psychology Associates
REFERRED BY: Child's Therapist

BIRTHDATE: 4-6-81
AGE: 4-2   SEX: F
RACE: W
SCHOOL: Kiddie Corrall
GRADE: Preschool

REPORT TO: _Mother_

BEHAVIORAL OBSERVATIONS: Jessica was brought for evaluation at
the request of her mother to evaluate her ability to serve as a
witness in a trial involving sexual abuse case against her
natural father, in the event that her competency should become an
issue.   She was allegedly sexually abused by her father, a
psychologist in New Jersey, at eighteen months of age over a
three month period.   She subsequently moved with her mother, who
is currently working as director of public relations at a

Valdosta hospital, to Valdosta one year ago, where Mrs. Malvey's parents currently reside. Jessica has been in treatment with Pat Hastings in Valdosta to help deal with past and future experiences.

OBSERVATION OF BEHAVIOR: Jessica is a very attractive, verbally astute four-year-old child who was nicely dressed. She appeared rather cautious, tense and reserved during her interactions. She made little eye contact and maintained a serious look, at times appearing rather jumpy and tearful, never smiling. She seemed afraid of making a mistake, looking rather startled and searching the examiner's face for a reaction to her responses. She cried several minutes when she began to fail more difficult items on the Stanford-Binet. For this reason, testing was terminated before she reached her ceiling, although she of course was doing well.

SPIEGLE, Jessica
Page Two

TESTS ADMINISTERED:

STANFORD BINET

    Mental Age = 5-7
    IQ = 133

ROBERTS APPERCEPTION TEST
VINELAND SOCIAL MATURITY SCALE   5-0

FINDINGS: Based upon the clinical history I obtained from the mother, my clinical observation, and the clinical tests I administered, I have made the following findings:

1. Jessica Spiegle is a child of superior intelligence, with a Stanford-Binet IQ of above 133, which places her at the 98th percentile nationally.

2. Jessica Spiegle is a child of above average social maturity. She is slightly dependent, but superior in social poise, language, and basic communication.

3. Jessica Spiegle is a child with treatable but serious emotional problems related to the experience with her

father. She is highly anxious, mildly depressed, and significantly phobic about men. She is highly emotional, cries easily, but recovers swiftly.

4. Jessica Spiegle recalls events when she was under two years of age, in an age-appropriate fashion of pictures and sensations as opposed to cognitive or grammatical style.

5. Jessica Spiegle is overly dependent upon her mother, and has problems detaching herself from her mother in any nonusual settings.

Based upon these findings, I have reached the following conclusions:

1. Although Jessica was very young at the time of the events reported by her mother, she has clear eidetic (picture) memories from that period, and displays no evidence of these memories having been tampered with by an adult.

SPIEGLE, Jessica
Page 3

2. Although she is emotional, phobic, and highly anxious, as well as depressed, much of this is trial-related, and related to the trial anxiety of the mother and is treatable and should greatly improve in the post-trial period.

3. She is responding well to her current therapist, and that relationship should be maintained for a significant period after the trial.

4. Jessica is emotionally and intellectually, as well as socially, competent to serve as a states witness, and although it will be a serious trauma for her, she will certainly recover rapidly with treatment.

5. There is considerable evidence that standing her ground and completing this task will have very positive long-range implications for Jessica regarding the freedom to tell.

6. There is no evidence that any of her emotional problems

would contribute in any way to her making up or adding details to her memories.

Based upon these conclusions, I have the following recommendations:

1. She will make a competent, credible witness in spite of her emotional problems and her fearfulness regarding the courtroom experience.

2. Her memory of events at the time of this experience is highly credible because it is in the language of children, which is picture tapes rather than grammar.

3. She needs long-term treatment with her present therapist, if that can be maintained.

4. She will be able to recover quickly from the stress of the trial, if given supportive therapy.

5. Except for her attorney, the court, and her therapist, no one should inquire as to the events between her and her father.

Wallace A. Kennedy
Wallace A. Kennedy, Ph.D., ABPP
Clinical Psychologist

Robin McCallister
Robin McCallister, Ph.D.
Clinical Psychology Fellow

I was outraged. I immediately called the psychologist, Dr. Kennedy, in Florida, but he would not return my calls. I wanted to know how he could ethically write such a document. Toward the end of the week, I received a letter from Dr. Kennedy of Psychology Associates. It appears here as Exhibit E1. The second sentence immediately caught my eye. It informed me that this examination was done at the request of the Prosecutor. That was very interesting, since the Prosecutor had argued in court against an examination. This letter clearly contradicted what the Prosecutor had told the judge. Somebody was lying about who initiated the examination.

EXHIBIT E1

PSYCHOLOGY ASSOCIATES OF TALLAHASSEE

CLINICAL PSYCHOLOGY CONSULTANTS

904-878-3571
130 Salem Court
Tallahassee, Florida 32301-2810

WALLACE A. KENNEDY Ph.D., ABEPP
T. WAYNE CONGER, Ph.D.
PAUL S. DEITCHMAN, Ph.D.
BARBARA F. YOUNG, Ph.D., ABEPP

LAURA C. ROGERS, Ph.D., CLINICAL FELLOW
ROBIN McCALLISTER, Ph.D., CLINICAL FELLOW

August 27, 1985

Dr. Lawrence D. Spiegel
40 Baldwin Road
Parsippany, NJ 07054

Dear Dr. Spiegel:

I received your letter of August 14th. Since I performed my evaluation at the request of the office of the prosecutor, I requested his opinion. His office furnished you a full copy of my report, and I judged from the nature of your inquiry to both me and our clinical fellow, Dr. McCallister, that you have already obtained that report. If you have further need of material, I presume that you can obtain a proper subpoena and your attorney and the state prosecutor can litigate the matter.

Sincerely,

Wallace A. Kennedy, Ph.D., ABPP
Clinical Psychologist

WAK/clb

I looked again at the original examination. Sure enough, in black and white at the top of the page, it stated "Report to: Mother." But Kennedy's letter to me said the examination was done at the Prosecutor's request. Then why wasn't the Prosecutor's name on the report, instead of Valori's? How could the Prosecutor say to the newspapers that the defense had "shown no reason for having an examination," yet order one performed? Or was it Valori who played the psychologist against the Prosecutor and got the examination performed without appearing as if she was the instigator?

Later we obtained copies of correspondences between Kennedy and the Prosecutor. In a letter to the Office of the Prosecutor written by Dr. Kennedy and dated August 28, 1985, he concluded by saying something extremely interesting. It appears in his final paragraph and is noted here as Exhibit E2.

EXHIBIT E2

```
Janet Rapisardi
Re:  Jessica Spiegle
August 28, 1985
Page Two


The  only  problem  that I see in the whole issue  is  that  Mrs.
Mulvey  assured me that the prosecuting attorney of the State  of
New  Jersey had requested the evaluation of Jessica in  order  to
determine her ability to participate in a trial, both in terms of
her  emotional capacity to withstand testimony and her ability to
give coherent testimony.  I have never received a specific court
order or request to that effect.

Very truly yours,
```

Wallace A. Kennedy, PhD

Wallace A. Kennedy, Ph.D.
Clinical Psychologist

WAK/lk

The Prosecutor's office wrote back to Kennedy two days later and stated that their office did not request an examination. Their letter appears here as Exhibit E3.

EXHIBIT E3

LEE S. TRUMBULL
COUNTY PROSECUTOR

OFFICE OF THE PROSECUTOR
COUNTY OF MORRIS
COURTHOUSE
MORRISTOWN, N. J. 07960
201-829-8100

JOHN J.   REILLY
FIRST ASSISTANT PROSECUTOR
KAREN LEE BARRETT
DEPUTY FIRST ASSISTANT PROSECUTOR
CHARLES H. COE
CHIEF OF INVESTIGATIONS

August 30, 1985

Dr. Wallace Kennedy
c/o Psychology Associates of Tallahassee
130 Salem Court
Tallahassee, FL   32301-2810

Dear Dr.'s Kennedy and McCallister:

Please find enclosed two subpoenas in reference to State vs. Spiegel. Please be advised that you are witnesses for the State of New Jersey and that you may be called at time of trial.

I would further request that Dr. McCallister send me curriculum vitae. Additionally, I would like copies of Dr. Kennedy's 1984 writing concerning the psychologist in court and his 1985 writing concerning the psychologist as an expert witness.

Although our office did not request that you conduct an examination of the victim in this matter, I intend to use the information at the time of trial. Discovery rules in New Jersey require the State to provide the defense copies of your report, which has been done. I am aware that the defendant has continued to harass you, both telephonically and through the mail, in an effort to

circumvent the rules of discovery. I would suggest that, if you have further
contact with the defendant, you contact my office, so that I may take appropriate
action.

I will advise you when I am aware of a specific trial date, and look
forward to meeting you.

If you have any questions or wish to speak to me, please feel free to
contact me.

Very truly yours,

MICHAEL M. RUBBINACCIO
ASSISTANT PROSECUTOR

MMR:cg

I was being set-up again, that was for sure. It was difficult to tell
who was doing what. One thing was certain, somebody was lying.
Whether it was Valori or the Prosecutor remained, for now, a mys-
tery.

Herb needed to know about this exchange of letters and their
contradictions. I went to his office. I saw a gleam in his eye when he
realized what was happening. I asked if he was going to call the
judge. He sat back, smiled and then said, "Nope."

"Why not?" I screamed, in my fury to expose this situation.

"Because I'm going to keep this up my sleeve and bring it out
when I have the Prosecutor's pants down."

I wasn't sure exactly what that meant, but I knew Herb would
use this information in the most effective way. Yet without my
knowledge, Herb had already called Mr. Wahl and asked him if he
had advised Valori to have this examination, as the Prosecutor had
intimated to the judge. Wahl didn't seem to know much about the
matter.

A conference was convened at the end of the week with the
judge, the Prosecutor and Herb to determine who would conduct
the psychiatric examination. Herb again asked the Prosecutor to

reiterate how the examination in Florida had come about. The Prosecutor again asserted it had been done by Miss Mulvey, at the suggestion of her attorney. Herb then showed the judge the letter from Dr. Kennedy.

Judge Egan seemed infuriated. He declared that since the Prosecutor had the opportunity to choose his own expert, the defense should have that right as well, according to rules of fundamental fairness. He instructed Herb to choose an expert. The court would do likewise and both experts would examine Jessie. Another conference date was set to determine who the experts would be and when the examination would take place.

September and October 1985

Unfortunately, Judge Egan began a murder trial the next week and, consequently, the upcoming conference was postponed. This delayed my September trial date as well. Once again, we had to wait. I called Herb every day, asking if he heard from the judge. Had the psychiatrist or psychologist been chosen for the examination? Every day the answer was the same; nothing had been done yet.

I tried to concentrate on my work, seeing the few patients I had. Nick and I continued our investigations into the DYFS matter. There was always something to be done with VOCAL. In October, we were contacted by the *New York Times*. We spent many hours with the reporter and on Sunday, October 18, an article focusing on false accusations of abuse of children was printed. The issue remained in the public eye and it caused an increasing number of falsely accused to make their cases known to the press.

One Sunday evening I was home alone, depressed and feeling the futility of waiting for the judge to choose a psychiatrist. I was watching a movie on WOR-TV from New York. Ms. Penny Pinsker, Director of Public Affairs for WOR, came on with an editorial. The issue was sexual abuse of children. WOR was calling for background checks for all school employees. What bothered me was the fact that this was just another band-aid approach to the problem. I immediately wrote a reply and sent it the next day.

The following week, I received a phone call from Penny Pinsker. She informed me that they had received many responses to this editorial. The station had chosen mine as the editorial reply. Nick went with me for the filming. Consequently, Nick and I were asked to be guests on two of WOR's talk shows, "Face Off" and "Straight Talk." We recorded both shows shortly thereafter.

The editorial reply aired in October. WOR was not prepared for the response. Since they are part of the RKO network, the reply was seen nationwide. The station was flooded with responses, more than they could handle, more than they had ever seen. Many people supported my editorial and could identify with the problems of false accusations as I outlined them. Also, a great number of people wanted to know how to contact VOCAL.

It was quite a month for us in the media. "Face Off" was taped and given an air date of November 22. Penny had initially wanted a representative from DYFS to face me, but the department declined to appear. "Straight Talk" was recorded and given an air date of November 27. It featured Nick and the Acting Commissioner of Human Services, Mr. Perselay. The acting commissioner simply denied each point that Nick made. Nick publicly offered to show him concrete evidence of DYFS's wrongdoings, but the commissioner was not interested in seeing the proof.

Finally, in late October while I was involved heavily with the media, Judge Egan called a conference with Herb and the Prosecutor. The judge had chosen a psychiatrist in Morristown to be the court-appointed examiner. He wanted Herb to be prepared with the name of our psychiatrist by conference time. We had numerous conversations regarding our choice. Herb said since I was truly innocent and had nothing to hide, we should choose someone we did not know personally or professionally, someone with impeccable credentials. I agreed and Herb chose the psychiatrist a few days prior to the scheduled conference.

November 1985

Herb sent me a copy of the curriculum vitae of Alvin Friedland, M.D., the psychiatrist he had chosen. To say I was impressed would be an understatement. His vitae was seven pages long and showed flawless credentials. He was a Diplomate of the American Board of Psychiatry and Neurology. He had received the prestigious Golden

Merit Award and was named outstanding New Jersey psychiatrist in 1977. In fact, the judge and the Prosecutor were so impressed with Dr. Friedland's credentials, that no need existed for a court-appointed psychiatrist. The examination of Jessie was scheduled for November 7 in Dr. Friedland's office.

It was a strange feeling on November 7, knowing Jessie was in New Jersey, just fifteen minutes away. Yet, I was still not permitted to see her. The frustration was a bit more tolerable because I saw an end in sight. I had great faith in Dr. Friedland on the basis of his credentials and even greater faith in Jessie's inner feelings. I knew the depth of love we had shared and I believed those feelings would still be there despite what she had been told by her mother.

A week later I got a phone call from Herb. "I have the report. Come over immediately," he said.

The ride to his office was the longest twenty minutes I had ever experienced. I was literally shaking with excitement as he handed me the four page document. I had to read it twice to assure myself of its contents. The report was everything I had hoped for and more. Dr. Friedland stated Jessica showed no signs of having been traumatized or molested. He found she displayed no sign of being "deeply disturbed, phobic toward men, or even mildly depressed." Friedland stated the only time Jessie displayed any anxiety was when she told him her mother remembered something she did not. He made it clear that Jessie had no memory of any trauma, but was being told that something had happened to her by her mother. He said she displayed no fear of her father and considered me a part of her family.

Dr. Friedland closed his report with the recommendation that Valori receive counseling. No treatment was indicated for Jessie. Rejoicing erupted the moment I finished reading. Though I did not give any credence to the report from Florida, I had been worried about Jessie's psychological well-being throughout this ordeal. Now I knew she was all right. Janeen and Herb held everlasting smiles on their faces. I had not felt happiness like this in two years. Dr. Friedland's report appears here as Exhibit F.

EXHIBIT F

ALVIN FRIEDLAND, M. D.
A PROFESSIONAL ASSOCIATION
201 SOUTH LIVINGSTON AVENUE
LIVINGSTON, NEW JERSEY 07039

ALVIN FRIEDLAND, M. D., F. A. P. A.
(201) 994-1611

DIPLOMATE, AMERICAN BOARD OF
PSYCHIATRY AND NEUROLOGY, INC.

November 13, 1985

Herbert Korn, Esquire
20 Park Place - Suite 206
Morristown, N.J. 07960

re: Jessica Speigel
Birth Date 4/6/81

Dear Mr. Korn:

As requested, I had the opportunity to examine the above named 4½ year old girl in my office on November 7, 1985. She was accompanied by her mother and a representative of the prosecutors office, Ms. Janet Rapisardi.

Prior to my seeing Jessica, I reviewed the psychological report which was performed by the Clinical Psychological Consultants on Jessica on June 13, 1985. I also noted some brief details of the child's growth and development which were within normal limits.

At this interview, when I went to the waiting room to bring Jessica into my consultation room, she was extremely shy and reluctant. To get her to come with me I invited Mrs. Speigel and the representative of the prosecutors office to accompany Jessica. While Jessica was getting adjusted to the surroundings, I briefly spoke with Jessica's mother to ask her further questions regarding Jessica s background. She added that Jessica was born of a normal spontaneous delivery with no immediate perinatal or postnatal difficulties even though the mother had mild toxemia during the pregnancy. The apgar reading was within normal limits.

In time, Jessica became involved in making some drawings which gave me the opportunity to tell Jessica's mother to leave the room. However, Ms. Rapisardi remained as I continued speaking with Jessica until she became more relaxed and responsive. It was then I asked Ms. Rapisardi to leave and I spent the rest of the time with Jessica alone.

Jessica is an attractive well developed child who was appropriately dressed showing signs of good personal hygene. She presents no unusual physical characteristics or mannerisms. Her attitude and facial expression was compatable with the existing trend. She appeared age appropriate and very bright.

page - 2 -

re: Jessica Speigel
Birth Date 4/6/81

She presented no unusual behavior or conduct at this time. Throughout
this interview, she presented a full range of affect with general ease
of talking. There were no inappropriate emotions. There were also
no primary or secondary emotional reactions of any significance.

She appeared to comprehend reality and was well able to differentiate
fact from fantasy. She had an excellent intellectual grasp of reality
with good orientation and good knowledge of objects and persons.

Her overall speech and language was appropriate. Her thought processes
did not show any impairment and her form and content of thought was
not unusual as demonstrated by the dialogue and comments during this
interview.

In talking with Jessica regarding a fantasy regarding people living
in a home, she told me of a family consisting of a mother, a father and
a 4 year old child named Marie. The child kept herself busy by playing
school or else she played with her kittens. She went to sleep at 7:30p.m.
and woke up at 6:00a.m. The mother is always up with her but her father
slept late. On occasion she would visit with her "nanny and poppa" or
she would go to the store with her mother and father to buy food. When
she was with her friends she played legos (a childs construction game) or
else she watched television. She then told me that the child in this
family wished for puppies and money to buy food and to put into a bank.
She said the girl was never naughty and never angry but if there was any
difficulty, she was usually punished by being sent to her room for five (5)
minutes. She said that her daddy would sometimes use the same form of
punishment but <u>she was not afraid of him.</u>

When I asked Jessica where she was living, she said that she was in
Ridgewood and her "daddy was in New Jersey". <u>She said she does not
see him because he hurt her. She forgot what he did "I don't know -
I think about it at night - he did something - I don't remember in the
daytime - I could never remember but my mommy remembers and she will
tell you". Jessica than spontaneously said "he told a lie - he said
he did not hurt me but he did but I don't remember - he lied to my
mother - I don't remember that either I only remember it at night -</u>
but I don't remember in the morning - I don't know how I remember".

Jessica then said that she will "see him when he is good and than said
<u>"he got away with it - I don't know what that means - my mommy told
me but I forget".</u>

page - 3 -

re: Jessica Speigel
Birth Date 4/6/81

When I changed the subject, Jessica spontaneously told me that she was having a party on April 6th with her cousins. She than said that her daddy will not come because he is too busy - (I did not question her further regarding this but I did ask her if her parents were living together). She said "no my parents were divorced before I was born".

As mentioned, it is apparent that Jessica is a very bright, spontaneous child who can recall dates and details. She is able to be creative with good learning and adapting ability. There are signs of good self esteem and good inner organization. She appears to have an appropriate time sense which is very good for a child at this age. There are also feelings of adequacy and self reliance and certainly above average in being age appropriate in regard to her emotional content, language, body language and mental trend. She has good social awareness and self help functions.

Considering the findings at this interview, Jessica does not show any signs at present of having any emotional difficulties other than some confusion regarding her present family structure. She knows the contents of an intact family as well as mother-child and father-child relationships. She sees a father as a member of a family unit and certainly had no anxiety talking about this issue at this time.

It was difficult to understand how this child can emphasize and repeat how "her father hurt her" and say that she thinks about it at night but does not remember anything during the day only her mother knows. Certainly, there are no signs of her being significantly traumatized to effect her mental status. She is certainly old enough and spontaneous to recall traumatic events and dreams if they did exist.

In regard to the psychological examination performed on Jessica on June 13, 1985, I certainly can agree with the fact that Jessica is a child of superior intelligance with above average social maturity, appropriately dependant, superior in social poise, language and basic communication. However, I did not see a child with a treatable or serious emotional problems. She presented no signs of being highly anxious or mildly depressed or significantly phobic about men. When we were alone in the room, she was pleasant, responsive and cooperative. In fact, when the interview was over I had to take her by the hand out of my office as she wanted to spend more time.

Jessica at this time does not recall anything under two (2) years of age. Lastly according to findings of the psychological, I did not feel that Jessica is overly dependant at this time. She is attending a nursery and can be with other children and adults without her mother.

Also in regard to the psychological, Jessica does not have clear vivid childhood memories from "that period" which has been reported by the psychologist.

page - 4 -

re: Jessica Speigel
Birth Date 4/6/81

She presents no signs of any anxiety except that "her mother remembers
something but she doesn't".

Again, Jessica shows no signs of being "emotional, phobic or highly
anxious as well as depressed". She was upset at the begining of this
interview but quickly settled down and became most appropriate.

My response to the other findings of the psychologist is that the child
does not show any signs of having been "seriously traumatized". Even
if the child was "seriously traumatized" she would show some behavioral
signs in her mental status at this time. According to my findings, Jessica
does not.

The conclusions of the psychologist state that she would make a competant,
credable witness. I cannot comment on this remark since Jessica "does
not remember" if anything happened.

It is difficult for me to determine how the child reacted to the "picture
tapes" but certainly, in the child's concept of a family, there were no
signs of any pathology, anxieties or fears noted or related to the father
figure. And certainly, she was not fearful of me during our interview.
I don't see long term treatment indicated.

In conclusion, respecting the fact that the psychologist may have
interpreted some of the findings as being traumatic and considering the
very normal mental status of the child at this time and respecting the
mother's concerns of her child's welfare in regard to her father or "men"
may I suggest the mother receive guidance and counseling to help with
her child's normal growth and development since she is a significant
figure in the child's life.

As a last comment, in regard to the psychological report, the paragraph
entitled "behavioral observations" is not quite understood. Aside from
that, the paragraph entitled "observation of behavior" presents a child
who is tense and reserved, jumpy and tearful as well as fearful and
crying which did not allow the psychologist to complete her testing.
I don't know how the Roberts Apperception Test was completed for the
psychologist to list her findings, conslusions and recommendations.

If you wish any further information, or have any questions regarding
my report do not hesitate to get in touch with me.

Very truly yours,

Alvin Friedland, M.D.
Clinical Associate Professor of Psychiatry
Child and Adolescent
University of Medicine and Dentistry of New Jersey

/sk

The Beginning Of The End

With the report completed, a new trial date was set for December 2. Herb moved quickly, filing a pretrial motion. It asked Judge Egan to declare Jessica incompetent to testify. This motion was based on the psychiatric report which stated she had no memory of any traumatic events. In addition, Herb again asked that the condition of bail which prevented me from seeing her be lifted, since the psychiatric report indicated she experienced no anxiety related to her father.

The issue of Jessie's competency and the motion to change the condition of bail were scheduled to be heard as pretrial motions. That meant that my trial would begin with the court first addressing itself to these motions before it proceeded with testimony concerning the actual charges. According to Herb, that raised the possibility that the charges may be completely dismissed before a full-blown trial actually began. With Dr. Friedland's report in hand, we were optimistic that the madness could end shortly after the trial began.

Thanksgiving morning Janeen and I awoke about 9:00. She went into the kitchen to cook breakfast and I sat down at my typewriter to continue working on this book. I still had an overwhelming feeling that something was missing somewhere in my case. Knowing I might soon be on trial compelled me to review the mountain of files one more time. I began to skim through the court orders, transcripts and certifications.

I was drawn to my file marked "DYFS/Prosecutor." I pulled out the five or six hundred pages. Included were all the DYFS notes, records of the Prosecutor's "investigation," and old transcripts. I opened the transcript of the Grand Jury proceedings. How silly this was, I thought. I had looked at these files countless times. Yet the compulsion to look at them one more time was so strong, I began reading.

It was the testimony of the Prosecutor's investigator, Janet Rapisardi, that stopped me. There was something very strange which I had never noticed before. Each time a Grand Juror questioned Rapisardi about the initial filing of the complaint, Prosecutor Rubbinaccio would very carefully rephrase the question for her. She would actually answer his rephrased question, which differed slightly from that of the juror. "Why!" I screamed in my mind.

"Why did he do that?"

The Grand Jury seemed very intent on wanting to know who filed the initial complaint. Then, I asked myself, why hadn't the Prosecutor called Valori to the stand? Why hadn't the Grand Jury heard from her directly? After all, she was the first to hear Jessie's alleged complaints. Why put her aunt on the stand and not her? Suddenly it was clear. The Prosecutor had apparently shielded Valori's instrumental role in generating these charges.

Then it struck me that Valori, too, in one of her sworn statements had gone out of her way to make sure she was not connected to the filing of the sexual abuse complaint. I did not remember which certification, but I knew it was written shortly after my arrest. I pulled the folder marked "Valori's" certifications. It too, contained at least five hundred pages, consisting of fifty or sixty certifications as well as other miscellaneous papers and reports. I had kept them in sequential order as much as I could over the years. I went directly to December 1983, but didn't find anything there. So I flipped to January 1984. There it was, almost larger than life. It was the certification Valori had filed for my bail modification hearing, dated January 3, 1984. It is shown here as Exhibit G. These sentences rattled my mind.

EXHIBIT G

VALORI M. SPIEGEL,	: SUPERIOR COURT OF NEW JERSEY
	: CHANCERY DIVISION
Plaintiff	: MORRIS COUNTY
vs.	: DOCKET NO. M-03149-83
LAWRENCE D. SPIEGEL,	: CIVIL ACTION
	:CERTIFICATION OF VALORI MULVEY
Defendant.	: DATED JANUARY 3, 1984

Valori Mulvey, of full age, certifies as follows:

10. Although I am not the person who filed the complaint against the defendant nor did I have any participation in making the decision to bring the charge; I firmly believe that the

When Valori said she had not filed the charge and had nothing to do with bringing the charges, I was instantly reminded of the lines from *Hamlet*, "The lady doth protest too much, methinks." I looked again at Rapisardi's testimony in the Grand Jury transcript. A juror asked Rapisardi this question, "The child's mother is not the one who brought the information out. Is that it?"

That question was rephrased by Rubbinaccio. "Did the mother contact DYFS?"

Rapisardi responded, "The mother never contacted DYFS directly, no."

It was the word "directly" that screamed out at me. All this time I always assumed Valori had managed to get the priest, Father Frank, to call DYFS. Now I wondered. I read the rest of the Prosecutor's notes. Then another strange thing struck me. There was virtually no mention of Father Frank in any of the Prosecutor's reports, save one sentence. Kay Curtiss, the DYFS worker, told the Prosecutor the initial complaint came from Father Frank.

"Told," I thought. Where did it say that the Prosecutor talked to Father Frank directly? "Nowhere" was the answer. Nowhere in the entire investigation did the Prosecutor interview the individual who allegedly brought the entire matter to the attention of the authorities. Something was very wrong. Now I knew the missing piece was somewhere in the DYFS notes.

I spread the papers all over the bedroom. I had to go through the DYFS notes again. There were handwritten notes by a score of different caseworkers and supervisors. Some were from Morris County, some from Somerset County. There were typed reports, periodic assessment forms and intake reports. I spent several hours scanning form after form, not knowing exactly what I was looking for. I continued to read, trying to figure out what certain DYFS abbreviations meant. I wanted to understand totally what I was reading. I feared I would pass by the missing piece if I wasn't completely careful. I spotted a paper which I didn't remember seeing before, buried within the voluminous file.

It was dated 12/6/83 and marked Screening/Incident report. It was handwritten by a DYFS caseworker, Ann Battaglia. It was clearly the first DYFS report of the case. It came from the Somerset office. There in black and white was the notation that the initial call to DYFS came from an investigator from the Somerset County prosecutor's office. It stated that at 3:35 that afternoon, Investigator Linda Mundy of the Somerset prosecutor's office called DYFS and reported that Valori had called them at the suggestion of a Father Frank. This report, seen in Exhibit H, was then forwarded to Kay Curtiss, also of the Somerset DYFS.

EXHIBIT H

Alleged Perpetrator (name, address, relation) _Father_			
If any family member is known to DYFS: Name _Jessica Spiegel_	If known to Central Registry:	Reportable to Central Registry [X] Yes [ ] No	
Case Status _closed_ DO of Sup _Burlington_	Date _____	If Yes, Reason for Referral: [ ] 09 Emotional neglect [ ] 10 Physical neglect [X] 11 Abuse, physical/sexual	[ ] Other (enter reason code) ——
Case No. _KC 188150_ Worker _Franchetti_	DO of Sup _____		

Information Received by (SIGN BELOW)	Routed to (PRINT NAME):	Date:	Time:
1. _Ann Battaglia_	_S. Ken_	12/7	
2. _S Ken_	_K. Costin_	4/7	7:30
3. _S Ken_	_2 Oliv_	12/13	11:00
4.	_K Costin_	1:1	

Now I knew how the Grand Jury had been given a total misrepresentation of what actually occurred. It was clear how Investigator Rapisardi was able to say that Valori never contacted DYFS directly. What was omitted, however, was the fact that Valori had contacted the Somerset County Prosecutor before they called DYFS. Nevertheless, Valori started the ball rolling. So what had really happened? Was the Prosecutor's office and Investigator Rapisardi grossly incompetent or did they deliberately lie?

Before jumping to conclusions, I wanted to be sure these documents were what I thought them to be. Thanksgiving Day notwithstanding, I called a friend who worked for DYFS. She understood the urgency and went over the form with me on the phone. My friend from DYFS said, "Absolutely, Larry, that is an official, initial screening report and the person in the blank you are talking about is the first person to make the complaint."

Now there was only one element to check. I called information to get the number for Saint Mathias Church. It was time to speak directly with Father Frank. Unfortunately, according to Father Peter, Father Frank was out for the day, but he would ask him to call me back. It was almost 2:00 p.m., time to leave for Janeen's parents' house and Thanksgiving dinner. Now it really felt like I had something to be thankful for.

When we returned home that night, Father Frank had returned

my call and left his private phone number. I called him first thing the next morning. He verified that he did not make the call to DYFS, but had suggested to Valori that she call DYFS or the Prosecutor if she felt abuse had occurred. He was reluctant to discuss specifics since he observed the confidentiality of matters like these. He did say that the advice he gave to Valori was advice he would give to anyone in such a situation. He added that he thought someone from DYFS and/or the Somerset Prosecutor's office had called him, but he didn't really remember anymore.

I thanked him for his help. I hung up knowing I had all the pieces. The Prosecutor's office had seemingly misled the Grand Jury. Why? What made this case so important to them?

I had no idea what value this information was to me legally, since my case now rested on Jessie's competency. I was certain Herb would not attempt to call a halt to the current proceedings and challenge a two-year-old indictment. Nevertheless, I immediately told him what I had discovered. He assured me he understood the significance, but like any excellent trial attorney, he would not allow it to distract him from the matter at hand on Monday. He would remember this information and use it at the proper time. The remainder of the Thanksgiving weekend was quite tense in anticipation of Monday.

Monday, December 2, 1985

After a sleepless Sunday night, Janeen and I were inside the courthouse by 9:00 a.m. for the start of my trial. Herb immediately handed me a pile of papers, five different motions from the Prosecutor. They were requesting closed-circuit television, the exclusion of any information about our divorce, the exclusion of prospective jurors who read *Psychology Today* or *Omni* magazines and a host of other things. Their nonsense had begun already.

Herb said the motions indicated "they" were grasping at straws. The State was taking no chances. They probably wanted to delay the proceedings. They had to be worried about going to trial. They hoped more delays would break me financially and emotionally. Since I was already over $80,000 in debt and Herb was working for free, it was a senseless strategy. Emotionally, I was determined to make it through anything. Yet I didn't know how cruel things were really going to get. I didn't know I would soon be pushed to the brink.

It took several hours for the prosecution and the defense to present all the motions. These motions were actually the ground rules for the trial. When all motions were heard, a lunch recess was called. We were told to be back in court by 1:30 p.m. The Judge would then rule on all the pretrial motions and from there the trial would proceed.

We left the courthouse for lunch. The familiar routine brought back memories of the past three years of legal struggles. I couldn't help but think of the accused who were not self-employed, who could not make their own hours, who did not have family or friends to help them financially. This was the reason so many victims of false charges take plea bargains. They simply cannot afford to go on fighting the battle. They plead guilty to a lesser charge, even though they are really innocent. This gives the Prosecutor a conviction to add to his "body count." But it leaves the victim guilty for life.

We reconvened and Judge Egan moved through the motions. The judge said he would decide on our motion to exclude Jessie's testimony later in the proceedings. He would take into account the psychiatric and psychological reports. Although the Appellate Court had cleared the way for Jessica to testify, the presiding judge could still exercise his discretion, and prevent her from testifying if he found her incompetent. If that were to occur, in all probability the Prosecutor would seek an appeal of that decision, hoping the Appellate Court would insist the judge hear testimony from Jessica. We would then have to go around the same legal circle we had looped already. This would delay my trial again for some time.

Judge Egan ruled on the Prosecutor's motion for an adjournment. He would not postpone the proceedings and ordered the Prosecutor to have his witnesses ready for next Monday. He then granted Herb's request that the Prosecutor instruct Valori not to talk with Jessie about the case. He instructed the Prosecutor to be prepared to go to trial or dismiss the charges, the moment he ruled on Jessie's competency. He would tolerate no further delays.

The Prosecutor requested Judge Egan not to admit into evidence a medical report from the Roxbury Pediatric Group and disallow any testimony regarding the divorce. The medical report, dated before my arrest, indicated Jessie had a prior history of vaginal rashes and irritations, which would be similar in appearance to the irritations which Valori identified as the result of sexual abuse. The marital history was crucial, of course, to show the bitterness and chronic visitation and custody disputes. Nothing escaped Judge Egan's attention. He denied these motions along with several others, e.g., excluding divorced individuals from serving on the jury. He told the Prosecutor in no uncertain terms that he was going to allow evidence the admittance of which might show an existing medical condition.

Finally, the judge instructed the attorneys to provide each other with a complete list of witnesses by the end of the week. All parties were to be present on Monday, December 9, 1985. Janeen and Herb immediately turned and looked at me. December 9, 1985 was two years to the day of my arrest!

Herb and I spent the next day preparing for the trial. Herb believed the Prosecutor would go to trial, even if the judge disqualified Jessie as a witness. It would be too embarrassing for the Prosecutor's office to just dismiss the charge after two years. We planned the order for calling the witnesses so that the jurors would gradually have revealed to them the whole "Set-up" now that it was finally clear to us. Herb arranged for subpoenas to be sent to each of the witnesses. There was nothing to do but wait until Monday.

Monday, December 9, 1985

Two years to the day of my arrest, all parties were in the courtroom except Valori and Jessie. They were in the Prosecutor's office. The judge announced that he wanted to interview Jessie before giving his decision on her competency. The interview would take place in his office and be recorded on videotape. Only he, the Prosecutor and Herb would be in the room with Jessie. I was to sit by myself in another room and view the proceedings on a television screen. After the interview, Judge Egan would listen to the testimony of the "expert witnesses": the psychologist for the prosecution and the psychiatrist for the defense. Then he would give

Herb Korn, my criminal attorney, knew I had no money left. I wondered how that would affect his thoroughness. It didn't.

his judgement as to Jessie's competency. We took a recess to have the video cameras put in place and to have Jessie brought over from the Prosecutor's office.

This was not what we expected. Herb assured me the judge was doing this for safety's sake. The Prosecutor would not appeal the ruling on Jessica's competency if the judge did a thorough analysis of the matter now. This was Judge Egan's way of preventing an appeal of his competency decision. But the idea of watching Jessie on television, after not seeing her for two years, was sheer torture. Yet it was better than having Jessie on the witness stand in a courtroom for public view.

For close to ninety minutes, I sat alone and watched Jessie and Judge Egan. Jessie looked the way I remembered her, just a little bit bigger. She was still carrying her doll around with her. At first she was a bit shy, but soon warmed up to the judge. She sounded like the Jessie I knew — chattering away and seemingly not the least bit self-conscious. The judge finally got around to the important questions — what's the difference between the truth and a lie? What happens when you tell a lie? But she did not want to talk about this and really said nothing direct. Finally, Judge Egan saw he was getting nowhere and decided to take a lunch break. He would talk to Jessie in the afternoon.

About an hour and a half later, after Jessie had had lunch with the Prosecutor, Valori and her parents, it was a totally different story. As soon as Jessie walked into the judge's chambers, she said, "I know who you are. You are Judge Egan." She also told the judge her mother was outside the door. The judge assured her Valori was in another room. Jessie would not be dissuaded and insisted her mother was outside the door. The judge told Jessie he would tiptoe to the door and open it. He seemed as shocked as the rest of us to find Valori with her ear to the door. Egan instructed Valori to wait in the other room. Jessie simply said, "I told you she was there."

Jessie had obviously learned a lot at lunch. In addition to knowing the judge's name, she gave all the magic answers needed to qualify her to testify. She told the judge that "Daddy" touched her "private parts," a term she never used before. She spontaneously added with no prompting, "My Mommy didn't teach me that.

The people who say Mommy teaches me that are bad." The judge asked how she knew that people who say that are bad. Jessie promptly replied, "My Mommy told me." With that, the judge ended his interview. The newspapers, as exemplified in Exhibit I, told the story.

EXHIBIT I

Girl queried on tape in sexual abuse case

By BILL RILEY

A 4½-year-old girl was videotaped yesterday as she was interviewed by a judge in a closed-door hearing to determine her competency to recall events that happened more than two years ago, when Morris County authorities say she was sexually abused by her father.

Superior Court Judge Charles Egan, sitting in Morristown, is scheduled to issue a ruling today on the competency issue, along with a decision on whether testimony from psychologists who examined the girl will be admissible.

Lawrence Spiegel, a Parsippany-Troy Hills psychologist, was charged on Dec. 9, 1983, with molesting his daughter during a weekend visit. He has denied the charge and maintained that his ex-wife filed the complaint out of revenge after a bitter divorce.

Egan met with the girl for 90 minutes in his chambers with Morris County Assistant Prosecutor Michael Rubbinaccio and defense lawyer Herbert Korn. The defendant was able to watch via the television camera set up to tape the discussion.

Stating he had the discretion to close a competency hearing, Egan said he will announce a ruling today.

Korn said he knows of no other case in which such a procedure has been used. He said the judge did not allow him to ask the girl, who lives in Georgia with her mother, any questions.

"I have asked for an opportunity to cross-examine, but no decision was made," Korn said.

The attorney said his impression of the girl's statements to the judge was they were "98 percent 'I don't remember' or 'I don't want to talk'" and "2 percent parroting."

In prior rulings, courts have said the girl can testify while sitting on her mother's lap. Korn, however, challenged her ability to recall events and distinguish memories of real events from fantasy or what her mother has programmed her to say over the years.

Public testimony was offered by a Florida psychologist, Wallace Kennedy, who examined the girl in June and September. He found that the child exhibited most of the eight characteristics displayed by children who have been sexually abused.

According to Kennedy, Spiegel's daughter has "superior intelligence" and can recall events from October through December 1983, when, authorities said, the molestations took place. He maintained that the child's memory of, and ability to communicate, what occurred would improve as she got older. Kennedy said the child described an oral sex act committed by her father.

Under questioning by Korn, Kennedy said he would "be surprised" to learn it was the first time the girl made such a statement.

Korn said a psychiatrist who examined Spiegel's daughter at the request of the defense is scheduled to testify today. He said the doctor found the girl displayed no signs of being traumatized by any incident with her father and has no ability to remember events that happened when she was less than 30-months old.

Tuesday, December 10, 1985

Shocking and agonizing describes the next day in court. We had to sit through more pretrial testimony from the experts to establish their qualifications. Dr. Wallace Kennedy, who had begun testifying on Monday, took the stand again. He was the psychologist from Florida who examined Jessica in June.

According to Kennedy, Jessica displayed the syndrome of an abused child. He listed symptoms of sexually abused children including: aggressiveness, sleep disturbances, sexual talk, dependency and several others. Such behavioral traits he attributed to abuse. Obviously, Dr. Kennedy never considered the possibilities that a child who was abruptly separated from her father and constantly told she was abused by him, might exhibit anxiety.

But Kennedy contradicted himself several times, especially when Herb began to cross-examine him. He stated on the two occasions he examined Jessie, he spent only twenty to thirty minutes with her and more than sixty minutes with Valori. Herb ended his testimony by asking several questions with regard to sexual abuse. The final question was, "If a father kisses his two-year-old on the tush, is that sexual abuse?" The answer was, "Yes." So much for Dr. Kennedy.

The Prosecutor also attempted to qualify Jessie's "current

therapist," Pat Hastings. She was a social worker from Georgia and clearly did not have the proper credentials to testify as an expert. Judge Egan disqualified her after Herb had completed his cross-examination. During the past two years, Jessie had been taken to five or six therapists, who had investigated or treated her for a trauma which never occurred.

Later that day, Dr. Friedland testified. His examination revealed that Jessie displayed no sign of trauma. He also had the opportunity, at Herb's request, to view the videotape of Jessica's interview. He stated that Jessie's spontaneous reply, "My mommy didn't teach me that," troubled him. He felt that this was some indication that she might have been programmed.

Wednesday, December 11, 1985

On Wednesday, the unthinkable happened. The judge had read Herb's comments about the trial in the newspaper and was annoyed. He felt statements given to the newspaper made it more difficult to find impartial jury members. He was also concerned about the trial starting so close to the Christmas holiday recess. All things considered, Judge Egan postponed the trial until the new year. Before dismissing the court, he ruled Jessica was competent to testify. In addition, he was considering videotaping her testimony from a private room.

A few minutes later, I found myself out of the courthouse with my trial postponed until after the holidays. I went home to face a third Christmas without Jessie.

7

WHAT ARE WE DOING HERE?

Stage 7: The Resolution

The courtroom felt austere and foreboding as I sat in the defendant's chair on Monday morning, January 6, 1986. Herb spoke softly to me, "Be yourself but remember, no displays of emotion, no shaking your head in despair." I nodded in response and thought about the decision the jury would soon make — an innocent man, free to see his child or a prisoner for fifteen years in a state penitentiary.

This wasn't the first time Herb had spoken these words. He and Steven had prepared me to the point where I had control over my frustration, anger and fear. I'm not certain whether their talks were prompted more by their legal experience or our friendships. But they had worked with me long enough to control my every emotion. In preparation for the case, when I lost my temper or appeared exasperated at one of them, either Steven or Herb would inevitably say, "That's exactly what you will not do in court. If you have trouble with what I say, think what the Prosecutor will do to you."

Herb and Steven had prepared me well. Inside I was nervous and jittery, but I did not show it. Even seeing the packed courtroom did not disturb me as it had in the past. Behind me sat many of my friends and family, along with the familiar faces of ex-students and others who had followed the case and supported me. I glanced toward the back rows. The reporters were already at work, writing furiously in their pads. There were more of them than ever before.

My attention was drawn to the judge as he took the bench and immediately spoke. He said the network news affiliates had requested permission to film in the courtroom. I feared that would create a circus-like atmosphere and distract us. After some discussion, it was decided that only print media would be allowed.

The decision that Jessie would testify had already been made before the holiday recess. If the decision had been the opposite, we would have been involved in further appeals by the Prosecutor which would have resulted in more delays. But her testimony would be given before a video camera in the judge's office with only Herb and the Prosecutor present. Jessie would not be physically present in the courtroom. In effect, this would be a repeat of Jessie's competency interview made with Judge Egan in December.

With the preliminaries completed, the judge banged his gavel and declared the trial underway. The first hour was filled with last minute rulings and explanations of procedure. The judge finally announced the start of jury selection. He instructed the bailiff to bring in the first group of prospective jurors.

A few moments later, the doors swung open and about thirty people entered. They varied in age and dress, some in jeans and T-shirts, some in suits and ties. The older women sat with serious looks on their faces and hands folded on their laps. They were a true cross-section of people, yet there were more older people than younger. I thought to myself that many younger people must wiggle their way out of jury duty due to work obligations.

Hour after hour the jury selection continued. The bailiff rolled a wooden drum filled with numbers which corresponded to a number on each prospective juror's name tag. The jury box filled with people, only to empty after countless questions from the judge, Herb and the Prosecutor, Mr. Rubbinaccio. The questions flew across the room. Have you read anything about this case? Have you seen anything on television? Were you or any member of your family ever involved in a criminal proceeding? Would you dismiss the word of a four-year-old, just because she is four? Would you have a problem with the sexual nature of this case? Do any of you know the defendant as a teacher or psychologist or personally? Would anything interfere with your ability to render a fair and impartial verdict?

Individuals who raised their hands to any of these or other questions were ushered into the judge's chambers for private consultation with the judge and attorneys. More often than not they never returned to the courtroom. Each time the supply of prospective jurors dwindled, the judge would call for a new group and more would stream into court. I sat silent and watched, feeling petrified inside, but looking cool and collected on the outside. The day ended when the judge adjourned the court about 4 p.m.

"We are still far from selecting a jury," said Herb, once we were back in his office. I began to complain; the tension had worked me into a frenzy. Herb responded, "You'll just have to bear with it. This could take another whole day." We talked for a few more minutes and with his final words of encouragement, I left for home.

While driving, I wondered if my exterior calm could last through another day of jury selection. Could I continue to sit motionless hour after hour while jurors were asked the same questions again and again? I really didn't have much choice; I would just have to hold on. Herb and Steven had told me the jury selection would be difficult and repetitive. They were correct.

Tuesday, January 7, 1986

The next morning, before 8:00 a.m., John and Nancy Reber came over with a pile of newspapers which contained the first of what was to be the daily blow-by-blow coverage of the trial. Virtually all the articles concentrated on Jessie's forthcoming testimony via videotape. Judge Egan's telling remarks regarding Jessie can be seen in Exhibit A.

EXHIBIT A

Judge finds 4-year-old competent to testify

By BRIAN MURRAY
Daily Record Courthouse Writer

A 4-year-old girl will be permitted to testify, via television, against the psychologist charged with molesting her two years ago.

The psychologist, Lawrence Spiegel, 39, of Flanders, goes on trial today in Morris County.

"I would admit, quite frankly, there are some very genuine problems with (her) reliability, credibility ... but I simply cannot rule as a matter of law she is incompetent," Superior Court Judge Charles M. Egan said yesterday, denying defense demands that the girl not testify against Spiegel.

"So I'll rule only that she is competent to testify and will be allowed to do so."

Spiegel is accused of molesting the child on Dec. 3, 1983. He denies the charges and contends that the girl has been coached and "programed" by her mother.

Egan interviewed the child yesterday and Spiegel's attorney, Herbert Korn, cross-examined her in the judge's Morristown chambers. Korn has contended that the girl has no independent recollection of what occurred two years ago and is incapable of testifying properly before a jury.

"There is a tendency to confuse the competency of this girl to testify ... and her reliability, her credibility," Egan said. He added that she appears able to testify, although the information she offers about the alleged incident may be questionable.

"I recognize there are indications the girl has been, although I won't say programed by her mother, encouraged by her mother," Egan said. "There is no doubt there is a credibility issue, but credibility is separate and apart from competency."

He said the child told him in private interviews that she does not recall facts about the alleged assault but that her mother does. He also said the child sometimes describes aspects of the alleged incident in terminology more indicative of an adult talking than a 4-year-old.

"It would suggest she's being influenced, whether maliciously or sincerely, by her mother," said Egan. He added, however, that the credibility of a witness is for a jury to decide.

Jury selection for the trial began yesterday and opening statements by attorneys and prosecutors could begin today.

Late that day, the final juror was chosen and both the defense and prosecution agreed to accept the jury. I looked carefully at the fourteen people, twelve regulars and two alternates, who would listen to the evidence and determine my fate. There were twelve men and only two women. The men ranged in age from mid-twenties to retired, although most were older. The women were middle-aged and one constantly sat with an angry look on her face. I worried about her.

Once the jury was selected, Judge Egan emphasized two points. The first was regarding the Prosecutor's desire to allow testimony from Valori's Aunt Abby who had appeared before the Grand Jury. Since her testimony did not include any direct knowledge of the charge, Herb felt it should not be allowed. Judge Egan said he would make a decision about Aunt Abby's testimony the following day. The second issue took everyone by surprise. The judge said he was going to give the jury a "preliminary charge," or set of instructions, before the testimony began.

This was extremely unusual. The judge was going to explain the nature of the law as it applied to this case in advance of any testimony. Herb was right, Judge Egan was taking no chances. He was covering every base at least twice, to insure an absolutely fair trial and to avoid any appeals. This unorthodox move generated more publicity, as seen in Exhibit B.

EXHIBIT B

By P.L. WYCKOFF
Advance Staff Writer

In what he termed a "rare" move, a state Superior Court judge decided he will give the jury in the Lawrence Spiegel case a preliminary charge in order for them to better deal with evidence in the case.

Judge Charles M. Egan Jr. said he would explain the law to the 12-man, two-woman jury Wednesday morning before they heard any evidence because "it helps clear up what the jury is looking for in terms of how the facts of a case relate to the law."

While he said that such a procedure is "very rarely done," Egan said he wanted jurors to understand the charges against Spiegel, a Parsippany psychologist who is charged with molesting his daughter two years ago.

The Judge outlined the upcoming sequence of events. He would give the jury this initial "charge." Then the attorneys would give their opening statements to the jury. Next Jessie would testify via closed-circuit television. Other witnesses would follow.

Wednesday, January 8, 1986

Herb had warned me not to be distracted by the crowd that would come to see Jessie's televised testimony. I prepared myself for a packed room as Janeen and I drove to the courthouse. The area outside the building did seem very busy that morning. People moved about; lawyers rushed up the front steps with slim brief-cases tucked under their arms or dangling from their hands. The world was very much on the move.

We parked the car and entered the building through a side door that a deputy had shown us. It led up the backstairs to Judge Egan's courtroom and enabled us to bypass the crowd, except for those gathered just outside the courtroom door. Frequently, the reporters stood there to ask a quick question as the deputies ush-ered us in. This day it took a few minutes to wade through the mobbed entranceway. I heard people call my name, but I did not turn to look or talk, as Herb had instructed. On one side of the hall was a class of high school students with their teacher. They had come to see firsthand the workings of justice.

Reaching the courtroom, an officer pulled the heavy doors open saying "Good morning" in his usual monotone voice as we entered. I was stunned. The room was packed. They were standing in the aisles, every seat was filled. Now I realized the huge crowd outside the doors were those who could not fit in the courtroom. I struggled to keep a sense of detachment from it all. I did not feel the shame or embarrassment I had feared. Instead, there was a proud fighting spirit in me, although I tried to let nothing show.

The courtroom was adorned with television monitors and long, thick cables. Technicians were making last minute checks. There was a small television on the judge's bench, an extremely large set in front of the jury box and a third set between the tables for the Prosecution and defense. The public would watch the attor-neys' screen as well. The room was buzzing with excitement as the judge entered. He asked both sides if they were ready to proceed. Soon we were underway.

Assistant Prosecutor Rubbinaccio made the opening statement. He told the jury that the State intended to prove I had molested my infant daughter. He said they would call a doctor who would testify about an irritation in Jessie's vaginal area — an irritation that looked like a dark oval ring, an irritation caused by my lips. The State would prove that on the weekend of December 3 and 4, I had sexually abused Jessica with mouth-to-genital contact. I listened impassionately. Herb had warned me about all this. He sat absolutely unaffected. Occasionally, he glanced at me to make sure I was not reacting. The jury listened intently, shifting uncomfortably in their seats.

Prosecutor Rubbinaccio spoke forcefully but said little, gestured boldly but proved nothing.

When Rubbinaccio was done, Herb stood and walked toward the jury box. He began by telling the jury that as the defense, we did not have to say or prove anything. It was up to the State to do that. If we wanted, we could sit silently. We did not have to say a word in our own defense. He raised his voice and said, "But we are not going to be silent. We are going to show the truth, pure and simple."

He walked back to our table, picked up a document, turned to the jury and said, "Some of you may be saying to yourself, if he is not guilty, why is he here? He must have done something or he wouldn't have been indicted."

He explained that the Grand Jury process leading to an indictment was an arm of the Prosecutor, not an indication of guilt. He said that neither I, nor he, were permitted to be present. The Prosecutor alone had complete control of the Grand Jury process, including what evidence was presented. Herb held a document directly in front of the jury. "I have a copy of the indictment in my hand and I want to show you how much weight you should give it." He slowly and deliberately tore it into little pieces, literally letting the scraps fall to the courtroom floor. As the last shred of paper floated to rest, he said, "That's what the indictment is worth and that's exactly how much weight you should give it." He concluded his remarks and we adjourned for lunch.

The afternoon session began with Jessie's televised testimony. This was the event that worried Herb the most. He had never cross-examined a little child. Prior to Jessie's interview in court in December, I had spent hours on the phone with a well-known child psychologist, Dr. William McIver. He had reviewed a variety of approaches which Herb could use to communicate effectively with Jessie. Herb had practiced them, but now it was for real and for keeps.

I sat facing the television screen, my back to the public gallery and the jury to my right. My eyes remained glued to the set. Finally, the screen filled with my little girl, Herb and Rubbinaccio. They wore headsets with mouthpieces so they could communicate with the judge. They looked more like pilots or TV sports commentators than lawyers.

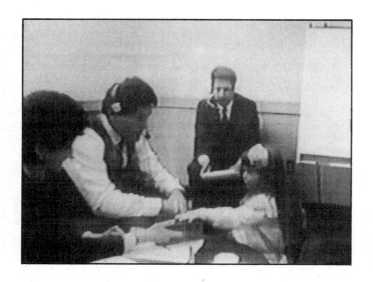

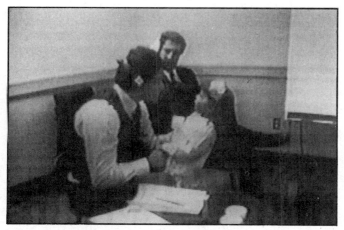

They swore Jessie in. She seemed confused as to what it all meant. It didn't take her long to demonstrate that she had no fear of men. She talked and played but it was officially called "giving testimony."

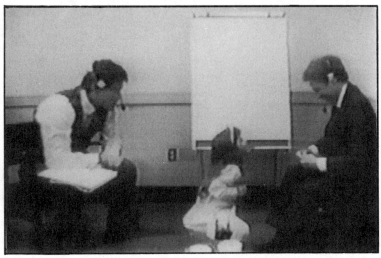

What Are We Doing Here?

The whole scene appeared bizarre. When the questioning began, I lost my calm detachment. Tears welled in my eyes. For two hours I fought to maintain my composure, but the tears ran freely down my cheeks. They were not tears of shame or embarrassment; they were tears of sadness at the reality of what was happening.

For almost an hour I listened to Rubbinaccio attempting to "question" my little girl. He began by asking Jessie about her home, her school, her mommy and her daddy. He gradually moved his questions toward Jessie's visitations with me. For a long time Jessie would not answer Rubbinaccio's questions. She talked, asked her own questions, became distracted, grew tired, acted silly and was more interested in the headsets worn by the two lawyers than in what was being asked of her. She repeatedly held Rubbinaccio's hand and hugged him several times during the questioning. If anyone had wondered about Jessie's fear of men since the alleged sexual abuse, they weren't wondering any more.

After forty-five minutes of prodding, Jessie told Rubbinaccio that I hurt her and added I was "bad" while changing her diaper and giving her a bottle. But her voice lacked any emotional stress, any trauma. She appeared to be a child who had been asked that same question repeatedly and now she had grown tired, perhaps even bored with the dialogue. Her attention became focused on Herb who had sat quietly several feet away absorbing the interplay between Jessie and the Prosecutor.

Herb moved immediately to establish a dialogue with Jessie. He used the playful style of questioning he had learned from Dr. William McIver from Oregon. Through long distance phone calls Dr. McIver had coached Herb on how to best question Jessie and, at the same time, avoid traumatizing her. Herb was able to clearly illustrate to the jury that Jessie's statements lacked credibility. At one point, Jessie said that her mother told her that I was "sick in the head." But when Herb asked Jessie for the meaning of that phrase, she didn't know what it meant. Herb was slowly unveiling Valori's two-year influence on Jessie. The jury had front row seats to see firsthand the damage done to Jessie and to me.

While sprawled across Herb's lap and giggling, Jessie told Herb, "Daddy hurt her in the bathroom, in the basement, in the attic, on the roof." To Jessie this entire affair was like a game. It was clear she had no recollection of any sexual abuse. After viewing her testimony, it was difficult to even perceive Jessie as a witness in this trial. It was even more difficult to view her as the victim. Exhibit C tells more about that day in court.

EXHIBIT C

Girl gives TV testimony against dad in abuse trial
4-year-old tries to recount incidents that took place more 2 years back

By BILL RILEY

A 4½-year-old girl testified via a closed-circuit television hookup in Morristown yesterday as the chief witness against her father, a psychologist accused of sexually molesting her more than two years ago.

In her statements, relayed to a 12-man, two-woman jury and a courtroom packed with spectators, the girl conceded she acted "pretty silly" while being questioned by Morris County Assistant Prosecutor Michael Rubbinaccio and defense lawyer Herbert Korn.

Korn is representing Lawrence Spiegel of Parsippany-Troy Hills on an aggravated sexual assault charge lodged by his ex-wife after he had a weekend visit with his daughter in 1983.

Holding Rubbinaccio's hand and going to him for occasional hugs at some points, while lying across Korn's lap at others, the child seemed more interested in the telephone headsets worn by the two lawyers than in their questions.

"Did he do anything to you when he put you to bed?" Rubbinaccio asked, referring to the allegations against Spiegel outlined by the girl's mother in prior hearings.

"No. He did hurt me. I remember he hurt me, but not when I was being put to bed," she replied, quickly adding her father was "bad" while changing her diaper and giving her a bottle.

When pressed, the child insisted she did not want to talk about it.

"It's scary to tell," the child said at another point.

The girl, questioned by Korn, referred to Spiegel as "Dada" and, giggling, reported her mother told her he was "sick in the head." She said she did not know what the phrase meant.

Spiegel, who has been allowed no contact with his daughter since being charged, cried as the girl hugged Korn and said she loved him and wanted to visit his house.

In his opening statement, Korn blamed a "sloppy investigation" for the charges against Spiegel, a former Morris County College psychology professor.

"They took the word of a 2½-year-old girl without any corroboration," he maintained, blaming Spiegel's ex-wife, Valerie Mulvey, for having a "mindset" against the defendant after a bitter divorce.

"Listen to the evidence and try and make sense out of it. What does this girl remember from two years ago? I think you'll agree it was something innocent picked up by Valerie Mulvey, who ran with it for a full 99 yards. Now's she's here today trying to score," Korn said, contending the woman influenced the girl's statements.

"Larry Spiegel hasn't been able to see, speak with, telephone or write to his daughter for two years. What does she think of him because of that? When she testifies, consider whether she really remembers if someone has been planting and reinforcing in her mind 'what daddy did,'" he said.

Rubbinaccio, referring to the child as "extremely bright" and "not easily manipulated," asked the jury to keep an open mind. "It's too easy to say you can't believe a 4½-year-old," he said.

Mulvey, now a Georgia resident, began testifying yesterday, admitting some statements she made at previous hearings were not accurate "because I was confused."

Thursday, January 9, 1986

Although Valori had testified briefly the previous day, the court had adjourned due to the late hour. Now the jurors watched her carefully as she returned to the witness stand. Herb was an expert at tripping up Valori. He once said to me, "It's simple, she's lying whether she knows it or not, which means she forgets what she has previously said."

At one point, Herb asked her about her feelings toward me. She got so angry she responded with, "I hated his guts." For the first time, the faces of the jurors seemed to reveal their inner feelings and the astonishment was evident in most of them. Valori contradicted testimony she had given at the June 1984 hearing. She blamed the confusion on the fact she was not prepared for that earlier hearing and had gotten her dates mixed. This day she could not remember what she said at that time. The newspapers immediately picked up on it as seen in Exhibits D1 and D2.

EXHIBIT D1

Hatred preceded accusation, ex-wife testifies

By P.L. WYCKOFF
Staff Writer

Lawrence Spiegel's ex-wife told jurors in Morristown Thursday that both she and her family had felt a great deal of hatred for Spiegel before she accused him of molesting the couple's 4½-year-old daughter two years ago.

Valori Mulvey, under questioning by defense attorney· Herbert Korn, said she had told a court official in 1983 of her hatred for Spiegel, while the couple was getting a divorce.

Mulvey detailed for Korn her feelings during the time since she and Spiegel separated in late 1982, and how she had filed a divorce complaint against him on grounds of adultery.

Spiegel, a Parsippany psychologist, was arrested outside his office on Dec. 9, 1983, a few days after his wife told state authorities that he had molested the then 2½-year-old girl. Spiegel has contended he is the victim of his ex-wife's vindictiveness.

Mulvey told Korn that shortly after the couple separated she got the flu and took her daughter to Burlington County where she stayed with relatives for three months. She admitted she did not tell Spiegel where she was going nor give him an opportunity to contact his daughter.

However, she testified that while she had discussed the divorce and the alleged molestation with the girl, she denied having influenced her to testify one way or another.

Mulvey said the girl had had "ambivalent" feelings about her father since the alleged incidents, and that she had tried to reinforce both the girl's feeling of love and of hatred for her father.

"She knows how I feel (about Spiegel) and I've protected her feelings from the divorce and throughout," Mulvey said of her daughter.

The girl testified Wednesday via closed-circuit television and, after prodding by Assistant Morris County Prosecutor Michael Rubbinaccio, said her father had "hurt her" and kissed her genitals while she was visiting him on Nov. 16 and on Dec. 3, 1983.

Spiegel sat quietly while his wife finished her testimony. "It makes me upset to see him. But I don't have the anger (anymore). I'm just agitated, I'm upset," Mulvey said.

EXHIBIT D2

Sex case testimony changed

By BRIAN MURRAY
Daily Record Courthouse Writer

MORRISTOWN — The former wife of a psychologist charged with sexually assaulting his young daughter contradicted previous testimony she had given against him in a Superior Court trial yesterday.

Valori Mulvey denied yesterday that she contacted the Somerset County prosecutor's office in December 1983, which, according to evidence, led to a Morris County investigation of psychologist Lawrence Spiegel.

Spiegel, 39, is accused of sexually assaulting the 2½-year-old girl in his Flanders home on Dec. 3, 1983.

Mulvey testified yesterday that the girl, now 4½, complained on Dec. 4, 1983, of her father "hurting her" during a visitation the day before. Mulvey said she suspected sexual abuse, took the child to a pediatrician on Dec. 5, and was later called by Linda Monday, an employee of the Somerset County prosecutor's office.

However, in testimony the day before, Mulvey had said she sought advice from a priest, was given Monday's phone number and called her, thinking Monday could offer counseling.

Asked by defense attorney Herbert Korn about the contradiction,

> Mulvey insisted she did not call Monday but that Monday called her.
>
> Mulvey's testimony on Wednesday, about her daughter allegedly being "hurt" by Spiegel on Nov. 16 and Dec. 3, 1983, also contradicted her testimony in a June 1984 court hearing.
>
> Confronted by Korn about the inconsistency, Mulvey said, "I was very confused at that (1984) hearing. I wasn't sure if I was going to be testifying at all."

Friday, January 10 through Sunday, January 12

The trial did not convene on Friday. Judge Egan had other legal matters to oversee. I met a few patients, several of whom had been in court all week. It was strange to begin a therapy session discussing their observations of my trial. Nonetheless, these people believed in me and were not hesitant to declare it openly. I sincerely appreciated all their support. When my professional work was concluded, I spent the remainder of the weekend in strategy sessions with Herb and Steven.

We expected the State to conclude their case on Monday. We would then present ours. Herb talked to all prospective witnesses, including Janeen, Debra, my ex-wife, Pauline, and our friends, Nancy and John. All had been at my house on the date of the alleged incident. Once again, Herb defined clearly the thrust of our case. He told them, "Most importantly, tell the truth. That's all we have to do. Don't embellish or add to it. I promised the jury the simple truth and that is what they are going to get."

Monday, January 13, 1986

On Monday, the State called their four witnesses in succession: Linda Mundy from the Somerset County Prosecutor's Office, Kay Curtiss from DYFS, Dr. Rogers, the physician who examined Jessie on December 5, 1983, and Dr. Wallace Kennedy, the psychologist from Florida. Dr. Rogers, under cross-examination by Herb, was asked if he ever described any irritation in Jessie's vaginal area as a dark oval ring. His response was "Never." When asked if Valori ever described it that way, his response was the same. Neither in direct examination by the Prosecutor nor in cross-examination, did he ever say this irritation was due to oral sexual abuse. He did say, however, such redness could be caused by tight clothing or coarse wiping.

Dr. Kennedy's testimony was even more harmless than his pretrial testimony. He again spoke of the characteristics of a "sexually molested child." But he admitted under cross-examination that these same characteristics could be found in children who had not been abused. The faces of the jurors reflected the vagueness in the doctor's testimony. Herb, as he did in the pretrial hearing, asked him if it was sexual abuse for a father to kiss his two-year-old daughter on the tush. Dr. Kennedy again said "yes," but qualified his answer, "Yes, if the mother is out of the room." At this, virtually everyone in the courtroom began to laugh. Once again, so much for Dr. Kennedy.

That concluded the presentation of the State's case. Herb immediately made a motion which is common legal protocol. He asked that the charges be dismissed. The motion was denied as we expected, but it was a way to reaffirm in the jury's mind that no case really existed. A reporter remarked to me while exiting for lunch recess, "We have to keep reminding ourselves we are watching the State's case." He concluded, "It seems more like the defense." That remark cheered me up. I thought to myself, now we can call our witnesses.

Once back in session, we began the defense. Steven took the stand first. He testified that he was my divorce lawyer and had overheard Valori on our court date of November 16, 1983, say she would, "Make sure that I never saw my child again." Mr. Rubbinaccio cross-examined Steven, but to no avail. Then Pauline, my first wife, who had visited on that December weekend testified. She was followed by Janeen and Debra. Nancy and John Reber, who had visited us on that Sunday morning, concluded the testimony. All of them said they had seen Jessie on the weekend in question and she seemed perfectly fine. Rubbinaccio went after them, searching for some angle of attack, but could not seem to find one. The newspaper coverage appearing in Exhibit E, tells the story.

EXHIBIT E

Judge denies request to dismiss sex charges

By BRIAN MURRAY
Daily Record Courthouse Writer

A Superior Court judge refused yesterday to dismiss charges against a psychologist accused of molesting his infant daughter, despite defense arguments that conclusive proof has yet to be presented against him in his trial in Morristown.

As the trial entered its second week, the Morris County Prosecutor's Office rested its case against Lawrence Spiegel, 39, of Flanders and defense attorney Herbert Korn charged that evidence presented by the prosecution has not substantiated allegations of sexual abuse.

Spiegel is charged with molesting his daughter on Dec. 3, 1983, when she was 2½ years old. Defense witnesses began testifying on his behalf yesterday after Judge Charles M. Egan refused to dismiss the case.

Spiegel has contended that the charges are a result of a custody battle had had with his ex-wife, Valori Mulvey of Georgia.

Egan, reviewing testimony introduced by the prosecution, refused to dismiss the case, saying, "The jury could find some reasonsable doubt (of guilt) ... but that doesn't mean they couldn't find the defendant did commit a crime."

Mulvey testified last week that the child complained to her on Dec. 4, 1983, that her father "hurt" her. The child, testifying via television, said at one point that her father "hurt" her and at another point that her father did not.

A pediatrician testified that he examined the girl on Dec. 5, 1983, and found her groin to be irritated. A psychologist testified that he interviewed the girl a year after the alleged incident and found her to exhibit signs of a child who had been sexually abused.

However, the doctors noted in their testimony that other things could have caused the signs exhibited by the child. Egan said that was for a jury to decide.

Among those who testified yesterday on Spiegel's behalf were his current fiance, Jineen Love, and his first wife, Pauline Spiegel, both of whom said they were with him and the child on Dec. 3, 1983, and that the child appeared happy, friendly and playful.

Other friends of Spiegel testified that they, too, observed the girl to be her "bouncy self" on Dec. 3 and Dec. 4, 1983, and not hysterical or withdrawn, as Valori Mulvey described her as being when she returned from a visit with Spiegel on Dec. 4, 1983.

Spiegel's trial continues today and could be put to the jury for a verdict before the weekend.

Tuesday, January 14, 1986

This is it, I thought as I turned off the alarm clock at 7:00 a.m. It took no time to wake up these days. Last night's conversation with Herb was still vivid in my mind. "It's up to you, now," he had said, as we sat in his office and reviewed the day's events. "The jury is just waiting to see for themselves what kind of person you really are. You have to maintain control of yourself on that witness stand. Don't let Rubbinaccio get to you. He'll try every trick in the book to get you to react to him. If you get angry or argue with him, you'll lose in the eyes of the jury. No matter what he says, you respond with 'Yes, sir,' 'No, sir' is that clear?"

I had never heard Herb so serious and grave. "Just stay with it for one more day," he had said as I left his office the night before.

"I will," I had called back, trying to reassure him.

I jumped out of bed, and into the shower. I talked to myself, stressing the need for calm. I was deathly afraid that the moment I stepped onto the witness stand I would lose it. Despite all the legal proceedings for the past three years, I had only testified once. I remembered being nervous then, when the consequences were much less serious than now. Then it was a matter of a visitation schedule. Now I was facing a minimum of fifteen years in prison and I would not get a second chance.

I took the familiar ride to the courtroom. The court was back in session and my anxiety disappeared as Dr. Friedland took the witness stand. He was our last witness before I testified. His silver-grey hair, tweed suit and horn-rimmed glasses gave a distinguished impression. He answered each question slowly and carefully. It appeared quite obvious he took no side in the case, he simply reported his findings. Jessie, in his opinion, displayed no sign of any trauma, did not remember anything from two years ago and showed no fear of men. He added a cryptic warning that although he had not seen a traumatized child when he interviewed her in October, she might well be traumatized as a result of this trial. On that note, Herb sat down and the cross-examination began.

Dr. Friedland remained unruffled by the Prosecutor's questions. The Prosecutor frequently shot the same phrase, "Isn't it true that . . ." and completed it with a "damaging statement." Friedland calmly responded with, "No, that is not true." The exchange continued for over an hour. The longer it continued, the more evident it became the Prosecutor was getting nowhere. Finally, he gave up as quickly as he began.

After a short recess, we returned to the courtroom. This is it, I thought. My stomach began to tighten. The crowd quieted as Judge Egan entered. The jury was brought in. "Call your next witness, Mr. Korn."

"The defense calls Dr. Lawrence Spiegel," Herb replied. I stood and walked toward the court clerk who was standing in front of the judge's bench holding the Bible. I took the oath. At that moment, the tightness in my stomach disappeared. My entire body was numb as I stepped onto the witness stand. I sat down and directly faced the jury for the first time. My pulse raced. Herb purposefully took time to give me a chance to get comfortable. Soon the familiar sound of his voice put me at ease and the dialogue began to fall into a comfortable rhythm.

Since I knew what would be asked ahead of time, Herb's questions were easy. At one point, when he asked how long it had been since I had seen Jessie, tears rolled down my cheeks. Herb quickly changed the subject and I regained my composure. I knew it would only be a few minutes before the Prosecutor would get the chance which he had wanted so badly for over two years.

Herb completed his questions and sat down. I waited for my

heart to begin racing again, but it never did. Rubbinaccio stood up slowly, looked me directly in the eyes with a cold stare and moved toward me. It was the first time I really had looked at him carefully. He was certainly a menacing figure — jet black hair, squared off jaw and the muscular body of a well-conditioned athlete. His eyes were dark, hard, and impersonal. He attacked with his questions.

I felt like I was on automatic. I heard myself responding with "Yes, sir," "No, sir," as the questions flew. In the corner of my eye I saw Herb nodding approvingly. I had no idea how I was able to stay so calm, but it began to feel comfortable after awhile. Don't get too self-confident, I told myself. That's what Herb told you to be careful about.

Rubbinaccio tried the same technique with me that he had used with Dr. Friedland. Almost every question was phrased with, "Isn't it true that . . ." and concluded with an allegation. This was already quite familiar to me and I found it easy to continue repeating ' No, sir, that's not true." Each time I did, he seemed to get progressively more frustrated. He knew this was his last chance.

Several times, Judge Egan warned the Prosecutor that his questions were getting out of line. Throughout the trial, the judge had been very specific in his instructions as to what kinds of questions he would allow and what he would not permit. One point which neither attorney was permitted to raise concerned alleged abuse prior to December 3, 1983. No evidence had ever been introduced to substantiate Valori's charges prior to that date. In other words, the abuse charge concerned the weekend of December 3 and 4 only. The attorneys were to direct their questions around events of those days. The judge reiterated several times that if either attorney raised the issue of abuse prior to that date, he might have to declare a mistrial. That could mean a new indictment, a new trial and more long delays.

I could see the frustration and exasperation in the Prosecutor's face. He walked to the witness stand and stood with his eyes about eighteen inches from mine. His look had changed from cold and impersonal to one of desperation. He knew he was losing it. He was begging me to lose my temper. His questions became more and more scattered as he continued. We covered every detail which Herb had reviewed with me. The training was paying off; I was calm and in control.

Rubbinaccio seemed bent on making something illicit out of games I played with Jessie. They were typical parenting games, but he used one innuendo after another to insinuate I had done something improper. Yet he was never specific in making a point. He just couldn't get to me because I knew the truth.

He walked to his counsel table, picked up some papers, turned and came right back to the witness stand. He asked if I recognized the document he held in his hand. He stepped right into the box and stood at my side, no more than twelve inches away. He handed me the papers.

It was the court order issued on November 16, 1983, requiring Valori to return from Ohio and bring Jessica to court. The date of the order was prior to the weekend of December 3, 1983. I became concerned about the strict guidelines of Judge Egan, which barred discussions of any accusation of abuse prior to that weekend. I was also mindful that Rubbinaccio was at the height of his frustration with me. Be careful, I said to myself.

"Yes sir, I do recognize it."

"Would you tell the court what it is?" he snapped.

"Yes, this was a show cause order which required Valori to appear in court with Jessica when she violated the court's instructions and left the State without permission. I was awarded joint legal custody as a result of her action."

"I didn't ask you that," he screamed at me and grabbed the document back. His face was bright red. He was fuming. Suddenly he said, "Isn't it true that Valori left the State because you had molested Jessica?"

Herb was on his feet instantly, "Your Honor!" Herb began to protest.

Suddenly I heard the loud crack of the gavel and Judge Egan was on his feet. He was fuming. For several moments I couldn't grasp what had happened or who the judge was screaming at. He shouted to the bailiff, "Get the jury out of here."

He remained standing, glaring at Rubbinaccio. The courtroom was absolutely silent, except for the sound of the confused jury making their way out of the room. Everyone was stunned, the whole room had suddenly plunged into a collective state of shock.

What Are We Doing Here?

The faces around the room told me that only the judge, Herb and Rubbinaccio understood what had happened.

The moment the last juror had left the room, Judge Egan let fly. Though I cannot remember his exact words, it went something like this: "You had to do it, didn't you? After all of these days in court, after all of the meticulous instructions I have given, you had to say that. Now, how am I going to instruct this jury to ignore that remark? How will we ever know if they did ignore your last comment, Mr. Rubbinaccio?"

Rubbinaccio stood with his head hanging down, staring at the floor. Then he responded, attempting to convince the judge that my statement, regarding the November 16, 1983, court order was not true. He intimated that the reason we had been in court that day was because of Valori's abuse accusations, not because she violated the court order as I had stated. Rubbinaccio was shifting the blame to me.

Judge Egan was in no mood for word games. He wanted to see what that court order said. He told the court clerk to call Judge Collester's chambers and have the entire matrimonial file brought upstairs to him. He would review the wording of the court order himself before determining what to do. The court would stand in recess. He cracked his gavel again, turned and walked into his chambers.

Several moments after he left, the room buzzed with voices and people moved about. Herb immediately grabbed my arm and we were quickly escorted out the back door and into a small consultation room. He closed the door and looked at me very seriously.

"Do you have a copy of that court order?" I looked at my stuffed briefcase. "It's in there somewhere," I responded. To reassure him I added, "I know that I outlined it accurately. What I said is accurate."

"We'd better find it," he stated, "and it better be what you said, to the letter, or we are in trouble."

I opened the briefcase and we began shuffling through the voluminous files. I pulled out one document after another. They were folded and bent, showing the wear of the last three years. As we searched, I asked Herb to clarify what was going on. He explained that if I had not told the truth, then the Prosecutor had a right to say what he did. If I had told the truth, then Rubbinaccio was in violation of the judge's directions. If that was the case, the judge might have to declare a mistrial. That meant the charges would be dismissed, but the Prosecutor could file them again. There would be no verdict, no exoneration by a jury.

I did not want that. I wanted my name cleared for my sake and Jessie's. Herb understood, but legal protocol dictated that if the judge did not declare a mistrial, we should motion for one. He said as a good defense counsel, it was better to push for the mistrial. The way things had gone, it was not likely the charges would be refiled against me. Herb saw the opportunity to end it all, here and now. He wasn't looking for a storybook ending, he was looking for an ending.

I didn't know what to think. I began to question the accuracy of my own testimony in regard to the language in the document. Although I believed I remembered the order correctly, I had to be sure. We could see the deputies walk by outside in the hall, carrying several large cartons to the judge's office. The matrimonial files were arriving.

We continued searching for twenty minutes, but could not locate the order. I was beginning to worry just as the bailiff entered and said, "The judge is ready to go back on the bench. He has the court order." Now we had to return to the courtroom without knowing where we stood. We would have to hear it from the judge like everyone else.

Tension filled the air. The jury had not been brought in yet. Judge Egan entered with the court order in hand. He looked directly at Mr. Rubbinaccio. He said the court order stated almost exactly what I had testified. He spent fifteen minutes giving the Prosecutor a thorough dressing down.

He told Rubbinaccio that he conducted certain aspects of this case disgracefully. If the Prosecutor truly had the best interests of the child at heart, he would never have pursued this case. He said Mr. Rubbinaccio did not care about justice or the child, just a conviction.

The judge concluded, "The bottom line is, the witness answered truthfully and you, Mr. Rubbinaccio, are out of order." He said, "A mistrial is always an abomination, but, in this case, it would be a travesty. Perhaps the mistrial should be granted, but I cannot bring myself to do it." He added that based upon the Prosecutor's attitude so far, he had no doubt Mr. Rubbinaccio would file charges again and he was not going to let that happen. He was not going to permit a situation in which Jessie might have to go through this whole ordeal again. He cared about the child. If the defense wanted to appeal this decision, it could do so. But for now, the trial would continue. With that, the jury was brought back in.

Judge Charles Egan, poignant and powerful, conducted a "no nonsense" trial.

Inside, I breathed a deep sigh of relief. I studied Judge Egan's face. I felt a growing admiration and appreciation for this man's compassion and wisdom. Thank God for him, I thought. As the bewildered jurors filed into the room. I resumed my seat on the witness stand. When they were seated, the judge spoke.

He told the jury I had answered the questions truthfully. To prove it, he read the November 16, 1983, court order. He also instructed them to disregard the Prosecutor's last remark and ordered it stricken from the record. Then he told Mr. Rubbinaccio to proceed.

Ironically, the Prosecutor had no more questions for me. He was not, however, finished with his case. He informed the judge he intended to call two rebuttal witnesses the following day, but would not disclose their names. Under law, he was not required to disclose the identity of rebuttal witnesses — those who ostensibly would contradict our witnesses' testimony in some way. We had no choice but to wait until tomorrow.

On our way back to Herb's office, we tried to anticipate who the surprise witnesses were. We were quite certain that one of them was Valori's attorney, Mr. Wahl, who would probably refute Steven's testimony. Herb was convinced the other would be Claudine, Lentchner's daughter and my baby-sitter. I did not believe the Prosecutor would bring Claudine from Florida. Besides, unless she lied, there was nothing damaging she could say.

"Would she lie if her parents told her to?" Herb asked. I did not think so. Nonetheless, I could see his concern. We would have to wait and see. I went home to face another anxiety-filled night. If everything went according to schedule, the trial would end tomorrow.

Wednesday, January 15, 1986

We had been right about the first rebuttal witness. The Prosecutor called Valori's attorney, Anthony Wahl. His testimony took all of five minutes. Mr. Rubbinaccio asked if Mr. Wahl had heard Valori remark to the defendant that he would never see his daughter again. Wahl said he had not heard that comment. When cross-examined and asked if he could be sure Valori did not make such a remark, he responded "No, I cannot be certain." He added Valori had bitter feelings toward me and he had spent much time in court making sure we did not get close to each other. This testimony certainly did not help the Prosecutor's case.

"Do you have another rebuttal witness, Mr. Rubbinaccio?" asked the Judge.

"Yes we do, Judge Egan. The State calls Claudine Hirsemann."

What Are We Doing Here?

Herb immediately stood and asked the judge if he could consult with Claudine and the Prosecutor prior to her testimony. This was normally done so the opposing legal side had some basis from which to cross-examine the witness. A conference was granted and the court stood adjourned for a short time.

I sat with Janeen in the waiting room, wondering what Claudine would say. She and I had been close since she was a baby. She had no reason to lie and I couldn't imagine her doing that. I had not seen her since she moved to Florida a year and a half ago. My thoughts were interrupted as the bailiff announced the judge was ready to begin.

The courtroom quieted, the judge entered and Mr. Rubbinaccio called Claudine. The Prosecutor asked a string of questions. Was Jessie's bedroom door open or closed? What time did she go to bed on Saturday night? Who put her to bed? What time did we have breakfast on Sunday? She looked uncomfortable, but responded honestly. The faces of the jurors told me they weren't hearing anything new. Rubbinaccio was not making any points. After thirty minutes, he completed his questions. Now came the cross-examination.

Herb was gentle in his approach to Claudine and showed none of the anxiety he had expressed to me the day before. After going over some preliminary facts, he got down to the crucial issues. He elicited the fact that she and Jessie were best friends. She had helped with Jessie almost every visitation weekend "On the weekend of December 3, 1983, did you notice anything out of the ordinary about Jessica? Did Jessie at any time seem upset, uncomfortable or act in an odd manner?"

"Never, she was her usual happy self all weekend," Claudine responded. So ended the drama of the rebuttal witnesses. The State had moved no closer to proving their case.

The court adjourned for lunch recess. That afternoon Herb and the Prosecutor would present their summations to the jury. The judge would then give his instructions to the jury. As usual, I didn't feel like eating, so I hung around the courtroom while Herb worked on his summation speech. We didn't know the Prosecutor had one more surprise.

Rubbinaccio dropped his final bombshell after lunch. Before

the summation began, he requested that the judge order the jury be removed so he could make a final motion. Herb and I looked at each other. Herb whispered he knew what was coming and told me to sit quietly. I had no idea what was happening.

I tried to follow the legal arguments. I could not fully understand, but I knew this was a last ditch attempt by Rubbinaccio to get me. He knew he had failed to prove the charge of first degree aggravated assault. Now his strategy was to "include all lesser offenses" when the judge gave final instructions to the jury. This meant the jurors would have the option of finding me guilty of a lesser offense, if they felt it applicable.

If there was doubt about my innocence, the jury could now find me guilty of a second or third degree crime. For the jury to have a middle of the road choice was a defense attorney's nightmare. Normally, the lesser charges are spelled out in the indictment if the Prosecutor wants to include them. In my case this had not been done. The judge was uncertain if the Prosecutor had the right to make the motion now. Herb argued against it, Rubbinaccio fought for it. The judge needed to research the case law so his decision would come the next day.

In the meantime, the trial would continue and the jury was returned to the courtroom. Judge Egan said, "Mr. Korn, you may proceed with your summation." Herb squeezed my shoulder to reassure me, picked up his pad of notes and walked toward the jury. He urged the jury to use their common sense, something he had asked them to do in his opening statement.

> I look for jurors who bring common sense with them to the courtroom and doesn't leave it at home because that's really what is important in deciding cases. You can't throw out your God-given common sense. You bring it with you and you use it. You use it when you analyze evidence, you use it when you analyze whether or not there is evidence, you use it when you talk about anything and everything, and that's common sense. How does it sit with you, how do the facts of this case sit with you? How do you feel about it? Are there questions that you have and if there are, that's common sense that is dictating your asking those questions. I know you all got it

and I want you to continue to use it.

He reviewed the testimony of each witness, separating the proven facts from the mountain of allegations. Dr. Rogers did not say he saw a dark oval ring. He said there was irritation inside the vagina. Dr. Rogers did not say this was caused by oral-to-genital contact. He did say this irritation could have been caused by wiping or tight underwear. His testimony was in direct conflict with Valori's statement that she "saw irritation as soon as she took Jessie's diaper off."

Herb showed the jury the drawings Jessie had made at DYFS on December 7, 1983, when her memory of what allegedly happened was fresh. She had marked virtually every place on the body with the exception of the genital area. Then after two years of programming, while being questioned by Herb, Jessie immediately put touch and kiss marks only on the genital areas. That was quite a change.

Then he came to Valori. He made it clear this was a case of her word against mine. If I was innocent, she was guilty of a very serious false accusation. No tricks, no fancy legal maneuvers, Herb came right out with it.

> Hell hath no fury as a woman scorned. You've all heard that before. And Valori Mulvey was angry, and Valori Mulvey was upset because Valori Mulvey had been jilted, jilted and her life was coming apart because of another woman. Valori Mulvey hated Larry Spiegel as only a wounded lover could hate. Larry Spiegel had it all. He had Janeen, he had a good relationship with his daughter, he had it all going for him, and what did Valori have? Sure, she has an agreement.

> So, what did Valori Mulvey do? Valori Mulvey either by design, premeditation or — and I say "or" because I don't know really what she was thinking — design or because of the blinders on her mind, because of her predisposition of this anger and hate for Larry Spiegel, made a mountain out of a molehill. And the best way to make a mountain out of

a molehill is to add a little dirt. And that is what she did.

There's a phrase that we learned in law school. We took some Latin, and it's called *falsus in uno, falsus in omnibus*. That means false in one, false in all. You can disregard the entire testimony of Valori Mulvey if you feel she was less than honest with you. If you feel that she got on the stand and took an oath and did not tell the truth, you can disregard her testimony because it's not worthy of your consideration. And I suggest that that is something that you should consider. I don't think — and I'm not bold enough to stand here and tell you that she lied. That's for you to consider. And I think it's something that has got to be considered very strongly. I'm just going to ask you a favor, ladies and gentlemen, and that is when Assistant Prosecutor Rubbinaccio gets up and closes and he sums up to you, you look him straight in the eye. He'll know that you are demanding of him — you have got a right to do this — you are demanding of him that he explain certain things to you. How about an explanation as to where, when and how this happened? An explanation as to what the proofs he's presented have shown as to when, where and how it happened. How about an explanation as to why it happened? How about an explanation as to how could Jessie be so happy, so carefree, so like Jessie on the afternoon and the morning after this allegedly occurred. Use your common sense. How could a child do that?

Then Herb hit upon the ultimate question, the question that several jurors, we later discovered, had been asking each other for almost two weeks.

You know sometimes I have had to ask and sometimes I did ask myself during this case, what are we doing here? Where is the evidence of anything? Accusations, insinuations, jumping from A to C without any logic, conclusions without any basis. What are we doing here! Where is the State's evidence of anything?

Then he talked about me.

> Larry Spiegel testified, ladies and gentlemen. Larry
> Spiegel is a broken man. Maybe you didn't get that from
> the testimony, but this is a broken man because for over
> two years he has not been able to walk down the street and
> put his head high. He's not been able to walk down the
> street and think about the last time he saw his daughter or
> the next time he'd be able to see his daughter.

> He hasn't had the opportunity to even talk to her. He has-
> been carrying this load on his shoulders, this scurrilous
> accusation that he molested his two and a half-year-old
> baby, for two years, and I say to you that the proofs that this
> State has come forward with to show that he did this hei-
> nous act are nonexistent.

> If you are to convict a man based on the type of proofs that
> the State has presented in this courtroom during the last
> week, God help us all.

Herb thanked the jurors and sat down.

Mr. Rubbinaccio followed. It was obvious he had abandoned
any hope of a first degree conviction. He used his entire summation to fill the jurors' minds with innuendo and insinuation. He
restated that Valori was a "concerned mother," that Jessie was an
"independent girl" and extremely bright. He restated that a crime
had been clearly committed. He presented no facts, no consolida-
tion of the "evidence" in the case. The newspapers carried the
arguments as seen in Exhibits F1 and F2.

EXHIBIT F1

Motives of ex-wife dominate closings in sex trial

By FRED SNOWFLACK
Daily Record Staff Writer

The motives of his his ex-wife dominated closing arguments in the Superior Court trial of Lawrence Spiegel, the Flanders psychologist accused of molesting the couple's 2½-year-old daughter.

Michael Rubbinaccio, a Morris County assistant prosecutor, said the ex-wife, Valori Mulvey, acted like a "concerned mother" when she spotted what was described as a red irritation mark in her daughter's genital area.

But Herbert Korn, the defense attorney, said that bitterness stemming from their divorce led Mulvey to accuse Spiegel, 39, of sexually abusing their daughter in November and December of 1983.

"Valori Mulvey was angry, Valori Mulvey was upset, because Valori Mulvey was jilted," Korn told the jury at the trial in Morristown yesterday. "Valori Mulvey hated Larry Spiegel like only a wounded lover could hate."

Korn said that Mulvey's resentment of Spiegel was such that "she saw what she wanted to see." He said the irritation mark in the girl's genital area cited in the trial could be attributed to other causes.

"Let's ask the question why," Korn said.

"Why would any human being, much less the father ... do this?" Saying such a person would be a "pyscho" or "the scum of the earth," Korn said the state has not proven Spiegel to be such a man.

Rubbinaccio said he did not have to show that Spiegel was a "psycho" but that he had committed a crime.

"He put his mouth on her vagina and hurt her," Rubbinaccio said. "That's not a game, that's a crime."

The prosecutor said Korn had painted a misleading portrait of Mulvey by describing her as a "flesh-eating monster." Rubbinaccio said, "Is that the type of woman you saw on the stand? She's a concerned mother."

The state is basing its case on the testimony of the girl, now 4½. Testifying by closed-circuit television, the girl pointed to the genital area of a drawing when asked where her father had hurt her.

Korn said the girl had been coached by her mother, and added it was virtually impossible for a 4½-year-old to remember an event that occurred when she was a "30-month-old baby."

Rubbinaccio said the girl was extremely bright.

"If you ask a child the right questions, you get the truth," he said. "She can't be manipulated. She's an independent girl."

Korn told the jury, which will begin deliberating today, that "Larry Spiegel is a broken man. For over two years, he has not been able to walk down the street and hold his head up."

EXHIBIT F2

Abuse case blamed on 'jilted' wife

By BILL RILEY

"Hell hath no fury like a woman scorned," a lawyer argued yesterday, contending that the former wife of a Parsippany-Troy Hills psychologist was out to ruin his life when she accused him of sexually abusing their young daughter.

"She was angry, upset and jilted. Her life was coming apart because of another woman, and she hated him like only a wounded lover can hate. He had it all: His lover, his job and the right to visit with their daughter. She was being left with nothing," maintained Herbert Korn, representing Lawrence Spiegel.

Spiegel was indicted and has been on trial since last week in Superior Court, Morristown.

Korn, making his closing argument in a packed courtroom, described his client as a "broken man" who has not been able to walk down the street with his head up because of "accusa-tions and insinuations made without any basis."

The lawyer maintained that the child has been "coached" for the past two years to believe that her father hurt her and that the various sessions with police, lawyers and psychologists have done more to traumatize the child than anything else ever could.

"Larry Spiegel has carried this scurrilous charge for the past two years. I say the proof does not exist. If you can convict a man on such evidence, God help us all," Korn said.

"This is a despicable, heinous charge. The only thing worse would be to convict an innocent man," he said, challenging the validity of opinions that the girl had been molested.

Assistant Prosecutor Michael Rubbinaccio maintained he had produced sufficient evidence, quoting the testimony of Spiegel's daughter, who testified in the case via a closed-circuit television hookup.

Although the girl was only 2½ years old when, authorities charged, she was molested, her recollection of "being hurt by daddy" during a weekend visit on Dec. 3-4, 1983, was strong enough evidence to convict, Rubbinaccio argued.

Judge Charles Egan is to charge the jury this morning.

Thursday, January 16, 1986

The moment I awoke on Thursday, I had a feeling of impending doom. I could not shake it. For the first time since the start of the trial, I felt extremely anxious. I waited for some calm to return, but it didn't. When we reached the courthouse, the proceedings began with Judge Egan explaining his research of the case law. My anxiety continued to heighten. The Prosecutor, by law, had the right to request the inclusion of the lesser charges. He would instruct the jury they had two alternatives in addition to the first degree charge. The worry in me was equally reflected in Herb's face.

Neither Valori nor any of her family was there. Apparently, they were not interested in Judge Egan's instructions. The jury was brought into the courtroom. We listened to the judge explain the law and the obligation of the jury. It was a detailed, deliberate and lengthy charge. He explained every point of law to be considered. He went over several points again and again. He used examples to clarify each point. He made sure the jury had no questions. As the clock approached 1:00 p.m., he asked them to go to the jury room to begin their deliberations. We were in the final phase of the trial.

I sat in a small corner of the hall, alone with Nancy Reber. Everyone else had gone to lunch and I had urged Janeen to go with them. Nancy was one of the few people who could handle me in a situation like this. I feared they would find me guilty of a lesser charge and had worked myself into a frenzy about it. Nancy gave me some space yet continued to talk calmly, no matter what I said. She was giving me real support. Around 1:30 p.m., we were suddenly surprised to see the jurors walking out. They were taking a lunch break. Great, I thought. This means they are going to be here for a long time. The anxiety of the entire experience had consumed me and I was splitting at the seams.

Herb had gone back to his office and I felt abandoned without him. I realize now I was almost in a delusional state. I decided to go to Herb's office. I literally ran there, arriving with my tie over my shoulder, my jacket half off and sweating profusely.

Herb's office manager took me by the arm. "Herb's on the phone," she said. I mumbled something about needing to write a document. She led me across the waiting room. "Here," she said, "You can sit and write here in Bernie's office."

As we passed Herb's office I heard him say to Steven on the phone, "This is the most depressing day of my life." That was all I needed to hear. My sanity suddenly and completely vanished. I sat down and began writing a document, to straighten out some personal affairs. I became completely absorbed in it. About a half hour later, I went into Bobby's office and she looked at me in surprise. "What are you doing here?" she asked.

"I just had to write this document, while we wait for the verdict," I responded. She kept trying to interrupt, but I would not let her. Finally, I glanced over to Herb's office and saw he wasn't there. "Where is Herb?" I asked.

"That's what I've been trying to tell you," she cried. "The court called five minutes ago, the jury is back."

"What! Why didn't he come and get me?"

"I guess he didn't realize you were here and I thought you had gone with him. You'd better hurry."

I ran all the way back to the courthouse, up the backstairs and through the courtroom doors. The crowd had returned to hear the verdict. When I finally got inside, Herb was standing in the center of the room. He had gotten up to look for me. When he saw me coming, he gave a disapproving look and motioned me to sit down. He looked at me and said, "Straighten up, what's the matter with you?"

I didn't respond. I just sat there while he pulled my tie up and straightened my jacket. The room quieted as the judge made his last entrance for this trial. He knew he would be free to exit after the verdict. Everyone else knew they would be free to go home. But what about me? That depended on the twelve people who now made their last entrance into the jury box. My whole body quivered with fear. Once they were seated, Judge Egan called, "Mr. Foreman, has the jury reached a verdict?"

"We have, Your Honor," came the reply.

Herb and I sat close to each other. My knees were literally knocking together. "Remember," he said, "No comments. No matter what they say, you don't say a word." I nodded my head. I was too scared to speak.

"What is your verdict, Mr. Foreman?" asked the judge.

"On the first degree charge of aggravated assault, the jury finds the defendant to be, not guilty." I waited for the next statement regarding a lesser charge. The jury foreman was silent.

"And with regard to the lesser charges," prodded the judge.

The foreman broke in, "I'm sorry, Your Honor, the jury finds the defendant not guilty on all charges." The courtroom erupted with sound, there was movement everywhere. At first I could not believe my ears. My eyes shot to Herb who sat smiling. The reality of it all struck me. Tears flowed down my face. I found myself wrapped in Herb's arms with the judge's gavel pounding that familiar crack through the commotion.

Judge Egan spoke. "Before I dismiss the jury, I want to say a few words." Though he tried to show no emotion, it was clear to me that he was pleased. In another rare move he spoke to the jurors after the verdict. "This has probably been the most difficult trial I have ever conducted." He said that this case had presented more problems than any other, including trials where the death penalty was involved. He thanked the jurors for their efforts and told them that they had reaffirmed his faith in the jury system. He concluded by saying the case against the defendant was dismissed and I was free to go.

My eyes caught a glimpse of the clock. I was a free man just passed 3 p.m. Including their lunch time, the jury had deliberated for only two hours. I was pulled into the pandemonium — surrounded by friends, relatives, reporters and well-wishers.

I tried to get to Herb, but he was surrounded by reporters. Judge Egan was still sitting on the bench overlooking the scene. I could not help but thank him. He responded, "Don't thank me, I'm just doing my job."

We began moving slowly through the crowd toward a back corridor, escaping the press and others. One of the Sheriff's Officers, John, who had stood in the rear of the courtroom during the entire trial, stepped forward and took my arm. "Boy, am I glad I didn't have to put these on you," he said, pointing to the handcuffs on his belt. "C'mon, we'll get you out of here. Follow me." He guided Janeen and me along the back corridors and staircases. Sheriff's officers, bailiffs, court clerks and secretaries were standing in doorways calling their congratulations. The last words I heard at the courthouse came from John as we reached a side door exit, "Okay Doc, you're on your own. Good luck."

With that I stepped out into a whole new world. Everything looked the same, yet it was all different.

EXHIBIT G

Psychologist Acquitted of Child Abuse

By Jay Mathews
Washington Post Staff Writer

A jury in Morristown, N.J., has acquitted a psychologist of sexual abuse charges after hearing his 4-year-old daughter testify about an incident that allegedly occurred when she was 2½.

The case had received national attention from fathers' rights groups, which saw it as a chilling misuse of the legal system by a bitter former spouse. The complaint by the child's mother, Valori Mulvey, 27, against her ex-husband, Lawrence Spiegel, 40, led to what legal experts said was the first time a child so young had been allowed to testify in such circumstances about such distant events.

Morris County assistant prosecutor Michael Rubbinaccio said his failure to win a conviction based on the girl's testimony indicates the difficulty in pressing charges against persons accused of molesting very young children.

Rubbinaccio cited the recent controversial dismissal of charges against five defendants in California's McMartin Pre-School case as further sign of a national legal quandary.

Spiegel, who said his clinical practice was severely damaged by the charges, said he was overjoyed at the verdict and planned to publish a book about his ordeal, "A Question of Innocence," on Father's Day.

Spiegel's attorney had objected to initial plans to allow bouncy, blue-eyed Jessica Spiegel to testify on her mother's lap to ease her fright. Appeals courts ruled that she could testify but the trial judge ruled out her mother's presence.

The girl instead testified via closed-circuit television with only Rubbinaccio, Spiegel's attorney and a camera operator present.

Alternately hugging and clinging to both lawyers, the girl told the prosecutor that her father had kissed her on the genitals and had "hurt me." She said her mother, whom Spiegel had accused of "programming" the child, had said Spiegel was "sick in the brain."

Spiegel said a family court judge will consider next week his request for temporary custody of his daughter. He has been denied normal contact with her for two years.

Psychologist found innocent of molesting daughter

By BRIAN MURRAY
Daily Record Courthouse Writer

Psychologist Lawrence Spiegel hugged his attorney and cried yesterday when a Morris County jury cleared him of charges he molested his 2½-year-old daughter.

But Spiegel, 39, of Flanders faces another legal battle in regaining visitation rights with the child, whom he has not been permitted to have contact with since 1983.

"A nightmare is over," Spiegel said after the jury of two women and 10 men returned from two hours of deliberations to announce to Superior Court Judge Charles M. Egan Jr. in Morristown they found Spiegel innocent.

Spiegel, who was charged with molesting his daughter in December 1983 when she was 2½-years-old, said he is now faced with financial ruin and a battle to restore a parental relationship severed with his daughter two years ago when he was charged.

The child, now 4½, is living with her mother, Spiegel's ex-wife, who Spiegel contends initiated the sex charges out of bitterness over their October 1983 divorce and to ensure he would never get custody of the girl.

"That's an issue I'm going to fight from now until I breathe my last breath," Spiegel said. He said his acquittal should permit him to see his daughter, but that his ex-wife, Valori

Mulvey, could file objections in Family Court.

Mulvey lives in Georgia and was not in the courtroom for the verdict yesterday.

Spiegel also announced yesterday that he has written a book on his ordeal, "A Question of Innocence," the proceeds of which will go toward paying his legal bills and as a donation to Victims of Child Abuse Laws, or VOCAL, an advocacy group for people deemed unjustly accused of abusing children.

"I've lost most of my private practice because of this trial ... and I've been financially devastated," he said, adding that Herbert Korn, his attorney, had done some defense work at no charge.

"The legal fees that will be collected will be substantially more than $50,000," said Korn, who represented Spiegel throughout numerous court hearings since January 1984.

A trial for Spiegel was delayed several times as Korn and Morris County Assistant Prosecutor Michael Rubbinaccio battled before appellate courts and the state Supreme Court over whether the child could testify.

The child eventually testified via television at the trial's start last week, after Egan ruled her competent and capable of relating facts to a jury.

"I would have to say this trial has been one of the most difficult I've conducted. ... This case has probably presented more difficulties for me than any case I've tried, including murder cases and death penalty cases," Egan told the jury yesterday.

"I decided to permit her to testify. Was I right? I don't know. In this case ... I was concerned in fairness to her that we should give it a try. ... I really agonized over that decision," he said.

Rubbinaccio expressed disappointment with the verdict and questioned whether prosecutors anywhere will be able to effectively prosecute accused child abusers when the child may be the sole witness.

The child testified that her father "hurt" her, but also said at one point he did not. The defense also contended Spiegel's ex-wife coached the child on what to say.

"In this case we had an exceptionally bright victim. A lot of prosecutors don't even have that advantage," Rubbinaccio said.

8

UNTYING THE LEGAL KNOTS

Stage 8: The Aftermath

Even though I had been acquitted of the criminal charges, the ordeal was not over as far as I was concerned. It would not end until my parental rights were reinstated and I could freely see Jessie. To do that, the law required me to go into Family Court. The issues of custody and visitation would be decided there. After a restful weekend, I was back in Steven's office on January 20. We were preparing the necessary legal papers calling for the reinstatement of my parental rights and the establishment of a definite visitation schedule.

In most states, the criminal and Family Courts have independent functions. Even after an acquittal in criminal court, the accusing parent can file motions in family court to prevent visitation. The Family Court decides the "best interests of the child," based upon its own hearings or trial. Thanks to VOCAL, my lawyers and my own research, we were aware of this procedure and were prepared to move swiftly into the Family Court hearings. Victims of false accusation seldom realize that the Family Court hearings are necessary before they have their parental rights reinstated. This even includes the right to see their children.

Valori, of course, filed papers which indicated she would fight my reunion with my daughter, despite the innocent verdict. In all honesty, we had expected nothing less. Her papers stated her conviction, "He did it and he got away with it." She, therefore, opposed any and all visitation. She also requested she be permitted to stay in Georgia with Jessie. So, once again, we prepared to fight it out in family court.

Tuesday, January 21, 1986

Strange yet familiar, was the feeling as I entered the Morris County Courthouse at 9:00 a.m. It was the same car ride, the same steps into the courthouse, but it was a different issue now. The legal battle for visitation and custody rights of Jessica was about to begin. Strange how things come full circle, I thought. The last time I had been in the family courtroom was in December of 1983 just after my arrest.

Valori purposely stayed in Georgia, forcing Judge Collester, the same judge who presided over the hearing in 1983, to demand that she return with Jessie. She knew her absence would delay the proceedings and that must have been her intention. At that hearing, Valori's lawyer objected to my demands for full parental rights. He contended that regardless of my acquittal, I was unfit to visit the child, let alone have custody. Steven countered by saying, "Every day is an additional harm. You can't give Jessica back to Dr. Spiegel when she was two and a half-years-old. You can't give her back when she was three or four." Judge Collester ordered Valori back to New Jersey with Jessie in one week. He would hold hearings on visitation the next Tuesday.

Friday, January 24

We held a news conference and announced we were preparing several federal lawsuits in response to the handling of my case by the authorities. Although I did not give specifics at that time, I did indicate that the defendants would include: Prosecutor, Lee Trumbull, Assistant Prosecutor, Michael Rubbinaccio, and their investigator, Janet Rapisardi. The charges would be prosecutorial misconduct and abuse of power. The newspapers carried the story as seen in Exhibit A.

EXHIBIT A

Mt. Olive doctor weighs suing state, local officials

United Press International

PARSIPPANY — A Mt. Olive psychologist acquitted on charges that he molested his 2-year-old daughter said Thursday he is considering filing a federal court suit against state and local officials "from Gov. Kean on down."

Lawrence Spiegel, who was found innocent after a two-week trial earlier this month highlighted by the testimony of the daughter, said he would seek damages from the Morris County prosecutor's office, state child welfare officials and others.

He said he is financially destitute and physically and emotionally exhausted after defending himself from the molestation charges, which he claims were concocted by his former wife.

Spiegel said he blames the New Jersey criminal justice system for his problems because of procedures which he said reward social workers for the number of cases they refer to prosecutors and prosecutors for the number of convictions they obtain.

Spiegel, 40, also said he was frustrated that, despite his acquittal, he must return to court seeking permission to visit his daughter, now 4 ½. He said he has not had visitation rights for 2 ½ years, and that the separation is emotionally more difficult to cope with than if his daughter was dead.

"With the death of a child, there's a finality you can accept and deal with," Spiegel said. "This is ongoing and the misery never ends."

The lawsuits served three purposes. First, I wanted to be certain that I had done whatever I could to put an end to this kind of atrocity. Second, I wanted those responsible for this disaster to be held accountable for their actions. Third and equally important, the lawsuits enabled me to seek financial recourse for my losses caused by the State. This was most necessary since I was financially ruined and facing legal debts nearing $100,000. My private practice had been reduced to shambles. Income lost in the countless hours spent in court, in hearings, in lawyer's offices, in bureaucratic delays and chasing Valori through several states should be compensated.

Tuesday, January 28

Valori and Jessie were still not in court. Valori's lawyer made some weak excuse for her absence, but Judge Collester wasn't listening to the nonsense. Instead he acted. He ordered them flown up from Georgia the next day. He appointed Katharine Sweeney, an attorney, as legal guardian for Jessica and ordered a psychiatrist, Dr. Steven Simring from the New Jersey College of Medicine, to evaluate Valori, Jessie and me. I knew this was necessary. Judge Collester wanted to know exactly what the Family Court had on its hands, and who was qualified to have what in terms of visitation and custody. Most importantly, Judge Collester gave me permission to visit with Jessie the following afternoon at Sweeney's office. I knew that I was not going to get much sleep that night. My scheduled reunion occupied my mind all day long.

Wednesday, January 29

Valori, by no choice of her own, finally appeared in court. Her testimony actually made matters worse for her. I felt some satisfaction, knowing she was damaging her own efforts at keeping me from my little girl. Under questioning by Steven, she asserted "He did it," regardless of the jury verdict. She could not let go of this idea, she was possessed by it. The more she testified, the more obvious her obsession became. Her testimony sometimes contradicted previous statements. This irrational thought process

His initial words to the court signaled the end of my nightmare. Family Court Judge Donald Collester declared, "There will be visitation".

seemed apparent to everyone. It alarmed me to think Jessie was influenced daily by this distorted view of events. Valori's emotional state underscored the need to have my full parental rights reinstated immediately.

The afternoon brought an unexpected and disturbing turn of events. By 2:00 p.m., Valori's parents were supposed to bring Jessica to the office of Katharine Sweeney who was to call Judge Collester's chambers and arrange for my visit with Jessie. I had anxiously anticipated our reunion and it was extremely difficult for me to concentrate on the court hearing. To say I was preoccupied with Jessie would be an understatement. I had waited over two years for this day. By 3:30 p.m. Sweeney had not called. I grew more worried as time passed.

Finally at 4:00 p.m., the call came. It was not what I had hoped. It was what I had feared. Sweeney told Judge Collester the visit should not take place that day. Apparently, by the time Jessie had arrived at Katharine's office, she was "out of sorts" and exhausted from the trip. In addition, Sweeney added that Valori's father had been uncooperative about my visit. He had given Katharine Sweeney a hard time. As a result, the judge ordered the visit postponed until the following day. In an unusual move, as a consequence of their behavior, Judge Collester decided Valori's parents should see the court-appointed psychiatrist as well. The newspapers captured the days events as seen in Exhibit B.

EXHIBIT B

Mt. Olive doctor's visit with daughter stopped by court

By P.L. Wyckoff
Staff Writer

Dr. Lawrence Spiegel, the Mt. Olive psychologist cleared of child abuse charges two weeks ago, did not get to see his daughter Wednesday.

State Superior Court Judge Donald Collester had ordered that Spiegel be allowed to see his 4½-year-old daughter in the office of

Morristown attorney Katharine Sweeney, whom Collester had appointed to be the girl's independant guardian.

But Spiegel said Wednesday that Sweeney told Collester the girl was upset and that her grandfather, who brought her, had acted "uncivilly." Spiegel said Collester ordered that a court-appointed psychiatrist to examine the grandparents.

Both Spiegel and his ex-wife, Valori Mulvey, are also to be examined in order to determine. if there should be any restrictions on Spiegel's visits with the girl and who should have custody of her.

Spiegel has not seen his daughter in over two years, since his wife accused him of sexually abusing the child. Spiegel contended the charge was concocted out of revenge for his divorce.

My worst fear throughout the last two years was that the separation might have hurt Jessie emotionally. Was she scarred by the experience? How would she react to our first reunion? Was her mood today an indication of her feelings toward me? I did not know what I was facing. I never felt comfortable with the idea of seeing her for the first time in two years in a strange office in the presence of a stranger, the court-appointed guardian. There had to be another way.

The answer came that evening. Janeen suggested I call the court-appointed psychiatrist and ask for his suggestions. Though I did not know him, there was no harm in seeking his advice. I called Dr. Simring and explained the situation. After some discussion he asked, "Who in your family would Jessica have only pleasant memories of. Who could break the ice for you?"

Immediately her Aunt Debra and Cousin Heather popped into my mind. I told him about them.

"That's perfect. Send them over first and let her establish a rapport with them. Then they can mention you and maybe even get Jessie to call you on the phone and ask you to come over."

It was an excellent idea and I thanked him for his help. I called Debra and she immediately pledged her assistance. She and Heather would be at Katharine's office at noon tomorrow. Janeen would go with them. This felt right and my anxiety began to dissipate.

Thursday, January 30, 1986

The Family Court hearing continued in the form of a conference which sought to develop the guidelines for custody and visitation rights. Both lawyers and the judge worked the entire morning on the details. Valori did not attend the session. I sat in the conference room reviewing my position with Steven every few minutes. I wanted nothing less than my full rights as a parent reinstated. The discussions continued, while just a few streets away, Dr. Simring's suggestion was working like a charm.

Debra, Heather and Janeen went to greet Jessie first. I called Katharine's office from the courthouse about a half-hour after they arrived. First I spoke with Katharine and then Debra. Finally Debra said, "There is someone here who wants to talk to you." I held my breath as she handed the phone to Jessie. Then I heard that familiar little voice and my eyes filled with tears.

"Hi, Daddy," as though I had spoken to her just yesterday.

"Hi, Sweetheart," I responded through the tears.

"You know what we're doing, Daddy?"

"No, Honey, what?"

"We're blowing up balloons," she said.

I heard Debra say, "Ask him if he wants to come over and help."

"Do you want to come over and help, Daddy?"

"Yes I do, Honey. I've never wanted anything more. I'll come right over."

"Okay, Daddy, I love you. Bye," and she hung up the phone.

I ran through the streets, crying the whole way. I got into the elevator and looked at my face in the reflective plate of the button panel. I wiped the tears from my eyes. My heart was thumping. Was it possible? Was she too young to really be affected by this ordeal? Did her own memories of me override her mother's programming? Was I still the Daddy she loved?

I walked quickly down the long hall and opened the door to Katharine's office. I had taken only a few steps when I saw her little figure appear at the opposite end of the office. We walked toward each other; then suddenly she began to run toward me. She stretched out her arm and put her little hand in mine. To her it seemed as if the past two years didn't exist. "C'mon Daddy, I want to show you something," she said happily.

Our reunion, a public moment filled with private feelings.

DAD D D Y

Jan 30, 1986 - Katherine Sweeney's office
1ST Visit

Jessie drew this for me several minutes later.

Katharine Sweeney, commented to the newspapers about the emotional atmosphere surrounding Jessica and my reunion. Interestingly enough, she focused accurately on the fact that the adults, even more than the child, were traumatized by this crisis. Newspapers focused on the proceedings in Family Court that Jessica and I attended together following our reunion in Sweeney's office. Exhibits C tells of these events.

EXHIBIT C

Acquitted psychologist greets his daughter at reunion

By BILL RILEY

Lawrence Spiegel was reunited yesterday in Morristown with his 4½-year-old daughter for the first time since 1983, when he was charged with molesting her.

Spiegel, acquitted of the criminal charge earlier this month, met with his daughter, Jessica, in the law office of a court-appointed guardian during the morning, after his sister-in-law, Debra Spiegel, and 5-year-old niece "broke the ice" for him.

"We spoke first on the phone, then she asked me to come to where she was to help her blow up a balloon," the smiling Spiegel said, recalling how his daughter "led him around and was introducing everyone to her daddy."

"It's hard to describe how I feel," Spiegel said later, stating the girl remembered him right away and showed no fear. "It's worth everything to see her again," he said.

Attorney Katherine Sweeney, acting as Jessica's legal guardian, said her office "became Romper Room" as the child and her cousin, Heather Spiegel, played, talked and wrestled with Spiegel before a court hearing on a visitation dispute between the Parsippany-Troy Hills psychologist and his ex-wife, Valori Mulvey, a resident of Georgia.

Sweeney said it was "very obvious" Jessica was not afraid of her father, as experts predicted she might be during testimony in Spiegel's criminal trial, and that she was "spontaneous and unrehearsed" in her behavior.

"She assumes they all love her, and she's right," Sweeney said. "It is obvious the traumatized people in this case are the adults, not Jessica," the lawyer said.

Jessica, who will be 5 in April, happily ate an ice cream cone when she appeared in the courtroom of Superior Court Judge Donald Collester and was offering hugs to relatives from both sides of her family as she bounced from lap to lap.

Collester said he is to decide today what kind of visitation rights are to be awarded Spiegel, who has also filed a claim for full custody of his daughter.

The judge said he will consider a suggestion from Sweeney that the visits be conducted at Debra Spiegel's Budd Lake residence.

In testimony Wednesday, Mulvey said she believes Spiegel molested their child during a week-end visit in December 1983 and fears he will do it again.

"He got away with it," she said, stating she is "strongly opposed" to unsupervised visits between Spiegel and her daughter.

Spiegel, who denied hurting his daughter, maintains Mulvey pressed charges against him as an act of revenge following a bitter divorce.

Friday, January 31, 1986

This day brought an end to more than the week, more than the month, more than the end of the visitation and custody hearings. This day brought the downfall of Valori and the exposure of the Prosecutor. This day revealed the source of the energy behind the false accusation.

Ironically Valori's obsession, which created this mess from the start, was the major factor in bringing it to an end. Valori was again testifying in regard to custody and visitation. She wanted only full-time chaperones present when Jessie and I were together. Steven kept up a barrage of questions, which more and more revealed her emotional instability. Finally, a suggestion from the judge, given in a spirit of helpfulness, oddly put an end to Valori's credibility and gave Steven an opportunity to go after the Prosecutor.

Judge Collester interrupted the questioning with a suggestion regarding supervision. He said, "Why didn't I think of this before." He turned to Valori and asked, "How do you feel about Janeen Love. I mean, beside the fact that she is now with your former husband, what do you think of her?"

"She's a liar," Valori screamed.

"What?" queried the judge.

"She's a liar. She stood there and watched him do it and then she lied about it."

The judge sat shocked by the response. He replied, "Did you

ever at any time before today tell this to anyone?"

"Yes," came the reply. "I told it to Janet Rapisardi from the Prosecutor's office."

The judge turned to the bailiff and told him to get Janet Rapisardi. He muttered something like, "We'll see about this." There was a recess to await Rapisardi.

Valori looked severely shaken. She seemed almost zombie-like as she walked from the room. Knowing Valori, I realized from the look on her face that she was scared. Somewhere in the back of her mind, she realized what she had done. Now for the first time in two years, a real look of fear flirted on her face. I thought, "This is a feeling I've lived with for so long. How does it feel, Valori?"

Steven was pretty wound up. He had been waiting two years for his chance to fight back. He wanted Janet Rapisardi on the stand. A short time later, not only Rapisardi but her boss, Rubbinaccio, came into the courtroom. Steven was flipping through papers, putting it all together. He wanted his questions to go to the core of the relationship between Valori and the Prosecutor's investigation. He was ready.

Judge Collester reconvened the court and saw Rubbinaccio sitting in the back of the room. Steven was intent on questioning Investigator Rapisardi and immediately began his efforts. The judge interrupted. "Mr. Rubbinaccio, I didn't request that you be here. I don't think either attorney intends to call you. I'm sure you have other things to do. You don't have to stay here."

Despite the invitation to leave, Rubbinaccio never responded and never moved. He sat listening to every word and scribbling notes in a pad.

Rapisardi's testimony helped crystallize my own thoughts. She provided the missing link. Now I fully understood how Valori's false accusation had become a two-year nightmare. Now I realized Valori's participation was only a small cog in a big wheel. For the first time, I clearly understood what happened to her psychologically — she was a victim, too. The Prosecutor's office, and DYFS had fed Valori's delusion after she made that initial phone call to the Somerset prosecutor's office. Valori's accusation was the spark, the authorities' power was the fuel for the fiery trials and I was the guy left to burn.

It all became clear as I listened to Rapisardi and watched Rub-binaccio. That was why he appeared so nervous, that was why he stayed after the judge invited him to leave. He wasn't here to pursue my case; he was here to protect his own neck. I focused on Steven asking why "they" had moved so quickly to arrest me, just one day after Valori's visit to DYFS. Was it Valori's request? Rapisardi answered, "No." Valori had asked that they not arrest me. There it is, I thought. The prosecutor just ran with the case right from the start.

Perhaps Valori realized that once the charges were filed, she was compelled to stick with her story. Otherwise, she may appear unfit to have custody of Jessica and open herself up to other serious charges. Perhaps she never dreamed at the very beginning that it all might get out of hand. She wanted to hurt me, to really scare me. She didn't know about over-zealous social workers or ambitious Prosecutors. To Valori, it must have been just another accusation, like the many which preceded it. To her, it was just another way to get at me in Family Court.

Steven continued to probe, asking again, "If Valori was not urging you to arrest him, why did it happen so quickly?" Rapisardi first said that Valori did not even know of the actual arrest until after it had occurred. Then she added that the arrest was made, "To prevent another visitation that weekend."

"You testified earlier that you were very familiar with the visitation schedule Dr. Spiegel had with Jessica, correct?" Steven asked.

"Yes."

"And you knew that he had visitation every Wednesday and every other weekend?"

"Yes."

"And you arrested him on Friday, December 9, 1983 for an act allegedly committed the previous weekend, December 3, 1983?"

"Yes."

"Then there was no visit scheduled for that weekend, was there?" Steven screamed. "It was every other weekend and you just testified you knew that, didn't you?"

Rapisardi's testimony was beyond my wildest dreams. Steven elicited so many contradictory statements that the judge halted the exchange. Judge Collester said, "These questions sound like a prosecutorial misconduct trial. That is beyond our scope here. If that is the case, Mr. Haft, I suggest you avail yourself of the proper forum for such a proceeding."

The room grew silent and still. Little else needed to be said. The cards were finally on the table. Yes, Valori started the ball rolling, but once the Prosecutor joined the game, there was no stopping it, no changing its direction. Apparently, Valori's delusions and hatred combined with the Prosecutor's lust for conviction, fed off of one another, and grew into a dangerous force which tried to turn an innocent man into a guilty criminal. It was not a case of the blind leading the blind, this seemed to be a case of the vengeful instigating the opportunist.

The questioning stopped, the hearing was over. The judge would wait to receive the psychiatrist's and law guardian's reports. Then the visitation and custody resolution would be finalized. Considering the fact that Judge Collester had presided over this testimony, I was more confident than ever that my full custody rights would be restored. I was given visitation rights with Jessie for the next two weekends. When would I forget this day? When would I forget this entire thing? Never.

A few weeks later, while the psychiatrist and law guardian were still preparing their reports, I received a call from a friend. She excitedly told me to buy the daily newspaper. She refused to say what I would find, but told me I had to get it. I did as she suggested. When I got home and scanned the pages, I discovered that Rubbinaccio had suddenly resigned. Strange coincidence, I mumbled to myself, his career as a prosecutor ending now, ending so abruptly. I wondered what effect the Family Court hearing had had on his decision. I wondered if my case contributed to this decision. If it did, so much the better. In my mind, our system of justice would be better off without him. I did not want to see him do to another family what he had done to mine. The papers were quick to report the news as seen in Exhibit D.

EXHIBIT D

Rubbinaccio to hang lawyer shingle

By BRIAN MURRAY
Daily Record Staff Writer

Assistant Morris County Prosecutor Michael Rubbinaccio, who successfully prosecuted James Koedatich for the murder of a Parsippany high school student, is trading his badge for a private practice.

"It was a rich, rewarding job, but there does come a time when you become too specialized," said Rubbinaccio, who is trying his hand at practicing civil law in Parsippany.

"The primary focus of the office is going to be corporate litigation, medical malpractice. I'm also assuming I'm going to be doing some criminal law," he said.

Rubbinaccio, 33, who has handled many major criminal cases during his five years with the prosecutor's office, officially resigns next Friday.

His most notable case was the prosecution of Koedatich in 1984. The Morristown man was found guilty in the 1982 abduction and stabbing death of Amie Hoffman. Koedatich's death sentence has been stayed pending appeals.

"Obviously the Koedatich case ... will be the most memorable," Rubbinaccio said, citing the publicity the case attracted and the emotional trauma he found in the victim's family.

"We as prosecutors deal a lot with victims of crimes ... and part of this job is dealing with their emotions and it definitely drains on you," he said.

Rubbinaccio said his decision to open private practice was prompted by a desire to expand his legal talents and a feeling that he had gone as far as he could in criminal law.

"I'll miss him," said Prosecutor Lee Trumbull. "He's been an important factor in this office since I got here. Maybe he'll be back as the prosecutor someday — if not in this county, in another."

A short while after, Judge Collester received the reports from the psychiatrist and law guardian. Both reports clearly pointed to Valori's irrationality regarding my relationship with Jessie. Both also urged the judge to ignore her requests. Below appears an excerpt from Dr. Simring's report:

> It is my opinion that Ms. Mulvey's recommendations for visitation are unreasonable and impractical. Given all the history, there is absolutely no justification to her demand for full time chaperones. I cannot see how Dr. Spiegel can reestablish his relationship with his daughter under such artificial and bizarre circumstances. Furthermore, I am aware of the geographical difficulties. Fortunately, both Ms. Mulvey and Dr. Spiegel have supportive families in New Jersey; there is really no one in Georgia. It would be quite unreasonable, in my opinion, to demand that visitation take place in Valdosta.

The report from the law guardian, Katharine Sweeney, was almost identical in content. Below is an excerpt from her report.

> I would further suggest that the meaningful visitation periods will necessarily be those in New Jersey. "Off site" contact between Jessie and her father just does not incorporate her in his life. The geographical distance is such that monthly visits as the norm are impossible. Luckily, Dr. Spiegel is on a teacher's schedule and can share vacation periods with Jessie. Ultimately I would assume that these will provide the source of most of their contact with each other if the residential custody is left unchanged.

On March 17, 1986, what remained of the black cloud which had hung above my head was completely blown away by the Family Court. Judge Collester entered an order, calling for joint legal custody, liberal visitation in my home and the reinstatement of full parental rights. I did not have to wait any longer, I could freely see Jessie from that moment on. I wasted no time. That night Janeen and I boarded a plane and flew to Georgia to take Jessie for a week of vacation.

Four weeks later on April 19, 1986, Jessie came home. I watched for signs of emotional damage and for a reluctance on her part to trust and love me. The door to her room was finally opened and I heard her voice, tender and filled with laughter, as she played.

I know I have had it bad — I very nearly lost my child and very nearly lost my mind. But the love between a parent and a child is a fulfilling love. Perhaps it can help us repair any damage done through these past several years. That hope was evident in our faces as the camera clicked our picture. That photo is on the front cover. It is strange to say after all this, but it is true — I am a lucky man.

EXHIBIT E

Dad regains right to visit daughter

From The Record's wire services

A Superior Court judge in Morristown yesterday restored visitation rights to a psychologist who previously had been acquitted on charges of sexually abusing his 4½-year-old daughter.

Dr. Lawrence Spiegel, 40, of Parsippany-Troy Hills, said he was elated with the decision and would immediately fly to Georgia to take his daughter to her grandparents' house in Florida for a visit.

He called Judge Donald G. Colester Jr.'s decision an "enormous victory for the cause" of parents who are acquitted of crimes against their children but have difficulty regaining their parental rights.

"I'm just very happy that this judge took a stand," Spiegel said. "I feel this will help a lot of people that are in the same situation — who have been acquitted but have not had their parental rights restored."

Colester restored all of Spiegel's parental rights in awarding him joint legal custody, "based on the fact the court found no evidence to support my ex-wife's allegations of child sexual abuse," Spiegel said. The judge also approved a court order allowing Spiegel to pick up his daughter at her mother's house in Georgia yesterday, he said.

A former psychology professor at the County College of Morris, Spiegel had not been allowed to see or contact his daughter since his former wife, Valori Mulvey, who now lives in Valdosta, Ga., charged him with molesting her more than two years ago.

The girl, Jessica, was among the youngest children to ever testify in a New Jersey criminal court. The question of her competency to testify was finally decided by the Appellate Division of Superior Court, which ruled she could testify if she sat on her mother's lap.

Anthony Wahl, an attorney for Ms. Mulvey, could not be reached for comment.

Spiegel, who was acquitted in January, said he has seen his daughter once since his wife charged him with molesting the girl more than two years ago.

"This is the first time in the State of New Jersey," that a judge has taken such strong steps in awarding custody to someone previously charged with sexual abuse of a child, said Nick Andrian, vice-president of VOCAL, or Victims Of Child Abuse Laws. Spiegel is president of that group's North Jersey chapter.

"Usually, Family Court judges are quite reluctant to reinstate someone's rights after they've been accused," Spiegel said. "A lot of parents must see their children only under supervision years after acquittal."

Spiegel said his former wife will have custody of the girl during the nine-month school year. He will have custody of her the remaining three months and during some vacations, Spiegel said.

He said he was "a little concerned about going to Georgia," but felt confident his former wife would obey Colester's order.

Spiegel has written a yet-unpublished book about the case, He said part of the proceeds will go to VOCAL. which is based in Jordon, Minn.

PART TWO

Zeroing In On The Facts

9

PUTTING THE PUZZLE TOGETHER

An Overview

Time and time again I watched the question marks formulate in people's eyes when I told my story. They muttered the inevitable and disbelieving "What?" Yet many of them were thinking, "Maybe he actually did something. Such a thing couldn't just happen to an innocent person." Friends, close friends and even my own parents reacted that way when I first told them of my situation.

Always there were questions. How did it happen? How can a parent/child relationship be terminated without an investigation? Don't our constitutional rights protect us from such indiscriminate and irresponsible interventions of government? Why didn't they work? How could such a grievous situation continue for so long?

Victims of false accusations ask these questions a hundred times over. From all over the country and from every race and social class, they reach for help. They desperately hope to solve their problem. All of them live in shock and disbelief; all of them desperately want answers. Since false accusations have reached epidemic proportions and have consistently uprooted the American family, we best find those answers now.

An equally important aspect to consider is the attitudes of our society toward child abuse allegations, especially sexual abuse.

The falsely accused not only face the "law," they face a powerful social attitude that casts them as "guilty" before the facts are even known. Corey Gordon, an attorney for many of the parents accused and acquitted in the Jordan, Minnesota, case, states in an article published in the *Minnesota Family Law Journal*:

> One of the problems frequently encountered by practition-
> ers in the area of custody is the unwillingness on the part of
> the judicial system, and indeed the general public, to
> believe that allegations of abuse, particularly sexual abuse,
> can be false. Historically, any allegations of sexual abuse
> were dismissed as fantasies. However, in recent years this
> notion has given way to a polar extreme: many people
> believe that "children don't lie" about abuse and, therefore,
> any allegations of abuse must necessarily be borne of
> truth. Accordingly, even in cases where the charging party
> is unable to demonstrate any tangible evidence of abuse,
> which is frequently the case in situations involving sexual
> abuse, many people are unwilling to say that the allega-
> tions have been demonstrated to be false, but merely that
> they are "unsubstantiated," implying that if more evidence
> was available, they would be substantiated.

The Underlying Factors

Lack of Accountability of State Agencies

In most states, child protection agencies have broad auton-
omy. They exercise authority unparalleled within state govern-
ments. Without a court order, a caseworker can remove a child
from your home. Yet caseworkers cannot be held personally
accountable for their actions due to governmental immunity.
Their information and records — unlike medical, police and work
records — are exempt from the Public Information Act. Even your
defense counsel cannot directly get access to their records if criminal charges are filed against you.

In almost every state, no clear limit of authority or accountability exists. Neither the Attorney General, the Public Advocate, the

Administrative Director of the Courts, nor the Governor exercise supervision in the operations of the child protection agency. Legislators in most states have no authority to monitor the actions of the agency. In essence, the agency has police-like powers to intercede in private homes without the consent or approval of any other body and is accountable to no one for their actions.

Case Overloads

Huge case loads prevent thorough evaluations. The Child Welfare League of America recommends a ratio of 20 to 30 cases per worker. But it is not uncommon to find workers assigned to 40 or 45 cases. In fact, some workers are responsible for 55 to 60 cases. This leaves little doubt that quality assessment of a case often loses to quantity.

Poor Measurement of Performance

The "body count" approach, the number of convictions for the prosecutor or the number of abuse cases uncovered by the social worker, becomes a measurement for job performance. As a result, subtle details which point to a false abuse case often go unnoticed. The need exists for an organized effort which pools the resources of psychiatrists, psychologists, child protection personnel and specially trained law enforcement investigators acting in concert.

Poor Checks and Balances and Poor Training

Caseworkers, seeing real human tragedy every day, grow overzealous in their efforts. Their emotional decisions, based on their desire to protect the child, sometimes result in the criminal prosecution of innocent people. Similar overreaction is also found in the slanted and biased reports of psychologists and psychiatrists. In seeking to help children, professionals, who are not fully aware of the consequences of their actions, can create disaster and break up the family.

The Professional Dilemma

Even more problematic is the task of the mental health experts, the psychologists and psychiatrists. In "False Allegations of Sexual Abuse, Have the Experts Been Caught with their Pants

Down?," in the January-February issue of *Forum*, forensic psychiatrist Dr. Lee Coleman described these problems.:

> Given this pressure from outside our professional ranks, as well as our own desire to help, it's not surprising we have responded to the call . . . . We offer our opinions in family and criminal court. Society calls and we respond. There seems little choice, given our appearance in so many other judicial proceedings and given society's assumption that we are the "experts." Do our evaluations really help? Are we able to bring special skills to the question of whether alleged molestation has taken place? Or, do our speculations, whether based on clinical interviews, play interpretations or psychological testing, merely provide protective service agencies with a false sense of security? Are our evaluations perhaps even discouraging social service agencies from doing a better job of factual investigation?

Gray Doesn't Equal Black and White

Additional overreaction springs from well-intentioned school programs, such as "good touch, bad touch." The self-consciousness these programs engender in children often leads a child to report a perfectly innocent episode as abuse. Sometimes a child even may use the abuse charge as a weapon against a teacher or adult. These actions encourage the over-zealous teacher or school administrator to contact the over-zealous social worker, who may without sufficient investigation, report the event to the prosecutor. It is easy to see how this system becomes dangerous and self-perpetuating.

Over Reporting

For years many child abuse cases went unnoticed and unreported. Officials are now reacting to that negligence by fostering an environment of over reporting, a backlash resulting in innocent people being charged with a serious crime. In 1972, 610,000 cases of child abuse were reported in the country. In 1985, that number had mushroomed to 1.7 million. Yet in that same year, 65 percent of all reports were unfounded.

Administrative Paranoia

As a result of the pressure exerted on the child protection agencies to do a competent job, there exists an outright fear within the agency of failing to properly protect the child. Administrators pressure supervisors, supervisors pressure caseworkers to document, through hundreds of agency forms, the handling of each case. Once a case is opened, even if the initial investigation reveals no abuse, it remains open for a prolonged period of time. Administrators fear additional claims of abuse will be filed after the case is closed, thus pointing to their incompetence.

The policy within the agency often becomes one of "cover yourself" rather than "protecting" the child. Countless cases which should be closed, remain open. They take the caseworker away from children who really need attention. But "on paper," the agency can look thorough, competent and very, very busy.

Long Term Solutions

Reduction in Case Loads

False accusations must be perceived as potentially dangerous to the affected family. Every individual should be made aware that false accusations weaken the family and can damage parent/child relationships. Top level government officials and those responsible for our social agencies must recognize this. Funding and personnel must be made available to implement constructive changes in our child protection procedures. Such changes include reducing the number of cases each worker must oversee. This would allow a more qualitative investigation of each case.

Early Psychiatric/Psychological Intervention

In addition, well-trained psychologists and psychiatrists must become part of an initial response team. The investigation of any abuse complaint should be conducted by a team, not an individual. Each member should review a specific aspect. Social workers would then have a more immediate and comprehensive understanding of the situation before any serious steps are taken. Insight into the complaint must precede action taken. Otherwise, there is the risk of creating a problem that actually covers the underlying basis for the initial complaint.

Special Training

Child abuse specialists must protect the child, but also must consider the welfare of the family unit. In cases involving sexual abuse, a team of professionals must be specially trained to unravel the evidence quickly and accurately. Until the facts are clear, the professionals must seek ways to protect the rights and sensitivities of everyone in the family. Taking the immediate safety step of removing the child from the home can be a dangerous and short-sighted action. Obviously, in cases where abuse is self-evident, the child cannot remain in that household. Removal of a child clearly being abused provides the best protection for the child and family alike.

Confidential Not Anonymous Reporting

Child abuse cases can be reported anonymously. As a result, many families and individuals are thrust into an investigation by the child protection agency when no abuse whatsoever has taken place. These people are simply "victims" of harassment, yet by law the child protection agency must investigate the complaint. Often the case, despite any signs of abuse, remains open and the innocent individual remains subject to further intervention by the caseworker. Therefore, complaints filed with the child protection agency must be "confidential" not anonymous. That adds the much needed element of accountability which will help prevent the ease of filing false accusations.

Thorough Review of Complaint and Motives

Before an abuse case reaches the courts, certain indicative factors should be carefully reviewed. Is there a custody battle or divorce proceeding involved here? Is the family intact? Who filed the initial complaint of abuse? Did it emanate from the child, parent or someone else? What qualified professionals evaluated the case and when? Was a follow-up investigation with members of both sides of the family conducted? Were friends, neighbors, and teachers interviewed? Such steps would all but eliminate the involvement of the judicial system in false abuse cases.

Putting The Puzzle Together

Just in Case

But even when false abuse cases slip through and reach the courts, certain reforms are necessary to safeguard the innocent. Judges need complete and competent reports of the investigation. Automatic, ongoing court-appointed psychiatric evaluation should be ordered for all involved. This would enable court-appointed, qualified professionals to make assessments over a period of time in concert with the professionals from the response team. This is extremely important in cases where the allegations arise from divorce/custody disputes. Cases involving intrafamily abuse should be heard first in Family Court before criminal proceedings are even contemplated.

No conflict should arise over whose rights should be protected first. Instead, a thorough and systematic handling of the crisis should reveal the problem. The task is to bring a resolution to the abuse problem. To do so, professionals must work together and take the necessary steps to protect the abused, to safeguard the family and to prevent a false accusation.

Help Yourself

The Support System

A victim of false accusation needs a strong support system. It should include friends, relatives, lawyers and competent mental health professionals. Such a system enables one to survive the early stages of the False Accusation Syndrome and encourages the accused to reach the "fighting back" stage. The support system is often the only thing the accused can actually direct and control in an otherwise confusing and intimidating situation. The wheels of justice not only grind slowly, but also constantly keep the accused in a defensive posture. After all, there is a limit to what one can do to alter the actions of over-zealous prosecutors and social workers. The accused can, especially through the support system, learn to cope with outrage, indignation and depression.

As with any victim of trauma, the person's need is for support during the crisis. Support does not mean solving the problems of the accused. It doesn't even mean giving advice as many people seem to believe. True support is the ability to empathize and be compassionate, to be the optimist when you sense it is needed. It means just being there, just talking, just holding a hand or offering a shoulder to cry on. True support is the willingness and strength to be there for the individual. It requires a commitment that is far more taxing than giving advice.

Victims of a false accusation are constantly involved in grief. The lack of finality in the crisis makes grieving an ongoing process which continues until the entire ordeal has ended. It is necessary for the accused to strike a balance between expressing sadness and putting it aside. Individuals who are part of the support system, need the insight and ability to help the victim achieve a balance between grieving and other positive measures which lead to a resolution of the problem. Competent mental health professionals can aid greatly in achieving this balance.

The self-imposed isolation of a victim of false accusation can also be addressed through the support system. Initially, it may seem the accused feels sorry for himself/herself. However, self-imposed isolation is a reaction to the shame and embarrassment of just being associated with this crime. Such isolation actually prevents the accused from interacting with the vital support system. The support team must encourage, but not pressure, the victim into social interaction.

There may even be a sexual dysfunction in the accused which is reflected in impotence, frigidity or loss of interest in sexual relations. A loved one's awareness and understanding of this situation is vital to the support of the victim.

Guidance Through Experience

VOCAL should be made part of this support system. It can provide lists of attorneys, psychologists and psychiatrists who have expertise in this field. In addition, VOCAL has a good deal of literature and other resources which can very quickly help sophisticate the falsely accused and those in the support system. Through attending VOCAL meetings and interacting with other VOCAL members, victims can find ways through the stages of the False Accusation Syndrome.

Picking the Right Professional

A friend or relative can assist the victim in finding competent professional help, both legal and psychological. It is crucial these professionals be sophisticated in child sexual abuse cases and have experience in false accusations of abuse. It is likely the victim, especially during the "depression" stage, will lack the strength and resources to make the inquiries and find the appropriate professionals. Assisting the accused in gathering this professional help will comfort and reassure them and better their chances for a just resolution of their problem.

When deciding on a professional, whether an attorney or mental health practitioner, a person should not hesitate to ask for credentials and experience. Professionals claiming expertise in false accusations will understand fully the real concern. If the professionals become defensive or argumentative, they are not someone the accused needs. Questions should be asked and the selection of the professional carefully considered. Without the proper help, the falsely accused could settle for a plea bargain.

The Plea Bargain Pitfall

The innocent often fall prey to the waiting hands of the Prosecutor and plead guilty to a lesser charge, just to put an end to the ordeal and to the separation from a child.

Prosecutors, as a result of over-zealousness to protect the child, blind ambition to further a career or a number of other reasons, will do "strange" things for a conviction. It is always to the Prosecutor's benefit to get a guilty plea, even to a lesser charge. Sometimes the Prosecutor will wait until the accused is emotionally and financially drained, then the plea bargain offer is made. It typically sounds like this:

> Listen, you can save yourself and the State a lot of time and heartache, if you'll just admit that you behaved inappropriately. Maybe you didn't even consciously realize it. We'll let you plead guilty to lewd behavior, or sexual misconduct. All the other criminal charges, including aggravated sexual assault and other first degree felonies, will be dropped. You won't have any felony conviction on your record. You'll

just get probation and you'd be able to see your child. Doesn't that make sense?

Some falsely accused are so battered and beaten, they accept the humiliation and anger and take the deal. Often this occurs with the consent of the victim's attorney. What the victim and attorney may not know is that this lesser charge will land the accused right back in Family Court. That court could bar the accused from the child or require all visits to be supervised. The stigma of the bargain will remain forever.

Making a Difference

False accusations are a universal problem. The fundamental issue here is the survival of the family and one's right to live without unwarranted interference by the government. Despite the specifics of a false accusation, victims have much in common. Their response often follows the stages of the False Accusation Syndrome. They are forced to take similar legal channels to prove their innocence. They are forced to deal with the social service agencies, the authorities and the reactions of their friends, family and co-workers. A thin line separates a parent from an accused parent. Suddenly one day, you can find yourself, from no effort of your own, on the nightmare side of that line.

What is needed is the safeguarding of our constitutional rights. What is required is Federal legislation that addresses the problems inherent in our child abuse system and those who use the child abuse laws as weapons against others. An excerpt from my own Federal lawsuit, Exhibit A, clearly indicates the constitutional rights which are being crushed by the current wave of violations of civil rights by prosecutors and child protection agencies.

EXHIBIT A

```
    ... The United States Supreme Court in the landmark case of
Santosky v. Kramer, U.S. Sup. Ct. 88-5889 (1982) held that there
must be conclusive evidence beyond a reasonable doubt (not merely
```

a preponderance of evidence) to terminate a parent's rights of access to their child. This holding was predicated on the concept that there is a rebuttable presumption that, as a blood, biologically-related parent, you are entitled to remain a parent without interference by the State. The State's actions in depriving the defendant of his fatherly rights constituted a de facto termination without due process. The acquittal of the defendant clearly establishes that there was not conclusive evidence beyond a reasonable doubt to support the plaintiff's charges and to justify any further withholding of the child from the defendant. Therefore, this Court would be doing a great injustice if it failed to rule that the defendant's fatherly rights to which he is constitutionally entitled pursuant to the First, Fourth, Seventh, Ninth, Eleventh, and Fourteenth Amendments of the United States Constitution, (See Wilke v. Culp, 196 N.J. Super. 487 (1984) have been violated.

In addition, the Court in Wilke reiterated the well settled principle that the law favors visitation and protects against the thwarting of effective visitation (see also Daly v. Daly, 39 N.J. Super 117 (Cty. Ct. 1956) Aff'd. 21 N.J. 599 (1956) and In Re. J.S.&C., 129 N.J. Super 486, 487, 489 (Ch. Div. 1974) Aff'd 142 N.J. Super 499 (App. Div., 1976). In the case at bar, it is clear that it was the sole intent of the plaintiffs to thwart the fatherly rights of the defendant as to visitation. These actions by the plaintiffs are clearly contrary to the law and public policy of this State and thus said wrongs must be immediately remedied by this Court...

...In Conclusion, I quote the language of the Honorable Dallin Oaks of the Utah Supreme Court who in the case of In re.J.P. 648 P.2nd Utah 1364 (1982) stated:

"The parental right (to rear one's children) transcends all property and economic rights. It is rooted not in State or federal statutory or Constitutional law, to which it is logically and chronologically prior but in nature and human instinct."...

Constitutional rights are everyone's business. They are something we mistakenly take for granted. Sometimes we only come to value and understand them when they are violated or threatened. What single element moves us to resolve the tragedy of false accusation? Dedication — the kind which typically comes from being personally involved. As with most complex issues, it seems that God helps those who help themselves.

All too often, I have listened to victims and their loved ones bemoan their situation. They do not mobilize their resources to help themselves. Understandably, some face circumstances where they can do little. But they are a minority. Most victims need to take that first step — to think about what to do — then to begin trying things, piecing things together, until the complex and, most often, obscure circumstances become clear.

This can be done individually and collectively. To become active in VOCAL or another reform movement, can broaden your understanding of the problem and help you develop techniques to get at information while protecting yourself. Above all, do not allow bruised egos to stand in the way of getting things done. We must bear in mind, although we face similar situations, we are all different. Some people work well in groups, some do not. It doesn't matter who is president and who is not. These are not profit-making corporations; they are social reform organizations. The more room that is made for sensitive egos, the less room there is for constructive collaboration.

Each of us must find our own mission. Whether by filing a lawsuit, making a film, handing out leaflets or writing a book, the individual contributes to a group effort and the group helps the individual. Always, there is more to do; never are we finally done. It is not enough to buck the system; it must be changed. The only way out of the nightmare is through it. The more falsely accused who reach the other side, the greater are our hopes of eliminating this kind of tragedy.

We all suffer. Yet those who survive and learn how to work through the system become the most influential in changing it. Those with special professional training have an obligation and responsibility to use it. Constructive change comes through many variations on the same theme. We can help protect our rights and family relationships by pooling our efforts. Fundamentally, no one is safe unless everyone is.

Those who think only of themselves will find that no one else is concerned about them. Those who think only of others may make things worse for themselves. Those who think of no one will remain as they are. We need no sacrificial lambs, just a cooperative effort.

Following my acquittal, Reg Wells moderated a nationally televised discussion with Thomas Blatner, Director of NJ Division of Youth and Family Services (DYFS). More than ever, we need to safeguard our youth without jeopardizing the American family.

EXHIBIT B

Morris trial sets tone for abuse cases

Experts see repercussions from Mt. Olive doc's case

By P.L. Wyckoff
Staff Writer

Few criminal cases in recent Morris County history have attracted as much attention as that of Mt. Olive psychologist Dr. Lawrence Spiegel, acquitted last week of sexually molesting his 2½-year-old daughter in late 1983.

The case had all the ingredients needed to attract the attention of the media and the public: charges of a heinous crime by a professional man against his infant daughter, counter charges that the accusations were trumped up by a vindictive ex-wife and, most of all, the testimony of a 4½-year-old witness.

But while the trial itself and its attendant publicity is over, attorneys, doctors and other participants say the case may have lasting repercussions for the prosecution of child sex abuse cases in New Jersey.

And although they differ on just what those repercussions will be, members of both prosecution and defense agree that the importance of the case for New Jersey law centers on the testimony of Spiegel's 4½-year-old daughter, via closed-circuit television, that her father had "hurt her."

The case began in December 1983 when Spiegel's ex-wife, Valori Mulvey, alleged that the psychologist and Morris County College instructor had molested his daughter, then 2½, while the girl visited him at his Flanders apartment. Spiegel said he was innocent, that the story was concocted by Mulvey out of revenge for their bitter divorce and for his being awarded joint legal custody of the girl.

More than two years later, following a number of hearings, psychiatric evaluations of the girl, and a seven-day trial featuring testimony from the daughter, psychological experts and Valori Mulvey, the ex-wife, a jury of 10 men and two women found the 40-year-old defendant innocent.

While disappointed in the jury's verdict, prosecutors say the case broke new ground that could change the way authorities look at abuse cases involving very young children. "I think our case will make it easier for other prosecutors," says Michael Rubbinaccio, the assistant Morris County prosecutor who tried the case for the state. "It showed a young child can qualify as a witness and can testify."

Such testimony has not often been used in New Jersey, and until recently was not common anywhere, Rubbinaccio and his boss, Morris County Prosecutor Lee Trumbull, say.

"We are taught not to believe kids," Rubbinaccio notes. Combined with a tendency on the part of familys to "hush up" allegations of such incidents, the result was that few such cases reached authorities. And almost none went to trial.

No other child as young as the Spiegel girl has ever testified in a sexual abuse case in New Jersey, and perhaps not in the entire northeast, Rubbinaccio says. State Superior Court Judge Charles M. Egan's decision to find the girl "competent" to be a witness — that is, that she understood right from wrong and the importance of telling the truth — did not come automatically, however.

Prosecutors were ready to take the case to trial in the summer of 1984, when state Superior Court Judge Arnold V. Stein ruled the girl, then 3 years old, was incompetent to testify because she could not answer questions unless seated upon her mother's lap.

A state appellate court ordered Stein to hold a second hearing on the matter, and in August 1984 he ruled that the girl was competent because she understood the difference between telling the truth and lying and because she had promised not to lie. Spiegel appealed Stein's decision, but the state Appellate Division let it stand.

Then last fall, Herbert Korn, Spiegel's defense attorney, again challenged Rubbinaccio's decision to put the girl on the stand, contending that a psychiatric examination of the girl revealed she had no memory of the time when she was 2½.

But in early January, Egan met with the girl and the attorneys in his chambers and held a videotaped competency hearing, after which he ruled the girl was able to be a witness. The judge said it would be up to the jury to judge her credibility.

• •

The girl would not have to take the witness stand, however. To save her from the trauma of facing a courtroom packed with jurors, attorneys and the curious, Egan decided she could testify in a small conference room with only the prosecutor and defense attorney present. The jurors and everone else would watch on closed circuit televisions in the courtroom.

Although such a technique has been used in other jurisdictions, most notably in California during hearings on alleged sex abuse at a

Los Angelas area day care center, it had only been used in New Jersey in a recent Burlington County case involving an older child, Rubbinaccio notes.

The Spiegel girl testified for about an hour, with attorneys spending most of that time discussding innocuous subjects to put her at ease. Eventually, she did say that her father had hurt her, and drew circles around the genital area of outlines of human figures to show where.

"What you saw is that there is not going to be an automatic disqualification based on age alone," Trumbull says. "You can have people that develop earlier (than others their age), and children can be precocious."

• • •

While the judge's decison to allow the girl to testify is significant, the case also is important because of the use of expert testimony, Rubbinaccio says. Both sides called expert psychological witnesses to testify about whether there are behavioral symptoms exhibited by abused children, and about whether Spiegel's daughter exhibited them.

Judge Egan did not allow the prosecution's expert, Dr. Wallace Kennedy of Tallahassee, Florida, to testify whether he thought the girl had been abused, but Rubbinaccio and Morris County Prosecutor Trumbull still believe the case "broke the ice" for giving an expert a chance to state his findings about an alleged victim. "We're dealing with the threshold of information that the psychological profession can offer," Rubbinaccio says.

Trumbull and Rubbinaccio say the amount of information professionals have learned about child abuse and its symptoms over just the last five years is startling, and that as that information increases, expert testimony will take on an even greater role in such trials.

• • •

Not surprisingly, Spiegel, and his attorney, Herbert Korn, see the case differently.

Spiegel and Korn point to Egan's granting them permission to get a separate psychiatric evaluation of the girl as a victory. The defense expert, Dr. Alvin Friedland, examined the girl last November. His findings were almost directly opposite of those of the prosecution's expert. The girl was not traumatized, and had no memory from late 1983, Friedland reported.

But neither Spiegel nor Korn hold out much hope that the case will change procedures at the state Division of Youth and Family Services, to whom Mulvey originally made her allegations.

Spiegel contends that the division is too willing to blindly swallow charges made by a vindictive ex-spouse and that it has an automatic attitude that defendants are guilty until proven innocent.

"We're charged with the responsibility of protecting children," responds Charlene Brown, spokeswoman for the division."We, by law, are required to investigate every incident of child abuse.

"We interview a number of sources before proceeding to another stage," Brown says, noting that the division works closely with law enforcement officials and prosecutor's offices. "We do consider children to be credible witnesses in appropriate cases.

"It's the judicial system that has to protect the adults," she adds.

Spiegel's experience has prompted him to become the head of the North Jersey chapter of Victims of Child Abuse Laws, or VOCAL, and to write a book on his experience, "A Question of Innocence," which is due on bookstands on Father's Day.

The case has also prompted Trumbull and Rubbinaccio to consider proposing a new tool in cases involving very young witnesses: holding a videotaped hearing soon after a defendant is indicted and allowing attorneys on both sides to question the child.

This would "memorialize" the child's testimony at a time much closer to the date of an alleged incident, and counteract defense delays, which Trumbull and Rubbinaccio feel hurt the prosecution in Spiegel's case.

While no such tape has ever been shown to a New Jersey jury before, Trumbull thinks state courts would seriously consider using this technique in the case of a young witness.

And although the technique would be new to New Jersey, Kennedy, the prosecution's expert, says it has been frequently used in Flordia and Georgia.

• • •

Spiegel's acquittal has not caused the prosecutor's office to reconsider prosecuting in cases with very young witnesses, Rubbinaccio emphasizes. "Kids are not just going to be shunted aside because we're dealing with factors such as age and divorce."

Everyone connected with the case agrees that because of changing times and technology more such cases are likely to appear in the future. Both Korn and Trumbull say that while the amount of child abuse that takes place may not have changed much over the years people's willingness to report it has increased drastically.

Kennedy notes that courts are increasingly willing to take advantadge of modern technology, such as closed-circuit television, as that technology becomes more familiar. Kennedy and the lawyers also agree that the question of just how old a child must be to be able to remember alleged incidents and to testify is one the courts are going to see more and more.

"I think the courts are going to have to wrestle with some very difficult concepts over the next few years," Trumbull says.

In a rare statement to jurors, Judge Egan, after the case was over, told the 10 men and two women that the case had been one of the most difficult of his career as a judge. The legal issues and questions that had to be addressed were unparalleled in his experience, he said.

• • •

Egan also voiced another thought but this was during the trial and out of the jury's hearing.

The judge said from the bench that it seemed the girl had become "the forgotten third party in the case," and it seemed possible that two years of hearings, testimony and interviews with investigators and doctors had posed the danger of traumatizing the girl more than the alleged incident itself ever could.

10

WHAT TO KNOW, WHAT TO DO

Everyone is vulnerable to false accusations of child abuse. Certain situations, in particular, are spawning grounds for false accusations. Know these "high risk" situations. Make "caution" and "concern" your watchwords.

- Divorce, separation and/or custody disputes.

- A stormy marriage or an unsettled live-in relationship with children residing in the household.

- Professional careers that require daily interaction with children: teachers, day care center workers, nurses, etc.

- Chronic disputes with a neighbor and/or relative.

- Positions of responsibility; coaching, supervising, chaperoning etc.

- Households where discipline problems frequently erupt

between a child and a single parent. Children, especially teenagers, are becoming "wise" as to how they can obtain a quick change in custody.

- "Suspicious" injuries treated in a hospital emergency room or medical clinic. Certain injuries are associated with acts of child abuse. Involve your family doctor in medical emergencies.

- Watch for warning signs of the "Set-up" stage as described in Chapter One.

- Be alert to sudden changes in a child's vocabulary or behavior. This may indicate that a child is being "influenced" by someone, especially if the changes are sexually related. Such changes, however, may indicate actual abuse.

If you are falsely accused of child abuse your initial responses to the charge are of paramount importance. Know what to do and what not to do. Informed decision-making can prevent you from making matters even worse.

- Treat the accusation very seriously. Find the money to defend yourself properly. Hire the best professionals you can find. The "good ones" often understand the situation and may be flexible when it comes to their fees.

- Get professional assistance immediately, both legal and psychological. Be certain the professionals are experienced in these matters. Check references through VOCAL.

- Do not waive any of your rights or sign anything without legal counsel. Do not be intimidated by threats from social workers or county prosecutors. Such tactics are designed to weaken you. Get legal counsel before you say anything.

- Reach out for support. Family, friends, medical doctors, psychologists, psychiatrists and VOCAL members can help. Do not isolate yourself completely or for long periods of time.

- Keep a daily journal of events. Do not trust your memory to reconstruct the facts. Remember, extreme emotional stress can distort your recollection of important information.

- Maintain files of all documents. Read and reread them. You may be surprised by what you have overlooked.

- Request through the courts that an independent psychiatric and/or psychological evaluation of the "victim" be performed immediately. You are entitled under the rules of fundamental fairness.

- Do not submit to a psychiatric/psychological evaluation for yourself before discussing the ramifications of this evaluation with your legal counsel. Such evaluations open the very dangerous door of "character testimony." The Prosecutor can enter into "evidence" its findings.

- Do not expect a "common sense" approach from the child protection workers or prosecutors. No matter how rational your explanations are, or how innocuous the situation seems, expect bizarre interpretations to be drawn from your statements.

- Record all interviews. Have your attorney or an adult witness present at all times when dealing with child protection agencies.

- Help your attorney gather information. Watch TV shows, news broadcasts, read current literature, become involved with VOCAL. Pass this information directly to your lawyer.

- Analyze the possible results of your legal moves. Good decision-making stems in part from your understanding of the "possibilities" of your actions.

- Avoid the plea bargain or a *nolo contendere* plea at all cost. It means "guilty" and could easily result in you never seeing your child again.

- File appeals immediately when your constitutional rights are violated. Conditions of bail or restraining orders can violate your rights. The appeals process takes a great deal of time so move cautiously but aggressively.

- Do not be afraid of the media. Consult with your attorney to prevent making public statements that could damage your case.

AFTERWORD

By Douglas J. Besharov, J.D., LL.M.*

UNFOUNDED REPORTS:
THE NEWEST DANGER TO ABUSED CHILDREN

For twenty years, children's advocates struggled to get child abuse recognized as a serious social problem requiring a sustained governmental response. They have succeeded beyond their wildest dreams. Every day seems to bring a new public outcry over a child who has been brutally beaten or sexually abused, and calls to "do something" about child abuse.

Unfortunately, this very success now threatens the future viability of child abuse programs. The understandable emotional impulse to "do something" about child abuse, fanned by repeated and often sensational media coverage, has led to an overreaction whose effects have actually been counterproductive. In 1975, about 35 percent of all reports turned out to be "unfounded," that is to say, they were dismissed after investigation. Now, ten years later, about 65 percent of all reports nationwide prove to be unfounded. This flood of unfounded reports is overloading the system and endangering the children who really are being abused.

The Background

A major impetus for the public concern was the federal Child

Abuse Prevention and Treatment Act of 1974. The most significant aspect of that law was a small program of federal grants (about $3.7 million per year) to states that met specified eligibility requirements. Only three states were able to satisfy these requirements in 1973, but in the following six years, state after state passed new child protection laws and established the comprehensive child protective systems needed to qualify for federal aid. By 1978, all but seven states had done so. Three more states qualified in 1984.

In a well-meaning effort to identify the greatest number of endangered children, one of the eligibility criteria included in the federal act was a requirement that states broaden their laws on reporting of child abuse. In particular, all forms of child maltreatment had to be reported, whether or not the child had been physically harmed. As a result, nearly all states now require the reporting not only of suspected physical abuse and sexual abuse and exploitation, but also physical and emotional neglect. In fact, the state laws go further, to include children who have not yet been either abused or neglected. Typical legislation requires a report in such cases as when the child's "environment is injurious to his welfare," when the parents are "unfit to properly care for such child," or, in a blatant tautology, when the child is suffering from "abuse or neglect." Many of these crucial terms are never adequately defined, or are defined using pat phrases and ambiguous indicators that do nothing to help professionals and the public decide whether to file a report. One state, for example, defines emotional abuse to include the failure to provide a child with "adequate love."

Under these state laws, medical, educational, social work, child care and law enforcement professionals face civil and criminal penalties if they fail to report suspected cases. The laws also include provisions that encourage all persons — including relatives, neighbors, and friends of the family — to report suspected maltreatment. In fact, nineteen states require all persons, even perfect strangers, to report suspected child abuse.

These mandatory reporting laws, and associated public awareness campaigns, have been strikingly effective. In 1963, about 150,000 children came to the attention of public authorities because of suspected abuse or neglect. By 1972, an estimated

610,000 children were reported, and in 1984, the figure was above 1.5 million. Federal and state expenditures for child protective programs and associated foster care services now exceed $3.5 billion a year.

Does this vastly increased reporting signal a rise in the incidence of child maltreatment? Some observers think so, and blame what they see as deteriorating economic and social conditions for the rise in the level of abuse and neglect. But there is no way to tell for sure. So many maltreated children previously went unreported that earlier reporting statistics do not provide a reliable baseline against which to make comparisons. However, one thing is clear: The great bulk of reports now received by child protective agencies would not have been made but for the passage of mandatory reporting laws and the media campaigns that accompanied them.

Unfounded Reports

The media have given substantial coverage to the dramatic increase in abuse reports, contributing to the sense of a "child abuse crisis." What they rarely mention is that as the number of reports has soared, so has the unfounded rate. For example, in New York State, which has one of the highest unfounded rates in the nation, the number of reports received by the state Department of Social Services increased by about 50 percent between 1979 and 1983 (from 51,836 to 74,120). Yet the percentage of substantiated reports fell by almost 20 percent (from 43 percent to 36 percent). In fact, the absolute number of substantiated reports actually fell by about 100. Thus nearly 23,000 additional families were investigated — while fewer children were aided.

Sometimes, of course, child protective workers wrongly determine that a report is unfounded, and sometimes they declare a report unfounded as a means of caseload control. However, the great bulk of today's reports involve situations that do not amount to child maltreatment, or for which there is no "credible evidence" — the legal test for determining the validity of a report. Many observers, however, believe that there is a higher likelihood of malicious reports in custody battles. Generally, reports involve an honest desire to protect children coupled with confusion about when reports should be made. A child has a minor bruise and, whether or not there is evidence of parental assault, he is reported as abused. A child is living in a dirty household and, whether or not his basic needs are being met, he is reported as neglected.

Some child protective specialists defend the current high rates of unfounded reports on the ground that a degree of overreporting is necessary to identify children in danger. To an extent, of course, they are correct. That is why the law mandates the reporting of "suspected" child abuse. But unfounded rates of the current magnitude go beyond anything reasonably needed.

Multiplied by the thousands, these unfounded reports have created a flood that threatens to inundate the limited resources of child protective agencies. Forced to allocate a substantial portion of their limited resources to unfounded reports, child protection agencies are increasingly unable to respond promptly and effectively when children are in serious danger. As a result, children in real danger are getting lost in the press of inappropriate cases.

Unfounded reports are also deeply unfair to innocent parents, and harmful to their children, as graphically illustrated by this book. The determination that a report is unfounded can be made only after an unavoidably traumatic investigation that is inherently a breach of parental and family privacy. If the case goes to court, the financial and emotional costs continue to escalate.

Laws against child abuse are an implicit recognition that family privacy rights are not absolute. But as Supreme Court Justice Brandeis warned in a different context, "experience should teach us to be most on guard to protect liberty when the government's purposes are beneficent." It is all too easy for courts and social agencies, in seeking to protect children, to trample on the legitimate rights of parents.

Each year, over 500,000 families are put through investigations of unfounded reports. This amounts to a massive and unjustified violation of parental rights. As more people realize that hundreds of thousands of innocent people are having their reputations tarnished and their privacy invaded while tens of thousands of endangered children are going unprotected, a backlash is sure to develop that will erode continued support for child protective efforts.

As discussed in this work, a national group of parents and professionals has been formed to represent those falsely accused of abusing their children. VOCAL, Victims of Child Abuse Laws, publishes a national newsletter and has about 3,000 members in nearly a hundred chapters formed or being formed, including ten in California alone. In Minnesota, VOCAL members collected 2,000 signatures on a petition asking the Governor to remove Scott County Prosecutor Kathleen Morris from office because of her alleged misconduct in bringing charges, subsequently dismissed, against twenty-four adults in the town of Jordan. In Arizona, VOCAL members were temporarily able to sidetrack a $5.4 million budget supplement that would have added seventy-seven investigators to local child protective agencies.

What Must Be Done

So far, most child welfare officials in federal, state, and local agencies have lacked the courage to speak up publicly about the inflation of abuse statistics by unfounded reports, fearing that such honesty will discredit their efforts and lead to budget cuts. But unless things change, the potentially valuable force of public concern will serve only to increase the number — and proportion — of reports ineffectually and harmfully processed through the system.

An important first step must be the development of practical guidelines about what should and should not be reported. The current approach in training sessions is to tell potential reporters to "take no chances" and to report any child for whom they have the slightest concern. This ensures that child abuse hotlines will be inundated with inappropriate and unfounded reports. Laws and educational materials should be modified to require reporting only when there is credible evidence that the child has been abused or neglected or is in substantial danger of being abused or neglected.

Reporting Suspected Sexual Abuse

This book is about one aspect of the problem — reporting the suspected sexual abuse of children too young to give independently sufficient testimony about the accusation and the abrupt severing of parental rights on the mere accusation of such abuse. In such cases, we must rely on circumstantial evidence of sexual abuse. For a child who was violently forced into sexual activity, there may be visible signs of the assault which should be reported.

The great majority of sexual abuse cases, however, do not involve violent, or forced, physical assaults on the child. The only physical evidence of non-violent sexual abuse, if there is any, is likely to be limited to signs of sexual activity, such as minor injuries or bruises to sexual organs. Physicians are becoming increasingly adept at finding such evidence, even when it is microscopic, and it can be an appropriate basis for a report.

In addition, in older children, many physical signs may just be evidence of sexual activity with peers. Whether we like it or not, young children today become sexually active much earlier than in past generations. Hence, for older children, signs of sexual activity should not be automatically interpreted as signs of sexual abuse. Unfortunately, there is no specific cut off between the age when one or the other is the case. Children under the age of 13 are unlikely to be involved in intimate sexual activities with their peers, but even here mores are changing. These borderline situations must be judged individually, taking into account the statements of the child and parents as well as the child's apparent maturity and social environment. In addition, certain behaviors of the child, though not an independent basis for an adjudication, can be helpful in assessing these borderline situations. However, their absence does not necessarily mean that the child has not been abused.

The statements of the child and others, and physical and medical indications are the only sound basis of a report. This does not mean that outsiders must wait passively until such evidence becomes available. Certain behavioral patterns, while in themselves are not grounds for a report, are, nevertheless, an indication that the possibility of sexual abuse may exist. To medical personnel, for example, they may suggest the need for a full physical examination of the child. For others, these behaviors are an indication that further inquiries about the child's situation may be necessary.

Attention to the issues raised here and efforts to implement the measures suggested may begin to balance the scales, so that human tragedies like the one described in this book will not be permitted to continue. The sanctity of the American family can be safeguarded while protecting children from abuse.

*Douglas J. Besharov, J.D., LL.M., directs a social welfare project for the American Enterprise Institute for Public Policy Research in Washington, D.C. He prosecuted child abuse cases in New York before becoming the first director of the U.S. National Center on Child Abuse and Neglect. He is on the adjunct law faculties of Georgetown and American Universities. His most recent book is *The Vulnerable Social Worker: Liability for Serving Children and Families.*

CHRONOLOGY OF EVENTS

1983

January 25 — Valori took Jessie and left our home, unannounced.

April 6 — Violation of visitation on Jessie's second birthday.

September 22 — Our divorce hearing.

October 20 — Divorce granted.

November 9 — Valori leaves the state with Jessica in violation of court order.

November 16 — Valori was returned to New Jersey by court order. Valori's attorney informed the court of sexual abuse accusation. Judge Collester dismissed the charge of abuse and awarded me joint legal custody.

December 3 and 4 — Weekend of alleged sexual abuse. Janeen and I set a date for our marriage.

December 7 — Valori took Jessie to Somerset DYFS and to Morris County Prosecutor's Office.

December 9 — I was arrested and charged with aggravated sexual assault in Randolph, New Jersey.

December 16 — Bail modification motions in criminal and Family Court. Motions denied in both courts.

December 22 — Valori's request to take Jessie to Georgia for holiday.

1984

January 24 — Indicted by Grand Jury in Morris County Criminal Court on count of First Degree Aggravated Sexual Assault.

January 30 — My partner, Dr. Lawrence Lentchner, resigns from the Integrative Psychology Institute. Several weeks later Lentchner is reinstated as Clinical Director of Institute.

March 16 — Motions to dismiss the indictment and modify the condition of bail. Motions denied.

April 17 — Trip to my parents' home in Florida.

May 3 — Second arrest on charge of threatening Dr. Lentchner.

June 8 — Motion filed to bring case to trial or dismiss it. Trial date set for June 18, 1984.

June 18 — Beginning of trial. Prosecutor attempts to qualify Jessie, at age three, as witness. Judge disqualifies Jessie as witness.

June 19 — Prosecutor appeals judge's ruling of Jessie's competency.

June 26 — Appellate Court rules judge should evaluate Jessie's competency if allowed to testify from Valori's lap.

August 3 — Judge rules Jessie can testify if permitted to sit on mother's lap.

August 16 — I file appeal on Jessie's competency as a witness and my condition of bail.

September 13 — Appellate Court denies modification of bail. I appeal to the State Supreme Court.

November 5 — Oral argument on competency heard by Appellate Court.

November 30 — Motion filed for one Christmas visit with Jessie. Motion denied.

December 12 — Supreme Court denies my appeal to modify condition of bail.

1985

March 25 — Appellate Court issues split decision allowing Jessie to testify from her mother's lap.

June 16 — Father's Day VOCAL demonstration at Governor Kean's home. The *Washington Post* publishes my case.

August 2 — Motion for independent psychiatric examination of Jessie heard in court.

August 10 — Motion for independent psychiatric examination granted.

November 7 — Psychiatric examination conducted. New trial date set for December 2, 1985.

December 2 — Start of pretrial motions in Morris County Criminal Court.

December 9 — Two years to the day after my arrest, the second trial begins. Second hearing held on Jessie's competency.

December 11 — Trial postponed until January 1986.

1986

January 6 — Trial begins in Morris County Criminal Court.

January 16 — Verdict - "Not Guilty" on all charges.

March 17 — Parental rights fully reinstated in Family Court hearing.

April 19 — Jessie came home.